EMPOWERMENT OF RURAL WOMEN IN INDIA

Empowerment of Rural Women in India

Edited by

Dr. Meenu Agrawal
Dr. Shobana Nelasco

KANISHKA PUBLISHERS, DISTRIBUTORS
NEW DELHI-110 002

KANISHKA PUBLISHERS, DISTRIBUTORS
4697/5-21 A, Ansari Road, Daryaganj
New Delhi-110 002
Phones : 2327 0497, 2328 8285
Fax : 011-2328 8285
E-mail: kanishka_publishing@yahoo.co.in

First Published 2009

ISBN 978-81-8457-151-6

PRINTED IN INDIA

Published by Madan Sachdeva for Kanishka Publishers, Distributors, 4697/5-21A, Ansari Road, Daryaganj, New Delhi-110 002, Typeset by Sunshine Graphics, Delhi, and Printed at Rajdhani Printers, Delhi.

Preface

Pt. Jawahar Lal Nehru's statement, made in an Annual Conference on Community Development, aptly sums up the importance of women empowerment in nation building: "In order to awaken the people, it is the woman who has to be awakened. Once she is on the move, the household moves, the village moves, the country moves and thus, we build the India of Tomorrow."

Empowerment of women consists of greater autonomy in decision-making to enable them to have greater control over their lives, which involves aspects such as economic opportunities, property rights, social equality, political representation, personal rights etc.

In India, total women population is 49.6 crore (48.26%) in which 9.2 crore women are living in urban areas while 39.1 crore in rural areas. Data shows that in urban areas 63.32 per cent women are educated while 38.33 per cent women are educated in rural areas. Thus, empowerment of rural women will not be possible unless they are properly educated. Some impediments that come in the way of female literacy are poverty, cultural traditions, household work, early marriages, distantly located schools, lack of female teachers etc. These factors play an important role in non-enrolment and faster dropouts of girls from schools. Policies have to be made in such a manner as to raise the literacy level among rural women.

An economic change in the life of women, especially of rural women, will be possible if they take up entrepreneurial, cottage, industry, agricultural and allied activities independently. These activities will generate employment not only for these women but for other women as well. These activities will generate regular income for these women throughout the year. If these activities are undertaken on the basis of proper planning and training, they can emerge as profitable ventures.

In rural areas, women have been participating in various agricultural operations such as sowing, transplanting, weeding, harvesting, manuring, irrigation, fertilizer application etc. They also participate in allied activities such as cattle management, marketing of produce, handicrafts production etc. Rural women mostly perform these activities on meagre wages or as unpaid family workers. Empowering rural women by implementing meagre income generation projects or plans will not be sufficient to ameliorate the prospects for a better life for them. Thus, their empowerment in all economic, social and political activities is essential.

It is a fact that rural women are invisible in statistics and remain unattended in planned development efforts as they have no control on or access to resources. In rural areas the participation of women in agricultural production and allied activities ranges from land owing status of the family to landless labourers. It is an established fact that unless the rural women are empowered in the earnest, rural development is not possible.

The prime objective of all rural development plans, programmes and policies should be the empowerment of rural women. Such plans and policies can ensure self-employment for women in rural areas. The main problem, therefore, is to find out such ways and means, which may empower rural women for their economic independence, decision-making, self-reliance, social rights and control on resources. It has been recognised that if rural women are empowered in the right direction and true spirit, their contribution will go a long in accelerating the pace of rural development in India.

Some International Institutions are also supporting the empowerment of rural women in India. The World Bank in 1997 announced the approval of a US$ 19.5 million credit to the Government of India for a Rural Women's Development and Empowerment Project. The project is the bank's first freestanding women's development project in India. The project's objective is to empower the poor rural women through self-help groups aimed at increasing control over resources, developing income-generating schemes, improving management and technical skills and gaining access to credit and social services.

An example of women empowerment: Beena Devi is one of the 1.2 million elected women representatives in rural India, the largest anywhere in the world. She was elected Sarpanch of Laharpura village in Bihar's Nauvada district. About eight years ago, she had never stepped out of her house. But today, she presides over countless meetings in the village, interacts with civil servants and politicians and travels across the country. She can debate with fierce confidence.

Ms. Rita Sarin, Country Director of The Hunger Project, an NGO working to Empower Women says, "In the initial stages of Panchayati Raj, it was common to have women as proxy members. But with time, those numbers are gradually decreasing. Though, there are still many who are 'Panch Patis' or women whose husbands take all decisions." Ms. Sarin believes that one day or the other, more women will come forward and they will be less dependent on their husbands or other male relatives for decision-making. Female panchayat head is very good because women are more conscientious than men. Their concern for sanitation, drinking water, immunisation and education means they prefer to spend panchayat money on this rather than the typical boy's projects such as building a panchayat ghar or a road.

As Mr. Mani Shankar Aiyar, Union Minister for Panchayati Raj, says proudly, "This scale of socio-politically empowered women cannot be found anywhere. Women have done much better than we ever envisioned. Women have been able to participate and this made them vocal and more confident. Public empowerment is leading to family empowerment and that's a big social change."

Dr. Meenu Agrawal
Dr. Shobana Nelasco

Acknowledgements

Firstly, we would like to thank Dr. Rita Bakshi, Principal, Ginni Devi Modi Girls (PG) College, Modinagar for allowing the use of college facilities and ensuring an environment conducive to creative thinking in the college.

We are also grateful to Shri Sudhish Aggarwala, Joint Director (R&D), Petroleum Conservation Research Association (PCRA), New Delhi for his creative suggestions, comments, cooperation and kind help.

We would like to convey our regards to our parents and family for their encouragement for writing and preparation of the book completed. They were a source of inspiration whenever we felt low.

Many friends and colleagues have enabled us to evolve our ideas and deepened our knowledge of the subject through discussions & criticism. We are deeply indebted to them.

We must express our sincere gratitude to the contributors who took the pain to write their investigative papers for the completion of this volume. Their names are listed elsewhere but their work is this book's core.

Finally, we are very much thankful to Shri Madan Sachdeva, *Kanishka Publishers, Distributors,* New Delhi, who readily accepted our proposal and saw the book through its many stages.

Dr. Meenu Agrawal
Dr. Shobana Nelasco

Contents

List of Contributors

Dr. H.M. Mittal, Assistant Professor in Law, University of Rajasthan, Jaipur.

Dr. Ram Naresh Thakur, H.O.D., Postgraduate Department of Economics and Director, Gandhian Study Centre, Samastipur College, Samastipur Bihar.

Dr. R.C. Agrawal, Principal, Ex-Dean, Faculty of Commerce and Business Administration, CCS University.

Dr. K.D. Gaur, Deputy Director, Indian Council of Social Science Research (ICSSR), New Delhi.

Prof. Rita Bakshi, Principal, Ginni Devi Modi Girls (PG) College, Modinagar, Ghaziabad, U.P.

Mr. Sudhish Aggarwala, Joint Director, Research & Development, Petroleum Conservation Research Association (PCRA), New Delhi.

Prof. M.C. Paul, Group of Adult Education, Jawahar Lal Nerhu University, New Delhi.

Juhi Gupta, Lecturer, Department of Management Studies, D.J.C.E.T., Modinagar and Research Scholar, Ginni Devi Modi Girls (PG) College, Modinagar, Ghaziabad, U.P.

Shubhi Agarwal, MBA, Research Scholar, M.M.H. College, Ghaziabad, U.P.

Dr. Manju Goyal, Reader & Head, Ginni Devi Modi Girls (PG) College, Modinagar, Ghaziabad, U.P.

Dr. Birendra Kumar Jha, Reader and Head, Department of Economics D.B.K.N. College, Narhan (Samastipur, Bihar).

Harender Kumar, Research Scholar (Economics), Ginni Devi Modi Girls (PG) College, Modinagar, Ghaziabad, U.P.

Dr. Pravesh Kumari, Lecturer Department of Political Science, Ginni Devi Modi Girls (PG) College, Modinagar, Ghaziabad, U.P.

Dr. Rupesh Tyagi, Ginni Devi Modi Girls (PG) College Modinagar, Ghaziabad, U.P.

Bhawna, Project Fellow, Economics Ginni Devi Modi Girls (PG) College, Modinagar, Ghaziabad, U.P.

Dr. Prabha Singh, Lecturer in B.Ed Department S.G. Degree College, Lucknow, U.P.

Dr. Babita Agrawal, Reader and Head Economics A.K.P. College, Hapur, U.P.

Aditi Tyagi, Research Scholar, Ginni Devi Modi Girls (PG) College, Modinagar, Ghaziabad, U.P.

Meenakshi Sharma, Research Scholar, Ginni Devi Modi Girls (PG) College, Modinagar, Ghaziabad, U.P.

Harsh Awasthi, Lecturer, Faculty of Management, Noida Institute of Engineering and Technology, (NIET) Greater Noida.

Dr. Neeraja Sharma, Lecturer, (PGDM) Galgotias Business School (GBS) Greater Noida.

Meenakshi Madan, Lecturer, NIET, Greater Noida, e-mail: choprameenakshi@rediffmail.com

Dr. Nadia Yusuf, Programme Director of Business Administration, Jeddah, Saudi Arabia, Associated to Lambton College, Canada.

Preeti Chhabra, Lecturer College of Home Science, Food and Nutrition Department, Ginni Devi Modi Girls (PG) College, Modinagar, Ghaziabad, U.P.

Priya Mittal, Lecturer College of Home Science Food and Nutrition, Department, Ginni Devi Modi Girls, (PG) College, Modinagar, Ghaziabad, U.P.

Rakhi Mittal, Lecturer in Home Science, Ginni Devi Modi Girls (PG) College, Modinagar, Ghaziabad, U.P.

Meenu Agarwal, Lecturer in Home Science, GDM Girls (PG) College Modinagar, Ghaziabad, U.P.

Lipi, Research Scholar, Ginni Devi Modi Girls (PG) College, Modinagar, Ghaziabad, U.P.

Roona, Research Scholar Ginni Devi Modi Girls (PG) College, Modinagar, Ghaziabad, U.P.

1

Dr. B.R. Ambedkar, Some Reflections on Dalits and the Indian Constitution: A Future Course of Action

Dr. H.M. Mittal

By independence we have lost the excuse of blaming the British for anything going wrong. If hereafter things go wrong, we will have nobody to blame except ourselves.

B.R. Ambedkar

ABOUT DR. BHIM RAO AMBEDKAR

Bhim Rao Ambedkar was born in 1893, in a Hindu, scheduled caste-Mahar family. His mother tongue was Marathi. He took his primary education at Satara and Bombay; Columbia University, New York City, M.A. and Ph.D. (Attended on a Scholarship of Gaekwar of Baroda) at University of London, D.Sc. Grays Inn. Bar in 1923. He taught at college level in Bombay. He was also a delegate to round table conference in 1930-32 and member Joint Parliamentary Committee on constitutional reforms. He was also Member of Parliament and a Member for Labour, Governor-General's Executive Council 1942-46. He was Minister of Law, Government of India for a period of four years, 1947-1951. He was a true leader of untouchables and an opponent of Gandhi and the Congress.

He authored several works on economics, finance, politics and the untouchables. In the Constituent Assembly he was Chairman, Drafting Committee. He was Member in Advisory Committee, Member C.A. Committee on functions, Member Union Constitution Committee. After dissolution of Assembly, he took retirement from public life, and convert to Buddhism.

When considering the effectiveness of a constitution, it must first be understood that it has real existence only in the way it is used. A constitution can be judged only by its adequacy to situations it was designed to meet – and by the extent to which the situations it might reasonably be expected to meet foreseen – and by the extent to which it commands the allegiance of those who are to govern themselves by it.

AMBEDKAR AND THE HARIJAN—AMBEDKAR IN A LETTER TO NEHRU 28 APRIL, 1948

Through his (Nehru's) co-operation, Ambedkar through the Harijan had got some safeguards in the Draft constitution which we might not otherwise have got. The Harijan need fear that the Assembly would make laws or frame the constitution in a manner prejudicial to their interest. Ambedkar believed *'what they had to fear about was bad administration ....which was due to the absence of man belonging to Schedule Caste in administration'*. Ambedkar charged the administration for being unsympathetic towards the SC because it was manned wholly by higher caste Hindu Officers who were partial to the higher caste Hindus and who 'practiced tyranny and oppression' on the Harijans. In Ambedkar's view, the best way to remedy this situation was for Harijans to become members of the various Governments in India and thereby to ensure that Harijans also become members of civil services.

WHETHER RESERVATION HAS MADE ANY SIGNIFICANCE DEVELOPMENT AMONG THE SC/ ST AND BACKWARD COMMUNITY

Very few people have been benefited by the reservation till date. The Supreme Court has also time and again observed in number of judgments that there should not be any compromise with the quality especially in super technical courses such as in Engineering, Doctor's Profession, etc. Therefore, government should make effort to develop the quality of the SC/ST and Backward community instead of conferring reservation benefit in employment or in admission.

FUNDAMENTAL RIGHTS AND DIRECTIVE PRINCIPLES OF STATE POLICY

The Fundamental rights and directive Principles of State Policy were included in the constitution in the hope and expectation that one day the tree of true liberty would bloom in India. The Rights and Principles thus connect India's future, present and past adding greatly to significance of their inclusion in the constitution and giving strength to the pursuit of the social revolution in India. The Fundamental Rights are to foster the social revolution by creating a society egalitarian to the extent that all citizen were to be equally free from coercion, restriction' by the state or by society, privately liberty was no longer to be the privilege of few.

The Directive Principles of State Policy are aimed at making the Indian masses free from the passivity engendered by centuries of coercion by society and by nature free from the abject physical conditions that had prevented them from fulfilling their best selves.

The essence lies in Article 38 of the Constitution;

> '..............*the state shall strive to promote the welfare of the people by securing and protecting as effectively as it may a social order in which justice, social, economic and political shall inform all the institutions of the national life.'*

To foster this goal the other provisions of the Directive Principles exhort the state to ensure that citizens have an adequate means of livelihood, that the operation of the economic system and the ownership and control of the material resources of the country subserve the common good, that the health of the workers, including children, is not abused, and that special consideration be given to pregnant women. Workers, both agricultural and industrial, are to have a standard of living that allows them to enjoy leisure and social and cultural opportunities. Among the primary duties of the state is the raising of the level of nutrition and the general standard of living of the people. The principles express the hope that within ten years of the adoption of the constitution there will be compulsory primary education for children up to the age of fourteen. The other provisions of principles seek equally to secure the renovation to Indian society by improving the techniques of agriculture, husbandry, cottage industry, etc.

AMBEDKAR'S OBSERVATIONS RELATING TO EQUALITY AND FRATERNITY

Ambedkar was aware that India was poor and impoverished and that the grant of political independence guaranteed only what the Indian people had the courage to salvage for them. ***He had been a revolutionary leader of the untouchables; and knew that his fight for his own people was not just with the states but with cruel forces in Indian society itself.*** Although a revolutionary, he had also suffered at the hands of the revolution. To him, it was never really a choice between the civil and political rights which gave protection to the struggles of the people and that true equality which makes people care for each other and their environment. Somewhat innocently, he may have believed that economic and social equity were possible even though those in power would surrender to it incrementally and to serve their own ends. But, if anyone did, Ambedkar knew that what was at stake was not just the equality that gives dignity to peoples' lives, but also fraternity that brought them together. His message seems remotely located in our contemporary past. Yet, we would be foolish to ignore it.

Dr. Ambedkar uttered a warning, which should be read as his prophecy. He observed:

> We must begin by acknowledging the fact that there is a complete absence of two things in Indian society. *One of these is equality*. On the social plane, we have in India a society based on the principle of graded inequality which means elevation for some and degradation for others. On the economic plane, we have a society in which there are some who have immense wealth as against many who live in abject poverty. On the 26th of January, *we are going to enter into a life of contradictions. In politics, we will have equality and in social and economic life we will have inequality*. In politics we will be recognizing the principle of one man one vote one value. In our social and economic life we shall by reason of our social and economic structure, continue to defy the principle of one man one vote one value. *How long shall we continue to live life of contradictions?* How long shall we continue to deny equality in our social and economic life? *If we continue to deny it for long, we shall do so by putting our political democracy in peril. We must remove this contradiction at the earliest possible moment or else those suffer from inequality will blow up the structure of political democracy which this Assembly has so laboriously built up.*

The second thing we are wanting in is recognition of the principle of fraternity. What does fraternity mean? Fraternity means a sense of common brotherhood of all Indians -- if Indians think of themselves as being one people. It is the principle which gives unity and solidarity to social life.............The sooner we realize that we are not as yet a nation and seriously think of ways and means of realizing this goal, the better for us............for fraternity can a fact, only where there is nation. Without fraternity, equality and liberty will be no deeper than a coat of paint?[1]

In the name of the human rights of the poor, the government demanded a massive and untrammeled empowerment of the state. Ostensibly to achieve the social justice goals of the constitution this empowerment became the property of the vast class of officials and politicians who were intermediaries between the state and the people.

But the massive empowerment of the state continued. The more it was empowered, the more it mindlessly abused its power, undermining its own legitimacy and corrupting its processes, loosing its sense of integrity and cohesiveness, and reconstituting itself as the unabashed instrument of those powerful enough to appropriate it?

Credibly, the judges resolved the issue of empowerment refusing to accept that 'socialism' was opposed to 'human rights'; and insisting that state empowerment had to be rigorously fitted into a framework of rule of law without becoming a bonanza for functionaries of the state or those who lived of its sins of omission and commission.[2]

Ambedkar's hope lay in Indian society creating a sense of fraternity which would pledge the nation not just to political but also social peace. That sense of fraternity which may perforce, find itself in the constant struggle of the oppressed was singularly absent in the highly individuated plans of government. The poor are forced to fight and compete with each other. Capacity has acquitted that dimension of a social virtue in a society which had learnt to respect consequential dividends more than issues of togetherness and moral equity.

India has been particularly defensive about its human rights record. Confronted with its lack of fraternity in so many spheres of human existence, India offers a flat denial. It is, after all, the land of dharma – the righteousness that brings people together. Yet artifact memories of the past cannot rescue India from the human rights indictment of the present. What we see is disconcerting enough: A manifest disrespect for the social dignity of persons and groups, ruthless oppression of the disadvantaged to prevent them from developing a capacity for resistance , brutality in society against the weak, oppressed and particularly, women, the elimination of peoples self definition to force them to face externalities on terms dictated by others.

Fraternity—both old and new—has not provided a protective umbrella of togetherness under which people can expect to be treated fairly. But what should frighten India is not just Ambedkar's consequential forewarning that the whole edifice of Indian governance might be 'blown up', but a sense of shame that we, in India, permit fellow beings to be treated in the way in which they are and do little to prevent the incoming tide of inequity and despair. Until this sense of honesty descends upon us in the full totality of its confrontation, the resolve with which we propose to tackle human rights issues will exist only amongst those who are forced to fend for themselves rather than as part of a priority agenda for Indian society as a whole.

What had to be assured to all subjects were the basic conditions under which they could define their being, with dignity both to themselves and in relation to others. Without this, they were condemned to live a disempowered life of social servility. The early drafts,[3] debates on the objectives Resolution,[4] the Advisory Committee,[5] the Draft Constitution,[6] the final round of amendments to the penultimate text,[7] and the final reading,[8] reflect this concern.

Credit goes to the Indian Judiciary that it has intervened in case concerning violation of human rights. Such as matters relating to right to protection against solitary confinement as in Sunil Bartra v. Delhi Administration,[9] right not be held in fetters as in Charles Sobhraj v. Superintendent, Central Jail,[10] the right against handcuffing as in T.V. Vatheeswaran v. State of Tamil Nadu,[11] the right against custodial violence as in Nilabati Behera v. States of Orissa,[12] D.K. Basu v. State of West Bengal,[13] matter relating to sexual harassment at the working place as in Vishakha v. State of Rajasthan,[14] are just a few pointers in that direction.

DUTY OF THE UNION TO PROTECT PROVINCE

In Ambedkar's view it the duty of Union to protect every province from external aggression and internal disturbance. The Union was given a constitutional responsibility for the good governance of the provinces. Ambedkar reiterated his belief that the union must have a clear constitutional responsibility to intervene in a province. Union action must not be a 'pure invasion' of provincial autonomy.[15] He further said that the provinces were in certain ways sovereign and had plenty authority to make any law for the peace, order and good government of the province. For a union to intervene in a province's government would therefore be a 'wanton invasion' of provincial affairs.

As regards the financial emergency Dr. Ambedkar introduced emergency provisions laying down that if the financial stability or credit of the nation or any province was in danger, the President could issue a proclamation to that effect and then take action in the same manner as under a proclamation of emergency, which would include directing provincial governments to observe unnamed 'canon of financial propriety.'

AMBEDKAR AND JUDICIARY

Ambedkar was perhaps the greatest apostle in the Assembly of what he described as one single integrated judiciary having jurisdiction and providing remedies in all cases arising under the constitutional law, the civil law or the criminal law. For him, such a judicial system plus uniformity of law were essential to maintain the unity of the country.[16]

The function of the judiciary is not to set itself in opposition to the policy and politics of the majority rule. On the contrary, the duty of the judiciary is simply to give effect to the legislative policy of a statute in the light of the policy of the constitution.

Courts of law are the products of the constitution and the instrumentalities for fulfilling the ideals of the state enshrined therein. Their function is to administer justice according to the law and in doing so, they have to respond to the hopes and aspirations of the people because the people of this country, in on uncertain terms, have committed themselves to secure justice-social, economic and political—besides equality and dignity to all.

Experience is the basis for the development and evolution of law, which cannot be allowed to remain static. Development of law by the Supreme Court of the United States would provide an apt example. In Dred Scott v. Sandford,[17] that court held that a 'negro' was the property of his master and a 'citizen' thereby legitimizing 'slavery' and discrimination on the grounds of 'colour and creed'. This doctrine was cast away; a century later by the same court in Brown v. Board of Education,[18] when it said that slavery is a de-humanizing despicable institution denying human dignity touch an extent that no court of law can uphold it and later that court gave it a decent burial in Bakke's case.[19]

CERTAIN ISSUES RELATING TO THE CONSTITUTIONAL MECHANISM

1. Whether Constitution has failed to work.
2. Whether Panchayati Raj System has brought the democracy at grassroot level?
3. What is the solution if the elected representative resigns from the party from which he has been elected and joins another party, defrauding with the voters?
4. Whether we have the democracy in real sense? Since representative is elected merely on the basis of 50 per cent or less votes cast?
5. What is the solution of corrupt practices in election, crime and violence is committed during election process, or booth capturing etc.?
6. Why persons having criminal background are entering in political arena?
7. Whether we have any full proof mechanism to examine the expenditure incurred by the individual MLA/MP for contesting the elections?
8. Whether we have been able to maintained republican character in our country?
9. How to check Maltreatment of Police and Jail authorities?
10. What is the solution for imposition of emergency in state/s or declaration of President Rule in state/s on falls pretext?
11. Whether problem of Un-touchability has been elimination from the society? Whether the members belonging to SC/ST and backward community have been brought to main stream of life in the country.
12. Caste politics has become a very derogatory practice for smooth workability of our constitution.

REFERENCES

1. XI C.A.D. 979-80 (B.R. Ambedkar).
2. See R. Dhavan, "Human Rights and Socialism" (Paper to a Human Rights Seminar at the Faculty of Law, University of Hong Kong, 1990).
3. II S.R. 69-80 (the Munshi Text); 36-55 (K.T. Shah's text); 84-114 (B.R. Ambedkar's text). The Munshi text formed the basis of the initial discussions of the Advisory committee.
4. I C.A.D. 57-107, 113-130,133-53,166-7.269-289,291-324 for debates on the Objective Resolution.

5. III C.A.D. 379-421,431-57,465-530; V C.A.D. 361-402 for debates on the Advisory Report.
6. The relevant debates on the fundamental Rights ch. Are to be found in the main at VII C.A.D. 473-606. Subsequent debates include IX C.A.D. 1191-311. IX C.A.D. 1496-570, XI C.A.D. 466-72, 531-36.
7. This was an interesting innovation to permit amendments between the Second Reading and the Third Reading .
8. The final reading was long and tendentious and to be found at XI C.A.D. 607-922,938-81.
9. 1978 (4) SCC 494.
10. 1978 (4) SCC 104.
11. 1983 (2) SCC 68.
12. 1993 (2) SCC 476.
13. 1997 (1) SCC 426.
14. 1997 (6) SCC 241.
15. Procedding of the Meeting 23 July, 1949.
16. CAD VIII, 37.
17. 15 L Ed 691 (1857).
18. 347 US 483 : 98 L Ed 873 (1954).
19. 438 US 265 : 57 L Ed 2d 750 1978.

2

Rural Women Empowerment in India

Dr. Ram Naresh Thakur

Empowerment of women involves many things such as economic opportunity, property rights, political representation, social equality, personal rights and so on. Historically the world over, either by law or by custom, the status of women is undermined by asymmetrical power relationships in decision-making, personal and social rights, access to resources and entitlement. Women in many countries still lack rights to inherit property, own land, get education, obtain credit, earn income or work outside home, control their fertility; they are still widely under-represented in involvement in decision-making at the household or social level. Empowerment by means of modest income-generation projects is clearly insufficient to ameliorate the prospects for a high quality of life for women.

UNDP Report indicates that while 67 per cent of the world's work is done by women, only 10 per cent of global income is earning by women and a mere 1 per cent of global property is owned by women.

According to Amartya Sen, "Women are less likely to secure favourable outcomes for themselves in household decision making processes. They feel that their long term security lies in subordinating their well being to that of male authority figures."

According to Bangladeshi Nobel Peace Prize winner Md. Yunus "Rural Development means development of weaker sections, low income groups, debar form development, depressed, exploited and livelihood needy like ST/SC, minorities, unemployed and women are needed sensitive Micro-finance and Micro-credit soft loan, without guarantor loan and financial assistance to needy person, than they can survive and develop."

In reality rural farmwomen are invisible in statistics, they remain unreached and unattended in planned development efforts and are with no access and control on the resources. Rural Indian women are extensively involved in agricultural activities. However, the nature and extent of their involvement differs with the variations in agro-production systems. The mode of female participation in agricultural production varies with the land-owning status of farm households. Their roles range from Managers to Landless labourers.

Women are acting in different roles in rural areas as:

1. Farm Managers
2. Farm Labourers
3. Post Harvest Processing and Farm Trade
4. Livestock
5. Fisheries
6. Group Organisers

Government has been implementing various programmes which support women to take up new ventures and start self-employment, which has been categorised under four heads:

1. *Empowering Strategies:* Indira Mahila Yojana (IMY), Mahila Samriddhi Yojana (MSY), The Rural Women's Development and Empowerment Project (RWDEP) now called as Swa-Shakti Project, Development of Women and Children in Rural Areas (DWCRA).
2. *Employment and Income Generation:* Training of Rural Youth for Self-Employment (TRYSEM), Swayamsidha, Swalamban, Support for Training and Employment Programme (STEP), Norwegian Agency for International Development (NORAD), Socio-Economic Programme (SEP), Condensed Courses of Education and Vocational Training (CCEVT), Swarnjayanti Gram Swarozgar Yojana (SGSY), Women's Vocational Training Programme (WVTP), Swarna Jayanti Shahari Rozgar Yojana (SJSRY), Urban Self-Employment Programme (USEP), Development of Women and Children in Urban Areas (DWCUA), Jawahar Rozgar Yojana (JRY), Trade Related Entrepreneurship Assistance and Development (TREAD), National Rural Health Mission (NRHM), National Rural Employment Guarantee-Scheme (NREG). Efforts are being made to merge STEP with other three programmes i.e. NORAD, SEP and CCEVT, thus

bringing out an umbrella scheme of "Training and Employment for Women."

3. ***Welfare and Support Services:*** Hostels for Working Women (HWW), Short Stay Homes (SSH), Swadhar, Creches/Day care centres for the children of working and ailing mothers.
4. ***Other Enabling Measures:*** Rashtriya Mahila Kosh (RMK), a national level mechanism to meet micro-credit needs of poor and asset less women in the informal sector. Also known as the National Credit Fund for Women (NCFW).

In India a large percentage to total population resides in rural areas as the following table says (Table-1).

Table-1
Percentage of Rural-Urban Population

Years	*Sector*	*Male*	*Female*	*Persons*	*% to Rural and Urban Population*
1951	Rural	153,444,642	145,199,739	298,644,381	82.71
	Urban	32,083,820	30,359,889	62,443,709	17.29
	Total	185,528,462	175,559,628	361,088,090	
1961	Rural	183,504,095	176,794,073	360,298,168	82.03
	Urban	42,789,106	36,147,497	78,936,603	17.97
	Total	226,293,201	212,941,570	439,234,771	
1971	Rural	225,319,943	213,725,732	439,045,675	80.09
	Urban	58,729,333	50,384,644	109,113,977	19.91
	Total	284,049,276	264,110,376	548,159,652	
1981	Rural	270,910,547	252,956,003	523,866,550	76.67
	Urban	82,463,913	76,998,634	159,462,547	23.33
	Total	353,374,460	329,954,637	683,329,097	
1991	Rural	324,321,614	304,370,062	628,691,676	74.29
	Urban	114,908,844	102,702,168	217,611,012	25.71
	Total	439,230,458	407,072,230	846,302,688	
2001	Rural	381,141,184	360,519,109	741,660,293	72.22
	Urban	150,135,894	135,219,060	285,354,954	27.78
	Total	531,277,078	495,738,169	1027,015,247	

Source: Census to India-2001, Population Tables.

The Table 1 shows that out of total rural population at around 50 per cent women lived in rural India. From the first Five Years Plan the development of rural women is the key factor for the programme planner, but it could not be completely achieved. The literacy rate of rural women is very poor as shown in Table-2.

Table-2
Male and Female Literacy Rates by Rural-Urban Division (in%)

Years	*Rural Male*	*Rural Female*	*Urban Male*	*Urban Female*	*Male*	*Female*
1951	19.02	04.87	45.60	22.33	27.10	08.86
1961	34.30	10.10	66.00	40.50	40.40	15.35
1971	48.60	15.50	69.80	48.8	45.96	21.97
1981	49.60	21.70	76.70	56.30	56.38	29.76
1991	57.90	30.60	81.10	64.00	64.13	39.29
2001	71.40	46.70	86.70	73.20	75.85	54.16

Source: Economic Survey 2001-02, Economic Division, Ministry of Finance, Government of India.

Although the Table-2 shows the rate of literacy both the rural and urban area. In past Couple of decade has gone up, but not very impressive. Despite rising figures, illiteracy is much higher in rural women than in urban women.

CAUSES OF RURAL WOMEN BACKWARDNESS

The major causes of rural women backwardness are:

- Illiteracy.
- Poverty in Rural Area.
- Child Marriage.
- Burden of Homely Works.
- Population Overloading.
- Lack of Natural and Human Resource in Rural Area.
- The Biased Vision of Society.
- Social Exploitation.
- Poor Health Rate.
- Dowry System.

Present law and order, also, are not favourable for them. It is far beyond to their imagination to take the help of law for the torture by their husband and Parent-in-Law. They are occasionally get sexual harassment, but owing to their sanctity and prestige they never reveal it. After all, the great evolution in medical the condition of women health is measurable and the root cause of their troublesome.

For the women empowerment particularly in rural area they should be educated and have to be conscious about their rights and role to build their future. They and only they will have to pay heed to their problems. It is the need of time they should take interest and play their role to form the government and their policy. In this direction the policy of newly formed Bihar Government about 50 per cent reservation for women in Gram Panchayat and local bodies is much affordable and commendable. Besides the equivalence of law, women should be taken in action after then the dream of women empowerment would be completed, and rural life would be prosperous. The real Empowerment of rural women can be achieved if every one accepts the truth that men and women are equal and their collective responsibility and duty makes a home, a society, a nation. Men should also have the respect to their heart. But by the time goes, the situation of women i.e., either urban or rural became increases. Most of the Non-Government Organisation made a great effort to redress these all problem. The Government should also afford these NGO's included with the fare planning and expenditure of government plans.

ROLE OF NON-GOVERNMENTAL ORGANIZATIONS (NGOs) IN RURAL WOMEN DEVELOPMENT

The major NGOs in Rural Women Development are: Bihar Rural Livelihood Promotion Project (BRLP), National Alliance of Young Entrepreneurs (NAYE), World Assembly of Small and Medium Entrepreneurs (WASME), Xavier Institute for Social Studies (XISS), Self-Employment Women's Association (SEWA) of Ahmedabad. 'Y' Self-Employment of Kolkata.

Association of Women Entrepreneurs of Karnataka (AWAKE), Rural Development and Self-Employment Training Institute (RUDSETIs) based in Karnataka.

FINANCIAL INSTITUTIONS

There are a good number of financial institutions that support women to start any new enterprises. Some of them are: Rashtriya Mahila Kosh (RMK), National Agricultural Bank for Rural Development (NABARD), Small Industries Development Bank of India (SIDBI), Council for Advancement of People's Action and Rural Technology (CAPART), Access to Credit through "Development Bank for Women Entrepreneurs" in small scale and tiny sectors, Reserve Bank of India (RBI).

In India, right from the beginning of Five Year Planning (1951-56) there has been endeavour towards the development of women. However, Sixth Plan (1980-85) has been marked by a clear shift in the approach, from 'welfare' schemes to 'development' oriented plans towards women. More recently the Ninth Plan (1997-02) made two significant changes in the conceptual strategy of planning for women development.

First, the Plan attempted what it called 'Empowerment of Women'. Second, it aimed at 'convergence of existing services' available in both women-specific and women-related sectors. The Plan directed both the Centre and the states to adopt the special strategy of 'Women's Component Plan' (WC) through which not less than 30 per cent of funds/benefits is expected to flow to women from all general development sectors. The ongoing Tenth Five Year Plan (2002-07) continues with the strategy of "Empowering Women" as an agent of social change and I development. For this purpose a sector specific three-fold strategy Social Empowerment, Economic Empowerment and Gender Justice has been adopted.

The National Policy of empowerment of women has set certain clear cut goals and objectives. The objective of the policy include:

- Creating and environment through positive economic and social policies for full development of women to enable them to realise their full potential.
- The de jure and de-facto enjoyment of all human rights and fundamental freedom by women on equal basis with men in all spheres-political, economic, social, cultural and civil.
- Equal access to participation and decision making of women in social, political and I economic life of the nation.
- Equal access of women to healthcare, quality education at all levels, career and vocational guidance, employment, equal remuneration, occupational health and safety, social security and public office etc.
- Strengthening legal systems aimed at elimination of all forms of discrimination against women.
- Changing societal attitudes and community practices by active participation and involvement of both men and women.
- Mainstreaming gender perspective in the development process.
- Elimination of discrimination and all forms of violence against women and the girl child; and
- Building and strengthening partnerships with civil society, particularly women's organization.

The approaches for empowerment of rural women can be divided into four broad heads:

(*a*) Educational Empowerment.
(*b*) Social Empowerment.
(*c*) Economic Empowerment.
(*d*) Technological Empowerment.

(*a*) EDUCATIONAL EMPOWERMENT

Education is the key, which opens the door to life, develops humanity and promotes national development. Education can be an effective tool for women's empowerment. It enables rural women to acquire new knowledge and technology required for improving and developing their tasks in all fields. Therefore, at least one Functional Literacy Centre should be opened in each Gram Panchayat area with a view to make all and rural farm women functionally literate and adult education necessary.

(*b*) SOCIAL EMPOWERMENT

Empowering women contribute to social development. Economic progress in any country whether developed or underdeveloped could be achieved through social development. Hence, women's empowerment cannot be ignored, while devising various policies for rural and socio-economic development.

(*i*) Status of Women

Even country has made progress in developing women's capabilities, but inequalities continue to exist between women and men. The low status of women is the outcome of a variety of causes in which patriarchal values reinforced by tradition, media and other socio-political institution play a major role. Thus, the institutional bases of women's oppression have to be sensitized to accept the gender equality and moreover, women's perception of themselves would also need to be changed.

(*ii*) Gender Bias

Cultural traditions and economic necessity have always mean a significant role for women in agriculture. In India it is not uncommon that women do not have control over the land. Even, where women constitute a larger share of a agricultural producers but, there are cultural constraints to easy communication between men and women, because almost all extension workers are men.

(iii) Health and Nutrition

Health and nutrition are two very important basic needs for empowerment of rural women. To achieve real and quicker development in health sector, an extensive as well as intensive "Health Education and Awareness Campaign" (HEAC) needs to be given topmost priority and it should mainly stress on nutritional education, benefits of immunization, family planning etc.

(c) ECONOMIC EMPOWERMENT

Empowering women with economically productive work will enhance their contribution to agricultural development.

(i) Access to Resources

The farm women need to have control over limited resources like land and livestock, so that they could take away decisions and implement them in any way that is required. Ownership and control over productive assets will create a sense of belonging and owning. It will thus help to take responsibility in family and local group activities. Other impact of control is to enhance their decision-making ability to meet some physiological needs like self-esteem and confidence.

(ii) Micro-Credit Programmes

Micro-credit programmes extend small loans to poor people for self-employment projects that generate income allowing them to care for themselves and their families. In most cases, micro-credit programmes offer a combination of services and resources to their clients in addition to credit for self-employment. Access to productive resources is critical for enhancing women's economic choices. Since, formal credit institutions rarely lend the poor, special institutional arrangements may become necessary to extend credit to those who have no collateral to officer their enterprises. In order to have access to credit, setting up self-help group, local banking system by women, Non-Governmental Organizations and provision of facilities by Government need to be established. The policy challenge is to support effective grassroots credit schemes and intermediaries and ensure that low-income have assured credit from the formal financial system.

(iii) Access to Co-operatives and Local Women's Organizations

Collectivization has been recognized as a tenet of women's empowerment. It has been defined as a process of bringing a group of women together at a base to become an integral part of an economic activity. Organizational efforts should be made for integrating farm women into development. Organization of Mahila Mandals, Co-operatives Societies and Discussion Groups. The control of these organizations should be in the hands of womenfolk themselves. Also, the present beneficiary approach to women's development should be replaced by participatory approach.

(d) TECHNOLOGICAL EMPOWERMENT

Though women are involved in almost all agricultural operations, in rural areas yet, they have inadequate technical competency due to their limited exposure to outside world. This has compelled them to follow the age old practices which in turn result in poor work efficiency and drudgery and needed computer, internet latest informations.

(i) Capacity Building

Capacity building and empowerment are important for which there should be decentralized capacity building among the rural women particularly farm women. Empowerment projects should go beyond the provision of basic social services for an. They should include components vital for enabling the poor to participate in economic activities. It is important to develop the skills among farm women in order to increase their productivity and to keep them abreast of modernization and technological changes for being competitive in the market.

(ii) Exposure to Mass Media

The transfer of technology approach, which mainly includes mass media are also not paying due attention towards dissemination, of adequate and timely agricultural and marketing information to the farm rural women. Therefore, there is outmost need to provide adequate coverage to the programmes related to women and they must get exposure to mass media for improving their communication and meditation skills to strengthen their capacity to contact and mediate with external world.

(iii) Appropriate Training Programme

Training is an important component of HRD which enhances knowledge, skill and attitude. For building technical competency among farm women, need-based skill-oriented training programmes to reinforce their role in farm activities need special attention. The training programmes should initially be organized on their felt-needs and then be switched over to unfelt but essential needs. To achieve this sacred task, infrastructure facilities in terms of more numbers of KVKs, FTCs and BRLP should be established in the district on priority basis.

(iv) Appropriate Technology for Women

In order to cater the technological needs of farm rural women, women specific technologies should be developed. While evolving agricultural technologies, indigenous practices used by women should be paid due attention for blending with the frontier ones for greater adoption. Also there is need to strengthen linkage between various research and extension organizations engaged in transfer of technology.

MEASURES TO STRENGTHEN WOMEN'S EMPOWERMENT AND RURAL DEVELOPMENT

Empowerment of women is the prime objective of all development programmes and policies. These programmes could be planned properly and implemented effectively in order to attain self-sufficiency and self-reliance. U.N. Commission on Status of Women says: Women constitute half of the world's population, accomplish about two theirs of its work hours, receive one tenth of the world's income following measures can strength self-employment in rural area in the service sector, which will generate additional income leading to economic independence of women:

- Identification and organization of innovative and high income generating activities suitable for women.
- Development of entrepreneurial abilities of women by organizing special type of training.
- Encouraging women to take up part-time jobs while being in the house itself, to earn additional income to support the family.
- Effective planning at the micro-level.
- Adequate representation of women experts in the case of women related development planning.
- Central and State Governments to place more emphasis on untouched areas in the service sector to involve women.
- Government can establish a separate mechanism levels to look after women's employment and their problems.
- Development of infrastructure facilities and supportive

services like land building, transport and also to look after the children.

- Encouraging women through formal and non-formal education to involve themselves in the service sector.
- Organising women service through women's associations, co-operative societies or Mahila Mandals, self-help groups etc.
- Establishment of supervisory bodies to monitor the implementation of Constitutional provisions related to.
- Steps to make women aware of technical and financial assistance available to women entrepreneurs, and to encourage them through concessions and incentives to enter into the service sector related to women.
- Government should encourage research and development in the service sector to find out high incomes generating activities suitable for women.
- Wide publicity to training programmes in the service sector.
- Creating awareness among educated and uneducated women about the availability of facilities and concessions for entrepreneurs.

As per the 2001 census, the total female population of India is estimated at 495.74 million. This is 48.3 per cent of the countries total population. The figure shows that women are vital human resources of the country. Thus they are considered to be the most critical determinant for its over all socio-economic development. According this census report, total number of rural working person was 31.06 crore in which male 19.92 crore and female 11.14 crore, where as in urban area total employed male 7.62 crore and female 1.15 crore out of total 9.18, crore working persons. This figure shows discrimination in employment sector. But a fact comes her that more working women are in rural area than urban area. These women are not engaged much paying jobs. Women in India form 89 per cent of informal and unorganized sector. Women's work participation rate is higher in rural areas. Women makeup for one-third of the labour force of India, where 90 per cent rural women workers are unskilled and 10 per cent women in urban area. In this regard 77 per cent women are in agriculture sector and in construction area only 10 per cent. In the organized sector up to 31 March 2002 in public and private both sectors the number of working women was only 49.5 lakh and number of men 6 times to women. It is 18.1 per cent of total employed persons in this sector. After micro analysis of working women, it is found the more women are working in social, service and personnel sector, it is 56.5 per cent in construction sector, 20.6 per cent agriculture and allied activities 9.4 per cent and insurance finance sector 5.2 per cent. Most of the Indian women are working on lower and general posts like clerks, Nurses and school teachers. Labour Ministry organized survey by National Sample Survey Organisation that calculated that total 11 crore 80 lakh women are working in unorganized sector. They are mostly agricultural labour, Khomachawala, working as casual labour, in construction works and domestic services on lower wages. Most of the key posts of any department in full of with male, very few for women. Women are 14.1 per cent supervisor and medium grade posts and only 4.3 per women are officers here. But only 4 per cent women are on apex posts on various departments. These statistics show the case of discrimination in employment sector not only rural area but urban area also.

Wage discrimination is common phenomenon for rural women. For every Rs. 100 earned by a male worker in rural India, a woman earned only Rs. 72 in 2004 05. She was better off in 2000-01, when she earned Rs. 75. The data for agricultural year 2004-05 and 2000-01, shows that in the agriculture sector, which is leading employer in the economy, the prevailing wage differential between male and female workers has increased. In 2000-01 the differential stood at 25.37 per cent but that has widened to the grim level of 27.6 per cent. It will give clear picture with the following table (Table-3).

Table-3

Average Daily Wages of Rural People (2004-05)

(in Rs.)

	Male	*Female*	*Wage Differential Per cent*
Agriculture	61.37	44.43	27.60
Sweeping	50.92	49.00	03.77
Unskilled labour	60.61	44.93	25.87

Source: Wage Report in Rural India, Labour Bureau.

Women are only dominant the low paying jobs like sweeping and provision of unskilled labour. Unfortunately even here there are wage differentials between men and women. While minor difference in wages was noticed for sweeping (3.77%), there was a yawning gap witnessed in the case of wages for unskilled labourers (25.87%).

Poverty distribution in rural area is gender biased because it is growing faster among rural women than rural men. Over the past 20 years, for example the number of women in absolute poverty rose by 50 per cent against 30 per cent of rural men. A poor woman involves herself in house making and rearing of hunger child, she does not spare time for searching the employment.

Rural women are subjected to some hindrances, which impose limitations on their potential to play their role effectively. Women are said to have equal status in the society, but when it comes to actual decision-making, men have final say while women have to accept a subservient status.

The poverty alleviation programme should form part of sectoral Programmes and area planning. The government agencies should be care on feminisation of poverty in rural areas. In this regard community based micro-enterprises like cotton coir rope making, coconut coir rope making, coconut leaf thatching, pickle manufacture, group leaf plate making, spices production, honey and food processing, agarbatti making etc. have proved to be most viable economic activities for rural women in the country to drive the beneficiaries out of the poverty trap. Here the products are produced according to local demand patterns and are consumed in the same locality.

REFERENCES

Acharya Sarthi (1989): Agricultural Wages in India, A Disaggregated Analysis, Indian Journal of Agricultural Economics, 44.

Adelman Inna and Morris Cynthia T. (1973): Economic Growth and Social Equity in Developing Countries, Stanford University Press, Stanford.

Agarwal Bina (1986): Women Poverty and Agricultural Growth in India, Journal of Peasant Studies, 13.

Dreze Jean and Sen Amartya (1998): India Economic Development and Social Opportunity, Oxford University Press, Delhi.

Annual Report, Ministry of Rural Development, 2001-02 to 2004-05.

Ministry of Rural Areas and Employment (1998): Evaluation Report of Employment Schemes, Government of India, New Delhi.

Surya Narayan M.V.A.N. 7and Nagalakshmi R. (2005): Role of Women in Rural Development, Kurukshetra, Vol. 54, No. 1.

Arthreya Venkatesh (2002): Gender and Survival in the Decade of Refonns: What does census 2001 Reveal, India Economic Association Conference, Thiruvananthapuram.
The Economic Times, Kolkata, 7 July 2006, p. 13.
The Economic Times, Kolkata, 27 September 2006, p. 10.

3

Impact of Unequal Healthcare Delivery System on Women's Health

Dr. R.C. Agrawal, Dr. Meenu Agrawal & Juhi Gupta

INTRODUCTION

The liberalization and globalization has impacted all areas of living setting in a chain of pervasive changes. The era of economic reforms in India since 1990 has had far reaching effects on issues of gender and society. Globalization is associated with free trade, free mobility of both financial and real capital, and rapid diffusion of products, technologies and information and consumption patterns.

In a democracy, the greatest good of the greatest number is the accepted guiding principle. Social and economic inequality is detrimental to the health of any society. Especially when the society is diverse, multicultural, overpopulated and undergoing rapid but unequal economic growth. There are obviously tensions within classes and communities, and therefore what ensures good quality for one group may not do the same for others. Gender inequalities pervade through the entire spectrum of society. The socio-cultural determinants of women's health have played a lead role in the persistence and strengthening of health inequalities. The primary challenge to health empowerment and socio-economic rights stems from poverty and underdevelopment.

The prevalence of a dominant family ideology, which strictly demarcates definite roles and obligations for girls and women, leads to their devaluation and marginalisation. The basic assumption is that girls are inferior, physically and mentally weak, and above all, sexually vulnerable.

That sixty-one years after independence, only a little more than a third of women are literate, is indicative of the overall attitude towards women and their roles. In addition, in keeping with the worldwide trend on exposing such data, information on violence against Indian women and girl children has brought into focus their extremely fragile position, both within the family and in public spaces. Yet, there has been slow progress in certain vital areas: female life expectancy at birth has risen, the sex differential in infant Mortality Rates is almost bridged, and an increasing number of women are joining the work force. The chief achievements of the last decade—and certainly among the most important features of the post-independence period—have been the 73rd and 74th Constitutional Amendments of 1993, which reserved 331/3 per cent, of seats for women in elections to local bodies in both the rural and urban areas.

In the years before the current phase of reform, there was enough evidence to suggest that poverty alleviation measures were not taken too seriously. Economist Pranab Bardhan has commented that while there was "some general progress over the years in the provision of public consumption and welfare measures for the poor" these remained woefully inadequate. He identified low investments, the absence of an adequate administrative machinery as well as organisational and managerial bottlenecks as being responsible. Further, during a financial crisis, "the axe falls most heavily on the social welfare programmes for the poor." That, in the post-independence period, investment and planning for the social sector has not been given the attention necessary for a country of India's size and dynamics is evident by a quick look at some figures: half a century after independence 130 million people in India do not have access to any kind of health facilities, 185 million have no access to drinking water and while the government claims that 80 per cent of villages have safe drinking water, a million children die each year from diarrhoeal diseases.

The incumbent package of economic reforms consisted of the four strategies of devaluation, privatisation, liberalisation and globalisation. All of these have, in one way or another, affected the life of the average household in a number of ways. The philosophy of open competition and privatisation has substantially permeated the social sector; as we shall see, in health care, a history of unsatisfactory state-run facilities has led to the burgeoning of the private sector. In the post-reform period this tendency is exacerbated, and, when combined with a de-regulated drug market, costs of health care shoot up. While advocates of the reform package do not rule out intervention on behalf of the poor, they assume that "the really effective weapon for poverty alleviation is accelerated economic growth."

HEALTH SCENARIO IN INDIA

In keeping with the World Health Organisation's definition, health is, viewed broadly as a state of mental and social well-being, to be regarded as a human and civic right. In India, the provision of basic health services is the responsibility of the State, where the Five Year Plans lay, down priorities and directions. The Constitution of India placed public health and sanitation in the state list; in other words, under the federal system of governance, the Indian states, rather than the Central Government have a primary obligation for these two aspects of civic life. While the idea of holistic health – preventive, curative and promotive – is a part of the current Indian development literature, actual implementation falls far short of people's needs.

Not unexpectedly, women and children (particularly those from underprivileged homes) are: easy victims of inadequate delivery systems and outreach programmes.

According to a recent policy document the Government of India admits that as human development indicators such as "life expectancy, literacy, school enrolment and medical care lag far behind those of most East Asian countries"; people who "are our most valuable resource" should be "at the centre of our strategy of economic reform". Pointing out that education and health care of the privileged have skimmed off a major share of budgetary allocations in these areas, the document argues for a redirection of priorities that will lead to "much higher shares of the budgets for education and health on primary education, basic health care and women and child welfare." Not unexpectedly, high birth and fertility rates are identified as major factors in this scenario of declining well-being and productivity: The document states quite, unequivocally that "the effectiveness of the family planning programme will need to be greatly improved" particularly in the high birth rate states of Uttar Pradesh, Bihar and Madhya Pradesh.

A large percentage of these funds are ear-marked for the, control of communicable diseases such as malaria, tuberculosis, leprosy, blindness and now AIDS as well as salaries and maintenance.

WOMEN: SOURCE OF A NEW LIFE

When, in 1975, Towards Equality, the Report of the Committee on the Status of Women in India, pointed out that demographic indicators suggested that "child bearing in India, for the majority of women, is more a health hazard than a natural function," it was recording an unpalatable fact of life: the average woman becomes pregnant about six to eight times within the 15-45 year age group. Thus, "of the total 360 months of reproductive life, 200 months or 50 to 60 per cent of the time are spent in pregnancy and lactation." Not unexpectedly, then, much of a woman's ailments are related to her reproductive history. Apart from this, women's heavy domestic-cum-work burden also makes them prone to a range of ailments.

The national health system is geared towards viewing the woman as mother and reproducer. Thus, "the health system has yet to waken to the fact that there are a large number of women in need of health care who are neither pregnant nor lactating." This attitude finds expression in inadequate sensitivity and training in non-maternity related health care issues as also in ill-equipped facilities and programmes. Both the private and the public health system's core attention towards women is viewing the latter as mothers. While the private nursing home sector comprises of maternity homes, the public health sector's major concern *vis-a-vis* women is to prevent them from becoming mothers.

Even for these limited programmes "health workers and infrastructures.... are grossly inadequate and of poor quality." When the facilities are not available, are too far away', and the personnel is unsympathetic, the opportunity costs in missing out on daily wages is too great.

Some analysts have also pointed to the fact that the majority of Indian babies are continue to be born at home. This fact brings into sharp focus three points: first, inadequate institutional facilities, second, a reluctance to use these facilities and third, the need to strengthen the indigenous system. Even when facilities are available why do Indian women prefer to have their babies at home, quite often attended to by barely competent helpers? Lack of faith in the public system is accentuated by shortage of medicines, distance, the need to have someone to go with and an overall belief that "we will not be treated as humans." While women seemed willing to go for prenatal check-ups to PHCs and municipal dispensaries, they drew the line at institutional deliveries. There were several women who went to the PHCs or nearby hospitals for prenatal check-ups and tetanus toxide inoculations. In addition to a fear of unsympathetic staff, many women felt that money which would have to be spent on medicines, injections, cotton wool and so on could as well be used for food and essential commodities at home.

Another important factor was the requirement of an attendant at the hospital or Centre: this meant that either the husband or someone else would have to take time off from work to be on duty in the hospital. Lack of childcare facilities meant that for the time that the mother was away, arrangements had to be, made-for other children. The Indian Council of Medical Research (ICMR) study confirmed the lack of many basic medicines in the PHCs resulting in patients having to buy them in the open market.

In a study in a Maharashtra village, out of 131 births in seven years, only one delivery was conducted in a PHC. Distance of the Centre, paying for a companion and the cost of food, medicines and other necessities led women to deliver at home. Further, there is also a fear of being coerced into sterilisation.

Both reproduction and reproductive health become major talking points in structural adjustment programmes as a fast growing population is viewed as being detrimental to economic development. Not unexpectedly then, of late, the State has decided to intervene more actively in reproductive control -through *(a)* disincentives and *(b)* experimenting with a range of new female-oriented contraceptives. Both are geared to the achievement of a Net Reproduction Rate (NRR) of unity by 2016 A.D. It is important to understand fertility and reproductive behaviour during a period of economic transition, as is the case with India today. By and large, "during the transition, population initially increases rapidly because the mortality rate declines well ahead of the fertility rate." In subsistence-level economies children are treated as commodities "who not only compete for scarce resources" but also help in the generation of these as well as of disposable income. There is evidence from developing countries that with an initial rise in incomes, fertility increases, only to decline later. An important input into all these debates is the employment status of the, woman: while data from industrialised societies indicate that there is a negative relationship between female labour force participation and fertility, the same is not true of many countries of the third world. Again there are important cultural factors such as producing sons for the lineage, which influence reproductive decisions. Above all, child mortality rates are of crucial importance.

In India, the infant mortality rate is declining every year, it is still extremely high. This results in several conceptions so as to ensure between 2 and 3 living children. The current thinking in family welfare and birth control strategies in India is an excellent testing ground for notions of intervention, boundary maintenance and sense of individual identity. Under the guise of providing more choices – and hence respecting a woman's sense of self – the State is seeking to intervene in her life through a series of invasive measures. It is not difficult to link the sudden frenzy surrounding new reproductive technologies and structural reform. As already pointed out, population growth has been identified as a major hindrance to economic development: A recent official document on the economic scenario has zeroed in on population growth as a "critical problem."

Clearly, the controversial issue of reproductive control and concomitant strategies impinge directly on ethical problems such as who makes the decision, the scope for choice-making, to woman's integral right to control her body and so on. Equally evident is the fact that in order to have an impact, the State, as the primary agency for effecting population control, has to work out carefully its policies and plans for implementation.

While the State has not felt obligated to act to improve the working conditions of the majority of women, its enthusiasm over new contraceptive technologies, a direct intervention in a very sensitive area of their lives is significant. In other words, the State is a selective interventionist. Even if it's accepted that due to the nature of women's work, the scope for intervention is limited, there are other areas, namely improved and extensive childcare and school facilities and access to health care, through which the State can improve the quality of Indian women's lives. There is little evidence, however, of these being priority areas. As a result, women combine their innumerable roles often with little or no support from the State. Expected help from family members shifts the responsibility disproportionately to female children.

The large majority of Indian women combine a multiplicity of roles, each with different health implications; however, the role of producer seems to dominate over other functions because women are producing most of the time. Either as home workers and managers, unpaid family labour or as workers in the competitive gender-biased employment market, women spend a major part of their lives in production. This aspect of existence occupies much more space and time than do consumption and distribution. It is also one where interfaces between different situations have not been worked out. In fact, while there is an abundance of women and work-studies, few look at the implications of hours of labour on a woman's body and mind.

Maternal Care Indicators

The three components of maternal care, that is, antenatal care, natal care and postnatal care are taken separately as dependent variables.

(a) Antenatal Care

- No antenatal care at all
- Minimum three antenatal checkups
- First antenatal check-up during the first trimester
- Two or more tetanus toxoid injections during pregnancy
- Received Iron Folic Acid (IFA) syrup or tablets for three months during pregnancy and
- Full ANC (Utilizing all the recommended antenatal care.

(b) Natal Care

- Institutional delivery
- Home delivery with the assistance of health professionals, and
- Home delivery without the assistance of health professionals.

(c) Postnatal Care

- Postnatal check-up within two months of delivery.

Women's Health Issues in the Era of Globalization

We now look at some trends in the post-reform period. Data from Sri Lanka that started on a programme of economic reform in 1977 indicates that an increasing awareness on health issues is coupled with the growing incidence of diseases associated with stress, particularly those of the cardio-respiratory kind. A similar pattern is emerging in India with the advent of tropical diseases like falciparun malaria and Japanese B encephalitis; stress-and-environment related cardiovascular complaints, respiratory and endemic intestinal problems as well as nervous disorders. It is likely that with continued rural-urban migration, the mushrooming of unhealthy towns and cities and the degradation of the natural environment combined with jobs which increasingly concentrate workers in industries, Export Promotion Zones and sweat shops, the range of diseases and illnesses will increase. Women and their health will be adversely affected as they form the basis of the pool of cheap labour, essential for the growth of EPZs.

In the context of the health sector it is important to look for growth per se, but for growth which is the result of a well-thought out strategy based on an assessment of felt needs.

In this case, attempts at satisfying safety net requirements by focusing on targets and numbers and thereby pumping more money into physical infrastructures and salaries and not human resources, means that the needs of the people have to be satisfied by the private sector: with the emphasis on privatisation, the marketised health sector is growing rapidly, putting, as we have seen, an increasing load on the family budget.

Growing dependence on the private sector in health is coupled with spiralling drug prices. In keeping with the reformist ideology, the New Drug Policy (1994) and the Drug Price Control Order of 1995 granted major concessions to the drug industry by way of reduced price and production controls. Not only is the consumer market flooded with drugs-many of which have registered a price increase of between 50-150 per cent after 1993 – but also quality control has been an early casualty. Health activist and, researcher Mira Shiva has commented that while a majority of the 80,000 drugs in the Indian market today are spurious, ineffective and even hazardous, the Drug Control Authority is so over-stretched that it cannot carry out basic quality control tests. The following studies show how patterns of health care have changed in the post-reform period in some selected areas. Among other things, due to an increasingly minimalist State presence, dependence on the private sector is growing.

EVEN BEFORE 1991, KERALA WAS THE BEST EXAMPLE OF AN INDIAN STATE WITH POSITIVE

Development indicators – and a high rate of use of available health facilities: female literacy is almost 90 per cent it is the only state with a sex ratio favouring women and lower than average birth and death rates. Recent surveys have shown that the state's population is extremely health conscious, with high percentages of child immunisation as well as institutional deliveries of babies, the figures for which are well above the national average. At the same time, it is also a state where death due to vehicular accidents and suicide are high; interestingly both these are major causes of mortality in developed countries. In a study of health status in Kerala, the increasing prevalence of deaths due to cancer, diabetes and disorders of the nervous system indicate that "diseases of poverty have been substituted by diseases of affluence."

Clearly, whatever the cause, the achievements of the state with regard to mortality decline can be heavily attributed to the utilisation of health services. Not only is health expenditure—at both the individual household, and state level-one of the highest in the country but also it is the growing private sector, which is being increasingly patronised. Due largely to foreign remittances, the average family in Kerala is able to afford health care and medical attention. At the same time, the state also has a higher than average morbidity rate, and sickness prevalence has increased as the mortality rate has decreased. This seeming paradox is easily understood if we take into account changing perceptions of health with higher levels of literacy and awareness is well as an "excessive concern with the health of children and pregnant women."

Another recent study of the post-reform period of 52 households in the semi-urban locality of Kozhikhode (Kerala) showed that the per capita medical expenditure has risen by 141 per cent in the 1991-94 periods. The expenditure on drugs per capita rose by 75.9 per cent for the same period; this rate was much higher than the overall consumer expenditure for all the households. In the present context it is particularly alarming that most of the expenditure is in the growing private sector where unscrupulous doctors with their arsenal of medical equipment, laboratories, tests, scans and so on are becoming increasingly popular. It need hardly be added that the entire public health system is not able to cope with the "increasing demands from a population which is conscious of the quality of care."

It is not difficult to extrapolate from the case of Kerala that in time the rest of India is likely to follow suit; however, what is even more disturbing is that even before other development indicators have caught up, a self-interested private sector in health care is likely-to take over. In other words, the inability of the State to satisfy a growing demand—which may be caused by a combination of better awareness as well as an actual growth in disease and illness—will result in an increasing reliance on whatever facilities are available. Our argument here is that there is enough evidence to suggest that with access to institutional facilities in either the public or private sector, not only do mortality and morbidity-rates come down, but also perceptions of health and general well-being improve.

According to some nutritionists the nutritional status does not depend on standard economic variables such as income, expenditure and consumption alone: for instance, the nutrition of a girl child, is determined not only by household income and its uses but also by "the educational level of her parents, the time-utilisation decisions of her mother, the number of her siblings, her vulnerability to gender discrimination, her activity level and exposure to social stimulation, the quality of the environment etc."

Health care together with nutrition is a household resource whose disbursement depends on perceptions of entitlements as well as the ability to satisfy these entitlements. While the internal dynamics and resources of a household are instrumental in determining entitlements, certain exogenous factors either facilitate or hinder these decisions. This means access to as well as ability to use institutions and opportunities, which will increase the resource base—material, emotional and otherwise—which underpin entitlements.

The following discussion will illustrate how child health is dependent on levels of maternal advancement, which are determined by factors—both endogenous as well as exogenous—to the household. Using the variables of women's educational, occupational and marital status as determinants for infant survival.

There is an urgent need then in the post-reform period to improve women's access to education, information and communications, through formal schooling, informally through community groups, NGOs and the National Literacy Mission; in the present context, it is of vital importance for the sustained health of not just the woman but also of her family members, and in particular the girl child. We would argue that it is of vital importance to understand the role of family and community traditions, local knowledge systems, word of mouth communications through voluntary organisations and NGOs, and indeed the State, on health status.

Clearly the Indian State is dragging its feet in the social sector both at the level of allocation of funds as well in an assessment of priorities. In doing so, it is limiting its competence in moving out of the endemic crisis situation in the social sector. The question is, why is the State reluctant to make the safety net work? India is a federal structure where financial responsibilities are shared between the Central Government and the states. A look at how states allocate their funds for the social sector becomes relevant in this assessment of priorities. In the post-reform period, most Indian states "have shown no marked thrust on public health." While states such as Kerala and Tamil Nadu "which have a strong political commitment to the goals of human development" had "protected" expenditure in the areas of health and education, this was not the case in the BIMARU states of Bihar, Madhya Pradesh, Rajasthan and Uttar Pradesh. As we have seen, these were already the states with low levels of achievement in development indicators. There is also information that these states have an above average annual increase of reported crimes against women. A study of 17 villages conducted to assess the impact of economic reforms on women's health indicated that women are now under increasing levels of stress and rarely have the time to visit a health centre or a doctor. In other words, though women's lives are becoming more difficult and they are subjected to increasing degrees of violence within the home and at the work place, strategies and policies are not fine tuned to these realities. An approach which takes into account voices from the grassroots is vital if the present crisis in the health sector is not to lapse into a phase of irreversibility. Such an approach would also take into consideration that access to a facility is dependent on a range, of factors, not unimportant among, which is the cost of the facility.

Despite its inadequacies and shortcomings, the State-run health care system is heavily subsidised; thus, access to it should be improved and not replaced by the private sector. Yet, under the economic reforms of the Congress Government led by P.V. Narasimha Rao, there, were ample indications that large-scale privatisation of health care was being seriously considered. In March 1995, a meeting of government officials, NGOs, health activists and others was convened in Jaipur to debate a recent World Bank document, Policy and Finance Strategies for Strengthening Primary Health Care Services. The recommendations of the meeting asked for more private sector involvement and experimentation with private contracting of public health services. The spirit of the meeting was clearly the need for alternatives to the fragile public health system.

The situation may be somewhat different now as it is unlikely that the United Front Government will push through privatisation of health services; the question is, will it empower the State to do more for the disprivileged? At the same time, it is clear that a structural Adjustment programmes will, at one point of time or the other, look to the marketability of a product or service. There is no evidence in the fifty years of India's Independence that its health sector has been 'marketable'; the question of course is, should health care policy be governed by market forces or by the needs of the large bulk of its population who are unable to afford private medical attention?

EMPOWERMENT, AUTONOMY AND ATTITUDE OF WOMEN: SOLUTION TO HEALTH PROBLEMS

Empowerment is a process, by which women gain greater control over material and intellectual resources which will assist them to increase their self reliance, and enhance them to assert their independent rights, and challenge the ideology of patriarchy and the gender-based discrimination against women. This will also enable them to organize themselves to assert their autonomy to make decisions and choices, and ultimately eliminate their own subordination in all the institutions and structures of society (Batliwala, 1995; Malhotra, 2002).

Many studies have identified education, work participation, exposure to mass media and household standard of living as determinants or factors or sources for empowerment. Education enhances a woman's position through decision-making autonomy, control over resources, knowledge, and exposure to the modern world and husband wife closeness. Female work participation in non-agricultural sector and level of wage are also considered as determinants of empowerment. Woman's gainful employment outside home exposes her to the outside world; delays age at marriage, provide a sense of financial independence and increase her bargaining power and autonomy within the household and society. Also, women's paid employment could alter the perception of women's value and motivate investment in the girl child's education and health.

The investment of power on a woman becomes evident through her participation in household decision-making, financial autonomy and freedom of movement. Lack of decision-making power by a woman could result into lesser timely health seeking behaviour and leads to greater adverse health consequences.

The input of empowerment also has to enhance her intrinsically by changing her attitude or ideology into egalitarian ideas, otherwise the power or autonomy she has gained, could not channel her to make welfare and developmental decisions. A fundamental shift in perceptions, or "inner transformation," is essential to the formulation of developmental choices. Non-egalitarian gender relations deny woman an egalitarian decision making role during health care need, and other family matters. Positive change in the attitude could alter the current submissive image of an Indian woman as only a reproductive tool, homemaker, caregiver and subordinate.

CONCLUSION

In the Country Report prepared for the Fourth World Conference on Women held in Beijing in 1995, the Government of India acknowledged that due to the new policies, over-all, the economic pressures may compel households to resort to various difficult survival strategies; further, the anticipated reduction in services implies that women may also have to allocate more time to activities that were previously at least partially provided by the state. Concluding that more research and time were necessary before the impact of structural adjustment programmes on women could be assessed; the document was hypothesising on likely fallouts. Clearly, if the Indian economy is to be competitive it has to liberalise and become a part of the global nexus. However, this does not mean that the State should be free to adopt an increasingly minimalist position in areas that determine the survival of a large bulk of its population. Health care is one such area; descriptions of the inner life of the household indicate how a complex interplay of factors determines entitlements and shares. The inability of the State to provide a workable system of health care only exacerbates the tensions experienced by underprivileged women whose daily lives are, in any case, becoming increasingly difficult. Any reform should be preceded by a period of intense debate, discussion and an elaboration of strategies and goals. It can be assumed that stabilisation and the structural adjustment programme were adopted after such exercises had been carried through. However, no such thinking seems to have influenced thinking on the social sector. At this point of time, there are no indications that it will not be the same story of more funds for a battery of new targets to be achieved. Those in positions of authority need to develop an unblinkered approach and look beyond their traditional information brokers and panacea of well-worn methods and approaches. A genuine commitment to distributive justice and equity requires much more than declining budgetary allocations; apart from a political will which means business it also requires the freedom and inclination to think of options and alternatives, to recognise that theories of rights and obligations will not work by maintaining a depersonalized, distancing attitude towards others. Above all for such a commitment to be meaningful, the State has to be prepared to listen to the multiple voices which question its policies; in other words, the State and its functionaries have to acknowledge the role of civil society in providing the 'human face', the critical edge, to reform and its often unacceptable assumptions about the citizens of a country faced with wide-reaching re-definitions of both their public and private spaces.

REFERENCES

Batliwala, Srilatha (n.d.). "Women and Health Care." Bombay: Foundation for Research in Community Health.

Bardhan, P. 1984. The Political Economy of Development in India. New Delhi: Oxford University Press.

Bidwai, P. 1996. "The Social Deficit—Need for Universal not Targetted PDS." The Times of India, August 2.

Chatterjee, M. 1983. "Women's Access to Health Care: A Critical Issue for Child Health," paper presented at the ICMR Conference on Child Health, Nutrition and Family Planning, Bangalore.

Dreze, J. 1993. "Nutrition and Health in Rural India", Economic and Political Weekly, February 13.

Duggal, R. 1995. "Public Health Budgets: Recent Trends", Radical Journal of Health, Vol. I new series No. 3, July-September.

1996. "Health Sector Financing in the Context of Women's Health", ISST, Occasional Paper No. 4/96.

Elson, Dianne. 1994. "Structural Adjustment with Gender Awareness?", Indian Journal of Gender Studies, Vol. I, No. 2, July-December.

George, Allen and Sunil, Nandraj.1993. "State of Health Care in Maharashtra—A Comparative Analysis," Economic and Political Weekly, August 8-14.

Ghosh, Arun, 1996. "Health Care and Globalisation—Case for a Selective Approach," Economic and Political Weekly, February 24.

Government of India. 1975. Towards Equality: Report of the Committee on the Status of Women in India, Ministry of Education.

Gunawardana, A.J.1995. "The Local Impact of Global Transformation the Sri Lankan Experiences", Mimeograph, Eighth Biennial AASSREC Conference, New Delhi.

Gupta, M., and Borkar A. n.d. "Women's Work, Fertility and Access to Health Care: A Socio-economic Study of Two Villages in Pune District," Bombay: The Foundation for Research in Community Health.

Indian Council of Medical Research. 1991. Evaluation of Quality of Family Welfare Services at Primary Health Centre Level, New Delhi: ICMR.

Irudaya Rajan and K.S. James. 1993. "Kerala's Health Status: Some Issues," Economic and Political Weekly, September 4.

Karlekar, M. *et. al.*, 1995. "Domestic Violence" unpublished report prepared for the Centre for Women's Development Studies.

Krishnan, T.N. and R. Kavita Rao. 1995. "Structural Adjustment, Globalisation and Social Development in India," Mimeograph, New Delhi : ICSSR.

Mathai, S. 1989. "Women and Health System" in C. Gopalan and S. Kaur (eds.) Women and Nutrition in India, New Delhi, Nutrition Foundation of India.

Ramalingaswami, Prabha. 1987. "Women's Access to Health Care," Economic and Political Weekly, July 4.

World Bank, The. 1996. Improving Women's Health in India, Washington: The World Bank.

4

Rural Women Empowerment through Self Help Groups

Dr. Shobana Nelasco & Junofy Anto Rozarina

Self Help Groups are the self-governed, peer-controlled informal group of people with similar socio-economic background, having a desire to come forward voluntarily for a mutual agreement of helping each other for productive or consumptive purposes.

Though the SHG is a common activity, generally in most of the cases just one person takes the initiative. The potential members of the community are generally invited to join. But the group elects leaders democratically and conducts meetings.

The purpose of this chapter is to examine the operation of Self Help Groups and to examine the comparative growth of Self Help Groups in India and Tamil Nadu.

Self Help Group concept is the brainchild of Grameen Bank of Bangladesh, which was founded by Prof. Mohammed Yunus of Chittagong University in the year 1975. The Self Help Group concept has got a mushrooming growth in various parts of the world in different forms.

In India, Self Help Groups (DWCRA Groups) are the sub-schemes of Integrated Rural Development Scheme (I.R.D.P.) started in the year 1982-83. The main aim of the scheme is to bring together the women members of rural families living below the poverty line with a view to generate self-employment on sustainable basis.

In India, the Self Help Groups are working under three major drives: They are self-driven Self Help Groups, Government driven Self Help Groups and Non-Governmental Organisation's (NGOs-voluntary agencies including many Catholic Churches) driven Self

Help Groups. The NGO driven mechanism is comparatively functioning very effectively. The motivation levels of NGOs are comparatively higher because of their efforts of survival. But it is also true that not all NGOs are sincere in their tasks, because for such NGOs, social outlook becomes secondary.

Formation of Self Help Groups

Generally one person takes the initiative of starting a Self Help Group. Interested people are motivated to join the team after clarifying the activities and mutual benefits. More likeminded members are promoted to come together for a common cause. Democratic elections are conducted to elect their leaders. Meetings are called on at regular intervals. Size of each group ranges from 12 to 20. NGOs are generally the steering instruments and motivating factors of these groups.

Activities of Self Help Groups

- Create a common fund through their regular savings.
- Organizing adult education centers.
- Organizing Mahila Mandals and Youth Clubs.
- Organizing Balwadis.
- Renewing the work of Jana Shiksha Nilayam—center for peoples education.
- Promoting Self Help Groups and their members.
- To promote themselves in Economic Activities.
- To help women in leadership position.

Mechanism of Operation

The methodology behind Self Help Groups is collective wisdom of the poor and the collective organizational capabilities.

Peer Pressure: Financial Institutions use social collateral in the form of peer groups to ensure loan repayment. The peer pressure encourages borrowers to be very selective about their peer group members and to repay loans in full and on time.

Peer Group Monitoring: The group members have an incentive to monitor one another to ensure timely repayment of the loan.

Mobilization of Saving: The Self Help Groups encourages group savings as collateral substitute of the loan.

Voluntary Formation of the Group: The groups are voluntarily formed by the borrowers. Use of self-selected groups of borrowers, generally consist of a minimum of five members, who guarantee each other's loan.

Joint Liability: The joint liability concept means that SHGs should be formed of likeminded people who would voluntarily take up joint liability for the group/individual loans.

Prasad Acharya (2004), in his study have analyzed the responses of women loan holders of the SEDP and have found out that most of the women felt that violence had gone down as a result of women's access to loans for a number of reasons: The easing of economic stress had reduced one of the causes of violence and the fact that women were now seen to be sharing the responsibility for family provisioning with men rather than constituting part of male responsibility. Women also felt that they had greater bargaining power within the family and could with hold co-operation if husbands proved extremely abusive.

According to Gurumoorthy (2000)[1], empowering women contributes to economic and social development. Economic progress in any country whether developed or underdeveloped could be achieved through social development. The self-help group disburses micro credit to rural women for the purpose of making them enterprising women and encouraging them to enter into entrepreneurial activities. Credit needs of the rural women are fulfilled totally through the self-help groups. SHGs enhance equality of status of women as participants, decision makers and beneficiaries in the democratic, economic, social and cultural spheres of life. SHGs also encourage women to take active part in socio-economic progress of our nation.

As according to Karmakar (2002), in India, in 1992-93 there were only 255 SHGs. But in 2001-02, it rose to a great height of 4,61,478 SHGs. Here the time series equation found for India is Y= -172552 + 50624.3 X. X being the years considering 1992-93 as the first year.

In Tamil Nadu, especially in South Tamil Nadu this concept has become a very popular concept among the rural poor. In Tamil Nadu, in 1992-93 there were 22 SHGs. From 1998-99, there is a steep rise. It rose to 2,633 SHGs. In 2001-02, it reached, 27,539 SHGs. Regression line of best fit for Tamil Nadu is Y= -2376.0 + 796.082 X.

Gurumoorthy, T.R., "Self-Help Groups Empower Rural Women", Kurukshetra, Vol. 48, No. 5, February 2000.

Progress of SHGs and their Bank Loans in India and Tamil Nadu

Year	India		Tamil Nadu	
	No. of SHGs	Bank Loan (in Lakhs)	No. of SHGs	Bank Loan (Rs. in Lakhs)
1992-93	255	3	22	2.239
1993-94	620	7	34	4.247
1994-95	2,122	24	203	20.994
1995-96	4,757	61	205	33.468
1996-97	8,598	118	408	59.520
1997-98	14,317	238	444	217.740
1998-99	32,995	571	2,633	558.935
1999-2000	1,14,775	1,930	7,715	1,958.237
2000-01	2,63,825	4,809	16,926	5,37.523
2001-02	4,61,478	10,263	27,539	10,463.598
2003-04	5,39,395	5,454	–	
Total	**9,03,742**	**18,034**	**56,129**	**1,84,56.501**
Compound growth rate	**119%**	**146%**	**124%**	**154%**

Source : NABARD Reports, 2006.

In Tamil Nadu, introduction of Self Help Groups were in three different phases. In Phase I self help groups were started in the year 1997-98 but the micro-credit was introduced in January 1999. The first phase has covered the following districts, Vilupuram, Dharmapuri, Namakkal, Cuddalore, Ramnad, Thiruvarur, Vellore, Madurai, Thiruvalur, Salem, Karur, ThoothukudSSi, Theni and Virudhunagar.

In Phase II, self help groups were started in the year 1998-99 but the micro-credit was given from January 1999 onwards. The second phase has covered the following districts. Sivagangai, Tirunelveli, Trichy, Thiruvannamalai, Pudukkottai, Nilgiris and Erode.

In Phase III, self help groups were started in the year 1999-2000. This phase covered Coimbatore, Kanchipuram, Kanyakumari, Perambalur, Thanjavur, Nagapattinam and Dindigul districts.

In Tamil Nadu Self Help Groups are growing at a faster rate. The Compound Growth Rate of Self Help Group in Tamil Nadu is 124 per cent, whereas the Growth Rate of Self Help Group in India is 119 per cent. Self Help Groups are growing at a faster rate in South Tamil Nadu when compared to North Tamil Nadu.

Self Help Groups are the agencies which are very crucial in promoting thrift and finance mobilization. The existence of Self Help Groups helps empowering women and empowering the poor. Through these groups lot of public works and social works can be implemented.

To conclude it was realised that Self Help Groups are still weak and are yet to train themselves in the field of micro finance. It was also found out that this concept is popular among the women. Men also should be included. Advertising and marketing strategies need to be adopted. The Self Help Groups are working at different levels and from different experiences independently. The Self Help Groups are working as different islands and sometimes there is competition and difference of opinion among them. And hence networking will be a good solution. At present the Self Help Groups are shelters of illiterates and hence efforts can be made to attract the educated unemployed also. Through Marketing and canvassing mechanism, efforts should be made to attract more educated members.

Swami Vivekanandha words are very powerful and sure will make any reader to think about, 'I ask earnestly to open girls' schools in every village. If women are educated ... culture, knowledge, power and devotion awaken in the land. That nation which does not respect women, has never become great, nor will ever in future ... the principle reason why our race has so much degenerated is that we have no respect for these living images of Shakti'.

REFERENCES

Fredrick. J. 'S.H.G.s Gateway to Success for Rural Women Entrepreneurs', Kissan World, September, 2005, Vol. 32, No. 9, p. 60.

Gupta. S.K., A. Shrivastava, 'A Study of Working of Self-Help Groups in M.P.', Indian Journal of Agricultural Economics, July-September 2001, Vol. 56, No. 3, p. 470.

Gurumurthy, 'Self Help Groups to Empower Rural Women', Kurukshetra, January 2006, p. 36.

Jayanthi .J, "Dairy as an Instrument of Women Empowerment: A Study", Southern Economist, August 15, 2006, Vol. 45, No. 8, pp. 17-20.

Natarajan, Dr. R. Ponmurugan, "Self Help Groups: Bank Linkage Programme" Kisan world, February 2006, Vol. 33, No. 2, p. 37.

Perumal, V.M.S., 'SHGs Empowering Women at Grassroots', Social Welfare, July 2005 Vol. 52, No. 52, No. 4, p. 5.

Prasad Acharya (2004), Micro-Finance and Women's Empowerment : Evidence from Bangladesh, A Paper Presented in the Seminar on Rural Women and Economic Empowerment of Women in South Asia at Social Science Institute, Allahabad, India.

Senthil Vadivoo and Sekar, 'Self Help Groups—A Movement for Women Empowerment', Kisan World, July 2004, p. 13.

5

Educational, Social and Financial Situation of Women in India

Shubhi Agarwal & Dr. Manju Goyal

You can tell the condition of a nation by looking at the status of its women.

—Jawaharlal Nehru

India is the original home of the Mother Goddess. The status of women in India has been subject to many great changes over the past few millennia. In our ancient history, we have many instances of women scholars and women rulers. Stories from mythology and folklore are recounted to prove that women in India have always been honored and respected.

Some scholars believe that in ancient India, women enjoyed equal status in all fields of life with men. Works by ancient Indian grammarians such as *Patanjali* and *Katyayana* suggest that women were educated in the early Vedic period. *Rigvedic* verses suggest that the women married at a mature age and were probably free to select their husband.

According to studies, women enjoyed equal status and rights during the early Vedic period. However, later (approximately 500 B.C.), the status of women began to decline with the Islamic invasion of Babur and the Mughal empire and later Christianity curtailing women's freedom and rights.

Although reformatory movements such as Jainism allowed women to be admitted to the religious order, by and large, the women in India faced confinement and restrictions. The practice of child marriages is believed to have started from around sixth century.

The Indian women's position in the society further deteriorated during the medieval period. Sati, child marriages and ban on widow remarriages became part of social life in India. The Muslim conquest in the Indian subcontinent brought the *purdah* practice in the Indian society. Among the Rajputs of Rajasthan, the *Jauhar* was practiced. In some parts of India, the *Devadasis* or the temple women were sexually exploited. Polygamy was widely practiced especially among Hindu Kshatriya rulers. In many Muslim families, women were secluded to *Zenana.*

In spite of these conditions, even then some women excelled in the fields of politics, literature, education and religion. Razia Sultana became the only women monarch to have ever ruled Delhi. The Gond queen Durgavati ruled for fifteen years, before she lost her life in a battle with Mughal emperor Akbar's general Asaf Khan in 1564. Chand Bibi defended Ahmednagar against the mighty Mughal forces of Akbar in 1590s. Jehangir's wife Nur Jehan effectively wielded imperial power and was recognized as the real force behind the Mughal throne. Shivaji's mother, Jijabai was deputed as queen regent, because of her ability as a warrior and administrator. In South India, many women administered villages, towns, divisions and heralded social and religious institutions.

The *Bhakti* cults tried to restore women's status and questioned some of the forms of oppression. Mirabai, a female saint-poet, was one of the most important *Bhakti* movement figures. Guru Nanak, the first Guru of Sikhs also preached the message of equality between men and women. He advocated that women be allowed to lead religious assemblies; to perform and lead congregational hymn singing called Kirtan or Bhajan; become members of religious management committees; to lead armies on the battlefield; have equality in marriage and equality in Amrit (Baptism). Other Sikh Gurus also preached against the discrimination against women.

During the British Raj, many reformers such as Ram Mohan Roy, Ishwar Chandra Vidyasagar, Jyotirao Phule etc. fought for the upliftment of women. Raja Ram Mohan Roy's efforts led to the abolition of the Sati practice in 1829. Ishwar Chandra Vidyasagar's crusade for the improvement in condition of widows led to the Widow Remarriage Act of 1856. Many women reformers such as Pandita Ramabai also helped the cause of women upliftment.

Rani Lakshmi Bai, the Queen of Jhansi, led the Indian Rebellion of 1857 against the British. She is now widely considered as a nationalist hero. Begum Hazrat Mahal, the co-ruler of Awadh, was another ruler who led the revolt of 1857. She refused the deals with the British and later retreated to Nepal. The Begums of Bhopal were also few of the notable female rulers during this period. They did not observe *purdah* and were trained in martial arts. Though Mahatma Gandhi himself married at the age of thirteen, he later urged people to boycott child marriages and called upon the young men to marry the child widows.

Women played an important part in India's independence struggle. The Rani of Jhansi Regiment of Subhash Chandra Bose's Indian National Army consisted entirely of women including Captain Lakshmi Sahgal. Sarojini Naidu, a poet and a freedom fighter, was the first Indian women to become the President of the Indian National Congress and the first women to become the Governor of a state in India.

There have been many changes in India since the country gained its independence from Great Britain in 1947, the most impressive being the rise of the Indian economy. India was one of the first countries in the world to give women the right to vote. The Indian Constitution is one of the most progressive in the world, and guarantees equal rights for men and women. The Constitution of India guarantees to all Indian women equality (Article 14), no discrimination by the State (Article 15(1)), equality of opportunity (Article 16), and equal pay for equal work (Article 39 (d)). In addition, it allows special provisions to be made by the State in favour of women and children (Article 15(3)), renounces practices derogatory to the dignity of women (Article 51 (A) (e)), and also allows for provisions to made by the State for securing just and humane conditions of work and for maternity relief (Article 42). The Government of India declared 2001 as the Years of Women's Empowerment (Swashakti). The National Policy for the Empowerment of Women came was passed in 2001. In 2005, the Women's Reservation Bill was passed, providing 33 per cent reservation for women in Parliament and State Assembly. Some of the notable women leaders in India include Sushma Swaraj, Vasundhara Raje Scindia, Sheila Dikshit, Jayalalitha, Uma Bharati, Mayawati, Mamata Banerjee and Sonia Gandhi. On July 25, 2007 the country's ever first women President Pratibha Patil was sworn in.

With the rise of a new wave of feminism across the world, a new generation of Indian feminists emerged. Women have developed according to their situations and have become advanced in various fields. Female activists united over issues such as female infanticide, gender bias, women health, and female literacy. Since alcoholism is often associated with violence against women in India, many women groups launched anti-liquor campaigns in Andhra Pradesh, Himachal Pradesh, Haryana, Orissa, Madhya Pradesh and other states. Many Indian Muslim women have questioned the fundamental leader's interpretation of women's rights under the *Shariat* law and have criticized the triple *talaq* system.

In 1990s, grants from foreign donor agencies enabled the formation of new women-oriented NGOs. Self-help groups and NGOs such as Self-Employed Women's Association (SEWA) have played a major role in women's rights in India. Many women have emerged as leaders of local movements.

Traditions such as *sati, jauhar,* child marriage, and *devadasi* have been banned and are largely defunct. However, some cases of these practices are still found in remote parts of India. The *purdah* is still practiced by many Indian muslim women and women in villages.

In recent times, contemporary Indian feminists are fighting for abortion, breast feeding, co-operation, control of the female body, diversity, divorce, education, equal pay, freedom, gender, independence, individual autonomy, maternity leave, nonviolence, reproduction, rights, sexuality, and tolerance and against discrimination, domestic violence, objectification, patriarchy, prostitution, sexism, and stereotypes. Medha Patkar, Madhu Kishwar, and Brinda Karat are some feminist social workers and politicians who continue their fight against fundamental casues of women's oppression in post-independent India. One of the most famous female business success stories is the Shri Mahila Griha Udyog, the makers of the Lijjat papad. In 2006, Kiran Mazumdar-Shaw, who started Biocon–one of India's first biotech companies, was rated India's richest women. Lalita Gupte and Kalpana Morparia (both were the only businesswomen in India who made our list of the Forbes World's Most Powerful Women), run India's second-largest bank ICICI Bank.

As per a synopsis by IndiaOne Stop.Com:

- India has the world's largest number of professionally qualified women.

- India has more female doctors, surgeons, scientists and professors than the United States.
- India has more working women than any other country in the world. This includes female workers at all levels of skill—from the surgeon and the airline pilot to bus conductors and menial labourers.
- Moves are underway to empower women. The most news-making development was the introduction of the Women's Bill in Parliament in late 1998: The Bill seeks to reserve a certain percentage of seats in Parliament for women. There is a National Human Rights Commission for Women that handle all human rights violations against women. There is a National Council for Women that advocate policy for Women. There is an entire ministry for women that formulates and implements policy for them.

Also some of the facts that further prove the rising status of women in India are:

- 1996: Indira Gandhi becomes the first women Prime Minister of India.
- 1970: Kamaljit Sandhu becomes the first Indian women to win a Gold in the Asian Games.
- 1972: Kiran Bedi becomes the first female recruit to join the Indian Police Service.
- 1989: Justice M. Fathima Beevi becomes the first women judge of the Supreme Court of India.
- 1997: Kalpana Chawla becomes the first Indian women to go into Space.
- 1992: Priya Jhingan becomes the first lady Cadet to join the Indian Army.
- 2004: Punita Arora becomes the first women in the Indian Army to don the highest rank of Lt. General.
- 2005: Manndhir Rajput, a 34-year-old women from Ludhiana, Punjab becomes the first Indian women to become an engine driver of trains with the New South Wales Rail Corporation, Australia.
- 2007: Pratibha Patil becomes the first women President of India.

The last few years have seen dramatic increases in the space available for women in Indian society—a consequence of affirmative policies and programmes by the government and initiatives by NGOs and other civil society groups. Most of all, these achievements are the result of years of determined advocacy, campaigning and action for change by women themselves. Women in India now participate in all activities such as education, politics, media, art and culture, service sectors, science and technology etc.

All this supports the contention that Indian women are free and equal members of society. Alongside this, however, is another body of evidence. The official statistics that are presented in government reports, the findings of local surveys and, most significantly, the daily experiences of women and men as documented in the media paint a very different picture.

While some women are emerging as strong and confident individuals, in control of their own lives and capable of raising their voices to demand their rights, others face a very different reality, promoting the question: Is the glass half full or half empty?

Not all facets of Indian women have enjoyed the same advancement in health, education and other human development issues. India will not realize the full benefit of an improving economy until the lives of the Indian people and especially Indian women improve. The inequalities that exist among region, social class and gender prevent the growth of the Indian economy from improving the lives of many everyday Indian people. Nowhere is inequality more evident than in the lives of Indian women, and likewise, there is no sector more affected by the lack of improvement in social issues. Perhaps the best evidence that women are not benefiting from an improved India is the fact that men outnumber women, whereas in most countries the opposite is true.

The most damaging denial of opportunity that women in India suffer is the ability to receive an education. The Indian Government is committed to improving the education of girls. Its constitution promises "free and compulsory education for all children until they complete the age of fourteen." Though it is gradually rising, the female literacy rate in India is lower than the male literacy rate. According to the National Sample Survey Data of 1997, only the States of Kerala and Mizoram have approached universal female literacy rates.

Despite the improvements in literacy, one of the main concern seems to be keeping girls in school. There are sometimes economic reasons for a girl to withdraw from school. She may need to help with family responsibilities, which may include caring for other siblings, cooking and cleaning. There is also the perception that educating a daughter will not benefit the parents and it may make it difficult for parents to find a match for their daughter. It is believed that a girl is best matched with a more educated husband; therefore girls are withdrawn from school at an early age. Another barrier to female education India is inadequate school facilities (such as sanitary facilities), shortage of female teachers and gender bias in curriculum (majority of the female characters being depicted as weak and helpless).

This low level of literacy not only has a negative impact on women's lives but also on their families' lives and on their country's economic development. Numerous studies show that illiterate women have high levels of fertility and mortality, poor nutritional status, low earning potential and little autonomy within the household. Additionally, the lack of an educated population can be an impediment to the country's economic development.

Contrary to the common perception, a large per cent of women in India work. In rural India, agriculture and allied industrial sectors employ as much as 89.5 per cent of the total female labour. However, there are far fewer women in the paid workforce than there are men. The majority of women in India are doing tasks that are not recognized by Indian society as meaningful. The majority of women work much longer hours then men, but much of their work is nurturing, and therefore not recognized as important. In the agricultural field, much of the work women do is pre and post-production, such as weeding, livestock rearing, and processing; and because economic value is placed on the actual ouput, the work is not seen as important.

In most Indian families, women do not own any property in their own names, and do not get a share of parental property. Due to weak enforcement of laws protecting them, women continue to have little access to land and property. The Hindu personal laws of mid-1956s (applied to Hindus, Buddhists, Sikhs and Jains) gave women rights to inheritance. However, the sons had an independent share in the ancestral property, while the daughters' shares were based on the share received by their father. Hence, a father could effectively disinherit a daughter by renouncing his share of the ancestral property, but the son will continue to have a share in his own right. Additionally, married daughters, even those facing marital harassment, had no residential rights in the ancestral home. After amendment of Hindu laws in 2005, now women in have been provided the same status as that of men.

Police records show high incidence of crimes against women in India. The National Crime Records Bureau reported in 1998 that the growth rate of crimes against women would be higher than the population growth rate by 2010. Earlier, many cases were not registered with the police due to the social stigma attached to rape and molestation cases. Official statistics show that there has been a dramatic increase in the number of reported crimes against women.

In 1961, the Government of India passed the Dowry Prohibition Act, making the dowry demands in wedding arrangements illegal. However, many cases of dowry-related domestic violence, suicides and murders are still being reported. Although amongst the urban educated, such dowry abuse has reduced dramatically.

India has a low sex ratio, the chief reason being that many women die before reaching adulthood. This can be attributed to female infanticides and sex-selective abortions. All medical tests that can be used to determine the sex of the child have been banned in India, due to incidents of these tests being used to get rid of unwanted female children before birth. Female infanticide (killing of girl infants) is still prevalent in some rural areas.

The incidents of domestic violence are higher among the lower Socio-Economic Classes (SECs). There are various instances of an inebriated husband beating up the wife often leading to severe injuries. Domestic violence is also seen in the form of physical abuse. The Protection of Women from Domestic Violence Act, 2005 came into froce on October 26, 2006.

The average female life expectancy today in India is low compared to many countries, but it has shown gradual improvement over the years. In many families, especially rural ones, the girls and women face nutritional discrimination within the family, and are anemic and malnourished. The maternal mortality in India is the second highest in the world. The average Indian women has little control over her own fertility and reproductive health. Women, particularly women in rural areas, do not have access to safe and self-controlled methods of contraception.

These differences in the health, education and standards of behaviour between the men and women of India, all contribute to the impairment of women's ability to improve their economic situation. The continued perception that women are not of value hinders women's ability to fully participate in the economy. The economic discrimination that the women of India suffer leads to a cycle of further discrimination in other areas and reinforces their low status.

Changes in the way Indian society views women will come through women's increased ability to participation in the economy, enhanced through education and legislation. Only when women are valued in their homes and communities will the lives of women in India improve, and when the lives of Indian women improve, those of their families will improve also. The change in thinking must begin in the minds of Indian women themselves. When women begin to see themselves as powerful, change will begin. India's constitution guarantees the rights of equal education and equal representation, but Indian women must have the courage to act on these rights when the oportunity is made available to them. Education will change the way women feel about themselves and the way they see their world. It is also important to increase the number of women participating in the political sphere that will make true change in the lives of everyday Imagine the growth that would be seen if every citizen in the country was given the dream, the change and the right, to full participate in the economy. Then India might truly become an economic superpower.

An UN Secretary General Kofi Annan has stated, "Gender equality is more than a goal in itself. It is a precondition for meeting the challenge of reducing poverty, promoting sustainable development and building good governance." This recognition is currently missing in India. Transforming the prevailing social discrimination against women must become the top priority, and must happen concurrently with increased direct action to rapidly improve the social and economic status of women. In this way, a synergy of progress can be achieved.

- As women receive greater education and training, they will earn more money.

- As women earn more money—as has been repeatedly shown-they spend it in the further education and health of their children, as opposed to men, who often spend it on drink, tobacco or other women.
- As women rise in economic status, they will gain greater social standing in the household and the village, and will have greater voice.
- As women gain influence and consciousness, they will make stronger claims to their entitlements-gaining further training, better access to credit and higher incomes—and command attention of police and courts when attacked.
- As women's economic power grows, it will be easier to overcome the tradition of "son preference" and thus put an end to the evil of dowry.
- As son preference declines and acceptance of violence declines, families will be more likely to educate their daughters, and age of marriage will rise.
- For every year beyond 4th grade that girls go to school, family size shrinks 20 per cent, child deaths drop 10 per cent and wages rise 20 per cent.
- As women are better nourished and marry later, will be healthier, more productive, and will give birth to healthier babies.

History proves that societies where men and women have played equal roles have been more balanced and prospered faster than those which have either been patriarchal or matriarchal. Women today more than even before will play a significant role in development of society.

Women are great carriers of value systems and it comes to them very naturally. Women are the one who will nurture the next generation, in whatever role they chose to be as a home maker or a professional. Women in India have made their mark in multiple fields—technology, literature, art, etc. There is hardly an industry/ sector where you wouldn't find women—and the women: men ratios are improving in all sectors in India.

Women would play an extremely important role in shaping the vision of a better India for an even brighter tomorrow—a country which is free from petty squabbles over caste, creed and religion, treats all its citizens with the same dignity and offers them equal opportunities at education and work.

6

Socio-Economic Condition of Rural Women in India

Dr. Birendra Kumar Jha

Because Women comprise half of human resources, they have been identified as key agents of sustainable development and women's equality is seen as central to a more holistic approach towards establishing new patterns and process of development that are sustainable. It needs hardly to be emphasized that human capital would be an extremely important, perhaps an inescapable input for the future of developing countries like India Human capital is already surging ahead to replace physical capital as the sole mover of the growth process. And so it has been recognized that all round development of human resources without any gender discrimination creates scope for speedy socio-economic development of a nation but unfortunately, gender discrimination prevails in the society and it is more severe in developing countries like India. Males dominate females in every sphere every where in the world. As a result men enjoy a higher status, while women have been leading a discriminated life. No doubt, biological distinction between man and women is found and women are physically weaker than men but there are no disparities in general intelligence between sexes; Gender equality is highly desirable as a feeling and realization of an equal status in all spheres of life, on the one hand, enhances the confidence and efficiency of a person and on the other hand, enables him/her to contribute in economic development of a nation and so realizing the need to improve the status of women and to remove the gender disparity, efforts are being made at national and international level.

In India, right from the beginning of Five Year Plan (1951-56) there has been endeavour towards the development of women.

However the Sixth Plan (1980-85) has been marked by a clear shift in the approach from welfare schemes to development oriented plans towards women although the consciousness generated by the report of the committee on the status of women (entitled' Towards Equality) led to changes in policies towards development of women in the Fifth Five Year Plan. In the Seventh Plan (1985-90) specific attention was paid to allocation for programmes/schemes which directly benefited women. The adoption of Women's Component Plan (WCP) is also traced back to the Seventh Plan which witnessed the initiation of a mechanism for identifying and monitoring schemes that extended benefits directly to women. In 1986, the Department of Women and Child Development (DWCD), under the Central Government's Ministry of Human Resource Development was entrusted the responsibility of monitoring 27 beneficiary oriented schemes under various sectors which directly benefited women. The Eighth Plan (1992-97) highlighted for the first time a gender perspective and the need to ensure a definite flow of funds from the general development sectors to women. The plan document made an express statement that "the benefits to development from different sectors should not by pass women and special programmes on women should complement the general development programmes. The latter, in turn, should reflect great gender sensitivity." The Ninth Plan (1997-2002) marked a significant progress in this regard. The plan adopted the Women's Component Plan as one of the major strategies and directed both the Central and State Government to ensure "not less than 30 per cent of the funds/benefits are earmarked in all the women's related sectors." The Tenth Plan (2002-07) marked another significant step forward as it envisaged "immediate action in tying up these two effective concepts of WCP and Gender Budgeting to play a complementary role to each other, and thus ensure both preventive and post facto action in enabling women to receive their rightful share from all the women-related general development sectors." The need for taking up Gender Budgeting was also felt in the National Policy for the Empowerment of Women, 2001 which observed, "Availability of adequate financial, human and market resources to implement the policy will be managed by concerned Department", and that the process will include, among other initiatives, "Assessment of benefits flowing to women and resource allocation to the programmes relating to them through an exercise of gender budgeting." The Eleventh Plan (2007-12) strategy for gender balancing takes care of the special needs of women. As a result of all these efforts discrimination against women seems to be declining in certain spheres, while in some other areas it is on an increase.

INDIA'S GLOBAL STATUS IN GENDER DEVELOPMENT

If there is gender equality, Gender related Development Index (GDI) and Human Development Index (HDI) would be the same but for almost all countries, the GDI is lower than the HDI indicating gender inequality everywhere (UNDP, 2002). Similar results appear (however with corresponding increased values of HDI and GDI) in Human Development Report 2005. GEM value ranges from less than 0.1 to more than 0.9 indicating enormous variation around the world in women empowerment (UNDP, 2005). The statistics in the HDR, 2005 reveal that the countries having a higher value of GDI (little lower than HDI) belong to the category of rich countries with a high GIP a high per capita income, lower percentage of population Below Poverty Line (BPL) and vice versa. While gender gaps in education are large in some countries and non-existent in some other, in economic participation and wealth sharing, gender gaps exist the world over. This indicates that women in almost all the countries are discriminated against and are leading a life with a lower socio-economic status as compared to men according to one or the other social, economic or political sharing indicator. While analyzing the status of women in selected twelve countries, (Harvinder Kaur, 2006) has found that GDI values are lower than HDI values and GEM values are further lower than GDI values irrespective of the human development category of the country.

What to talk of India and other poor Asian Countries, gender discrimination is quite glaring in economically developed countries. India is ranked 127 for Human Development Index out of 177 countries and 98 for Gender Development Index out of 140 countries in 2003 as reported in the Human Development Report, 2005 India is behind many developing countries including Sri Lanka, China both in terms of HDI and GDI values and ranks. It signifies that HRD and/or gender equalities are not the automatic process. The translation of growth to the HRD and/or gender equalities requires appropriate strategies for targeting particular groups. The performance of Sri Lanka or even Kerala at the regional level in India is akin to the developed countries in many respects of gender equalities because of the effective governance providing better education and health facilities to all. Even Bangladesh being the poor country is paying greater attention to the education of girls and involving the women in economic activities and thus improving its HDI and GDI ranks relatively at rapid rate 150 in 1997 to 139 in 2003 and from 123 in 1997 to 105 in 2003 respectively.

Table-1

India's Global Position in Gender Development

Country	*Human Development Index*		*Gender Development Index*		*Gender Empowerment Index*	
	Rank	*Value*	*Rank*	*Value*	*Rank*	*Value*
Norway	1	0.963	1	0.960	1	0.928
Australia	3	0.955	2	0.954	–	0.738 (2001)
United States	–	0.944	–	0.942	12	0.793
China	85	0.755	64	0.754	–	0.321 (2001)
Sri Lanka	93	0.751	66	0.747	72	0.37
India	127	0.602	98	0.586	–	0.176 (1999)
Pakistan	135	0.527	107	0.508	71	0.534
Nepal	136	0.526	106	0.511		
Bangladesh	139	0.520	105	0.514	79	0.218
Mozambique	168	0.379	133	0.365		
Ethiopia	–	0.367		0.355		
Niger	177	0.281	140	0.271		
United Kingdom	15	0.939	15	0.937		
Japan	11	0.943	14	0.937	43	0.534
Indonesia	110	0.697	87	0.691		
Thailand	73	0.778	57	0.774		
Nigeria	158	0.453	123	0.439		

Source: UNDP (2005) Human Development Report 2005 Oxford University Press, New Delhi.

The Table reveals the fact that the status of women of Niger is the worst whereas the status of women in Norway is far better. There is no gender gap in adult literacy rate in economically sound countries like Norway, Japan and United Kingdom and even in Indonesia whereas in the poorest country, Niger, the female literacy rate is the lowest i.e., only 9.4. In economically weaker Pakistan,

India and Bangladesh there is a very high gender gap. Demographic and economic features of Norway are also found most suitable for better status of women. Norway's population is very small (only 4.6 million), rate of population growth very low (0.38) and total fertility rate (1.7) lower than most of the Asian Countries. Economically, people of Norway are 6 to 10 times better than Asian Countries and more than 40 times better than African Countries. Thus, it is easy for government to provide facilities to manageable number of citizens and hence produce qualitatively better citizens (men as well as women) who helped Norway to touch heights (Harvinder Kaur, 2006). The huge population of India and its high total fertility rate are major hindrance in enhancing women's status to the desired level.

VIOLENCE AGAINST WOMEN REFLECTING LOWER STATUS OF WOMEN

One in every three women globally is subjected to violence during her life time. One in four women, men is exposed to domestic violence and this represents one of the main causes of injury and deaths among women world wide (Forum for Women and Development 2005). From womb to grave Indian Women face increasingly violent forms of gender bias. The violence against women takes many forms. They are killed in the Womb. They are traded for sex and labour. The NCRB report, Crime in India – 2005 observed that even though the share of violent crimes in the total number of crimes under IPC had declined continuously over 2001-05, the share of violent crimes affecting women had increased in this period, except for a slight decline in 2003. One would have assumed that given the constitutional framework, things would have changed in favour of women that has not happened. The economic reforms currently under way had not created the conditions for eradication of violence against women; if anything, it had generated more violence against women. Vibhuti Patel has drawn the picture in article' Globalization and Women'. Sex-Tourism in India has reached massive proportions with globalization. A new type of publicity material for foreign tourists shows scantily dressed women waiting for tourists at the beach or in the foyer of five star hotels. Worsening economic conditions force young, poor and lower middle class women to become prostitutes either for survival or by brute force. In last two decades, rich men from the Middle East, Scandinavia and Western Europe have been the main clients of the sex-industry. Now it is being geared up to accommodate an international clientele (Vibhuti Patel, 2007). It is but true that sex work in India, as in the rest of the world, employs a large number of females. Most of sex workers enter the profession involuntarily, being forced into either because of poverty, abandonment or violence by husbands or the other family problems. They are usually contractually obligated, in a form of bonded labour, to work in a brothel under the ownership of a madam or pimp. Not surprising, even those men who rent the services of prostitutes usually do not respect them and if prostitutes cannot win the respect of the clients they service, how can the rest of society be made to respect them? Reality lies in this fact that even in those countries where sex work is legal prostitutes do not command social respect but unfortunately, the overwhelming majority get sucked into sex work due to poverty related compulsion or absive family circumstances. This profession has received increased attention from social scientists and others in India where sex workers are at very high risk for the disease and transmitting it among other clients. Hereby, the findings of the oxford companion-the economics in India are worth rating. As per these findings sex workers with primary education earn about 4 per cent more than those with no education, while those with middle schooling earn about 22 per cent more. This reflects the segmentation of the market with more educated sex workers catering to more educated clients. Unlike other professions, age shows a sharp negative relationship with earning capacity. It is needless to say that the sex trade as a profession has thrived down the centuries across the world and India is not exception. People want it but condemn it, use it but damn it, need it but pretend otherwise. In a survey conducted by the National Commission for Women in 1997 among 200 Women in Tamil Nadu it was found that 50 per cent females had run away from home after sexual abuse within the family, 40 per cent completed secondary education, but started selling sex due to lack of other job opportunities, 63.3 per cent sold sex in additing to other work, 50 per cent started selling sex after desertion by husbands and 60 per cent were prostituting with knowledge of their families.

The Article 23 of the Constitution of India mandates prohibition of human trafficking as human trafficking for commercial sexual exploitation is one of the gravest violation of women dignity and their human rights. Such type of trafficking is demand driven. More demand, more crime. Another dimension is the vulnerability of trafficked females. Vulnerability, as often quoted, is not exactly poverty but it is a culmination of several factors, including lack of awareness of right, lack of access to rights, illiteracy, disparities on income, scope of exploitation, of poor law enforcement, lack of public awareness, existing culture of silence to violation of rights of other etc. undoubtedly, there is a momentum against human trafficking and one of the excellent examples is seen in the global initiative in fighting human trafficking initiated by the UNODC. The GIFT Asia Conference held in New Delhi during October, 2007 has been instrumental in creating tremendous public awareness and efforts by all concerned to bring AHT as everybody's business. But there is no need for us to be more hopeful in the nearfuture unless the present socio-economic condition of women prevail in the society.

What may be, when perpetrators are very family members, who are supposed to protect their women folk from such violence. When the protector turns predator the ultimate sufferers are women folk who endure the violence with great courage as she cannot speak out or walk out of the family in such situations. Only in grave situations such issues come to be known outside. Whatever data available is enough to throw light on the gravity of the problem. A case of Delhi which has got the dubious distinction of the rape capital of the country registered 599 cases in 2006 against 660 rape cases in 2005, recording 9.24 per cent decline in 2006 according to the Police Commissioner K.K. Paul. The table reveals the fact the fact that women are not safe anywhere.

Domestic Rapes			*By Acquaintances*		
Father	–	6	Neighbours	–	324
Step Father	–	5	Family/relative/ friend	–	43
Grand Father	–	1	Friend/lover	–	64
Brother	–	1	Servant	–	2
Ex husband/husband	–	3	Land lord/tenant	–	34
Uncle	–	11	Employer/co-worker	–	25
Cousin	–	5	Other known persons	–	42
Brother in law	–	19	Strangess	–	11
Father in law	–	3			

Source: Statistics released by the Delhi Police, Hindustan Times, January 6, 2007.

Generally, people do not register the crimes against women due to social stigma but the registered figures of crime against women reveal the fact that despite existence of special legislations providing protection to women, the proportion of crime against women as compared to total IPC crimes has increased from 3.5 per cent in 1998 to 9.5 per cent in 2004.

Table-2
Crimes Against Women Under IPC

Year	*Total IPC Crimes*	*Crimes Against Women Under IPC*	*% of Total IPC Women*
1998	1778815	119012	6.7
1999	1764629 (–0.8%)	123122 (3.5%)	7.0
2000	1771084 (0.4%)	128320 (4.2%)	7.2
2001	1769308 (–0.1%)	130725 (1.9%)	7.4
2002	1780330 (0.6%)	131112 (0.3%)	7.4
2003	1716120 (–3.6%)	131364 (0.2%)	7.6
2004	1832015 (6.75%)	1430615 (9.3%)	7.8

There has been an escalation of all forms of violence against women in India in the post two decades crimes punishable under the Indian Penal Code (IPC) namely, rape, kidnapping and abduction, homicide for dowry or dowry deaths, mental and physical torture, molestation, sexual harassment and trafficking of girls under 16 years, accounted for 93 per cent of the cases reported while the remainder came under special and local laws.

Table-3
Category-wise Number of Incidence of Crime

Type of Crimes	*1999*	*2000*	*2001*	*2002*	*2003*	*2004*	*Growth Rate 1999-2004*
Torture	43823 (32.28)	45778 (32.38)	49170 (34.19)	49237 (34.42)	50703 (36.06)	58121 (37.66)	32.6%
Molestation	32311 (23.80)	32940 (23.30)	34124 (23.73)	33943 (23.73)	32939 (23.43)	34567 (22.40)	7.0%
Rape	15468 (11.39)	16496 (11.67)	16075 (11.18)	16373 (11.45)	15847 (11.27)	18233 (11.81)	17.8%
Kidnapping/ Abduction	15962 (11.76)	15023 (10.63)	14645 (10.19)	14506 (10.14)	13296 (9.46)	15578 (10.09)	–2.4%

Contd...

Type of Crimes	*1999*	*2000*	*2001*	*2002*	*2003*	*2004*	*Growth Rate 1999-2004*
Sexual Harassment	8858 (6.52)	11024 (7.80)	9746 (6.78)	1055 (7.10)	12325 (8.77)	10001 (6.48)	12.9%
Dowry Death	6699 (4.93)	6995 (4.95)	6851 (4.76)	6822 (4.77)	6208 (4.41)	7026 (4.55)	4.9%
Traffic Act	9363 (6.90)	9515 (6.73)	8796 (6.12)	6598 (4.61)	5510 (3.92)	5748 (3.72)	-38.6%
Dowry Prohibition Act	3064 (2.26)	2876 (2.03)	3222 (2.24)	2816 (1.97)	2684 (1.91)	3592 (2.33)	17.2%
Other Acts	223 (0.16)	726 (0.51)	1166 (0.81)	2584 (1.81)	1089 (0.77)	1467 (0.95)	55.76%
Total	135771 (100)	141373 (100)	143795 (100)	143034 (100)	140601 (100)	154333 (100)	13.7%

Torture by husband and relatives accounted for the highest number of crimes against women. This category recorded an increase of 14.6 per cent in 2004 over 2003 while trafficking in girls as a percentage of total crime is low Torture accounted for 37.66 per cent of crimes followed by molestation which is 22.40 per cent in 2004. Both these crimes account for 56 to 60 per cent during 1999-2004. Rape, kidnapping and abduction cases accounted for 20 to 23 per cent while sexual harassment, dowry death and other accounted for the rest. Of the nine categories of violence all except sexual harassment have increased in 2004 over 2003. Sexual harassment has declined from 8.77 per cent in 2003 to 6.48 per cent in 2004.

Andrey Fernandes draws attention to a global level critique led by the U.S. and the Netherlands on what she says is a "dangerous theory towards violence against women in India. Some of these organizations say that because of female foeticides there is an increase in men who are young, poor and unmarried. They conjecture that these young men have high testosterone levels and this is one of the causes of violence against women (quoted by Lyla Bavadam 2008).

It is needless to say that a positive relationship exists among crime rate, literacy rate and per capita income.

SOCIO-ECONOMIC STATUS OF RURAL WOMEN IN INDIA

Gone are the days when people believed in the idiom, "Where women are celebrated, there resides the God." "Where women are respected,

Table-4
Status with Higher Number of Crimes Committed Against Women in 2004

Torture	*Rape*	*Molestation*	*Sexual*	*Down/Death*	*Kidnapping*
A.P.	M.P.	M.P.	A.P.	U.P.	U.P.
Rajasthan	West Bengal	A.P.	U.P.	Bihar	Rajasthan
West Bengal	U.P.	Maharashtra	Tamil Nadu	M.P.	Assam
Maharashtra	Bihar	Rajasthan	Maharashtra	A.P.	A.P.
U.P.	Maharashtra	U.P.	West Bengal	West Bengal	Bihar

there Gods delight, and where they are not, there all works and efforts come to naught." (Manu-Samita 111, 56). It was vedic era when women enjoyed a position of dignity in the society. In Vedic or Upanishadic era Maitreyi, Gargi and other ladies of revered memory have taken the places of rishis through their skill in discussing about Brahman. It is not true that in an assembly of a thousand Brahmanas who were all erudite in the vedas, Gargi boldly challenged Yajnalkya in a discussion about Brahman ? Undoubtedly, the Aryan and Semitic ideas of woman have always been diametrically opposed. Amongst the Semites the presence of woman is considered dangerous to devotion and she may not perform any religious function, whereas the Aryan's vision is found in favour of women. According to the Aryan a man cannot perform a religious action without a wife. In the period of degradation, when the priests made the other castes incompetent to the study of the vedas, they deprived the women also of all their rights. They were not allowed to touch the Shalagrama Shila or the household idol. Writing down Smrities etc. and binding them by hard rules, men have turned women into mere manufacturing machines. They have all the time been trained in helplessness, servile dependence on others. Some how or other man has dominated woman from ages past, and so woman was developed an inferiority complex. She has believed in the truth of man's interested teaching that she is inferior to him. She forgets the fact that she is not her husband's bond slave, but his companion and his helpmate, and an equal partner in all his joys and sorrows – as free as the husband to choose her own path. There was a time when women was so highly placed in the society that the children were named after their mothers as Kaunteya, Radheya etc. but a time has come when women lost their freedom. Manu wrote," In childhood a woman must be subject to her father, in youth to her husband, and when her lord is dead, to her sons. A woman must never be independent." Circumstances have forced upon us, for many centuries, the woman's need of protection. With foreign invaders the deformity in social structure began and women began to be treated as the weaker section of the society and as the assets of men. A criminal indifference on the part of parents have emerged. The parents deep their daughters utterly ignorant and illiterate and bring them up only for the purpose of marrying off to some young man of means as earlier as possible.

In the global era women of the Third World are seen as the most flexible of the World's Labour Force. The national and multinational corporations in the USA and Europe realized that the best way to reduce the wage bill and to enhance profit rates was to move industrial plants to poorer countries like India, Sri Lanka, Bangladesh, Indonesia, Philippines, Thailand etc. The cheap labour of docile, nimble fingered and flexible Asian Women - the last colony was found to be most attractive step to enhance profit margins. This policy was given the appealing little of 'Integration of Women in Development.' (Vibhuti Patel, 2007). Globalization is enjoying piggy ride over the backs of millions of poor women and child workers in the margin of economy economic as globalization, deep economic restructuring across countries and neo-liberal macro economic policies have led to increasing informalised and decentralised processes of production transforming labour markets and the World of Works in the industralised and the developing countries. In the name of flexibilisation; social security and statutory protection to workers have been dismantled.

Every women with a streak of individuality suffers from the painful feeling that she is forced to depend on others in her life. After long 61 years of Independence Indian Women remain underdeveloped; they are second class citizens, perceptibly behind their men in spite of many lofty and worthwhile legislation and equality rights and status guaranteed by the Constitution. Social and cultural conditioning makes men and men believe that women are physically weaker and they require protection. Indian culture has given our women a place in society of tolerance, self-sacrifice. It is a sad commentary of events, yet true that there is no section of our society more oppressed, more exploited and more neglected than women. In every segment, class or community, women suffer all the disabilities inflicted on that group and in addition, suffer also the consequences of gender discrimination. Yet, their contribution in economic life, social well-being, cultural continuity and ethical standards is far greater than their share of the population. Although women contribute much time and energy to keep the nation going, their contribution is scarcely recognized. As Jackon H. (1989) says "A women who created and sustains a home and through whose heads children grow up to be strong and pure men and women, is a creator second only to God." All nations have attained greatness, according to Swami Vivekananda, by paying proper respect to the women. That country and that nation which do not respect the women have never become great, nor will ever be in future. There is no hope of rise for that family or country, where there is no estimation of women, where they live in sadness. Undoubtedly, their contribution is quite substantial although it is a fact that the labour put in by women in discharging the economic and domestic duties hardly gets its due recognition. Women work for as many hours as men do, if not more yet their labour is counted as 'shadow work' giving them neither the due credit nor equal pay for the work done. Economic exploitation led to a more direct form of social oppression and women were made to pay a heavy price at the cost of their self-dignity and independence.

To Mahatma Gandhi, "Women is the companion of man gifted with equal mental capacities. She has the right to participate in all walks of life along with men. She has the same right of freedom and liberty as man's. She is entitled to a supreme place in her own sphere of activity as man is. By sheer force of a vicious custom even the most ignorant and worthless men have been enjoying superiority over women which they do not deserve and ought not to have." He has rightly observed that if by strength is meant brute strength then indeed is woman less brute than man. If by strength is meant moral power, then woman is immeasurably man's superior and so to call woman the weaker sex is a libel, it is man's injustice to woman. Has she not greater intuition, is she not more self sacrificing, has she not greater powers endurance, has she not greater courage ? Gandhiji decried discrimination against woman as an anachronism 'I fail to see any reason for jubliation over the birth of a son and for mourning over that of a daughter ! But the reality lies in this fact that girls are victims of discrimination based on gender, right from birth or say before birth. As per report of Human Development in South Asia,

2000 it is highly shameful to a take down that 84 per cent gynaecologists in Mumbai admitted to performing sex-determination tests resulting in continuous decline in sex-ratio of India, from 972 to 930 women per thousand men from 1901 to 1971. In 1991 census it came down to 927 per thousand. However, there has been marginal increase in India's ratio in 2001 i.e. 930 per thousand. Male preference adversely affects female through inequitable allocation of food, education and health care, a disparity frequently reinforced throughout life and for this, they are also been adopting the methods of foeticide.

In the male dominated society the status of women has had its social and historical peaks and troughts. Paradoxically, even while women continue to be worshipped as goddesses, they are relegated to a lower social status and are victimised in the name of social norms, cultural traditions and the associated prejudices; though women are considered key factors in the process of family socialization and its general uplift, yet they are accorded on unequal status and are often discriminated even in regard to food distribution and general well-being within the family; most rural women, by and large, represent the poorest of the poor and yet they have had the gratification of presiding over the fortunes of nation states and economic venture; biologically, women are a stronger lot with a high life expectancy all over the world and yet have a lower life expectancy and an unfavourable sex ratio in India; exceptionally, literacy and general health statuswise, women of North East India and the status of Kerala and Tamil Nadu have showed higher levels of achievement and yet most women in other parts of the country are illiterate and high health risk prone (P. Durga Prasad, 1995).

Indian Women are also victims of social discrimination and have a low status within the family. The logic behind such discrimination is such that girls appear as a libility for the family as they have to be married off, often with huge dowry, whereas boys are considered an asset as they carry on the family lineage and support the family in times of financial need and bring in dowry (Human Development in South Asia, 2000, pp. 122-23) The National Family Health Survey–2 (NHFS-2) (1PS, 2000) provides ample evidence of this neglect of the girl child. The infant mortality rate in the decade prior to the survey i.e., 1988-98, was slightly higher for boys than girls 75 and 71 infant deaths per 1000 live-births, respectively but female mortality i.e. below five years was slightly higher than male mortality rate because of the neglect of girls in juvenile ages 1-4. As against, as many as 105 female children who died per 1000 female children born alive without celebrating their 5th birthday, the number of male children who died was 97. The survey report assures us that this gender bias was evident much more in rural than in urban India. A World Bank Report on Women's health status in India, released in 1996, has girmly catelogued the variety of ways in which women are discriminated against. As girls, they get less vaccination, less education and less nutrition than their brothers and when they grow up, they are less healthy than their male counterparts and succumb more easily to sickness and disease. On the other side the intra-house hold distribution of labour and resources is loaded against women who work more or get a lesser share of food, health care, leisure and play. It is studied that in rural Punjab 21 per cent of girls in poor families suffer severe nutrition compared to 3 per cent of boys in the same family. Indeed, poor boys are better fed than rich girls (UNDP, 1995).

Poverty accentuates gender gaps and when adversity strikes, it is women who often are most vulnerable (UNDP, 1997 P 64) India continues to have the highest concentration of poverty accounting for almost one third of those with an income of less than one dollar a day, and it is estimated that women account for 93 per cent of those below the poverty line. It is becoming more evident that poverty among rural women is growing faster than among rural men. Over the past twenty years, for example, the number of women in absolute poverty rose by 50 per cent as against some 30 per cent for rural men (M.L. Narasail, 2006). There is no surprise when we find that whatever food is available tends to distributed disproportionately between males and females in poor households but even households that have enough, women are disadvantaged in term of food consumption because of traditional notions of what food women must not eat or that women must eat last. Income poverty explains about 10 per cent of the variation in child nutrition (Mahbub Ul Haq, Development Centre, 2000). Thus, females are basically discriminated because they are females and they are often underfed and even neglected when sick, leading initially to higher levels of undernutrition, resulting ultimately in higher female than male mortality. It is but true that Indian Women, regardless of their caste, religion or class, never enjoy equal status in the family or society and the neglect of girls in some regions is known to lead to sex selective foeticide and even infanticide (Kumar, 1989).

The most visible evidence of the neglect of girl child or say discrimination against women is the lower school attendance ratios of girls compared to boys although the Indian Constitution has expressed a strong commitment towards education for all, however, India still has one of the lowest female literacy rates in Asia. UNICEF advocates quality basic education for all children-girls and boys-with an emphasis on gender equality and eliminating disparities of all kinds. India is one of such countries which still do not have equality of education. According to 1991 literacy rate among men was 64.13 per cent and that among women was as low as 39.29 per cent. The disparities in the literacy rate between men and women seemed to have narrowed down to some extent in 2001. While male literacy rose from 64.13 per cent to 75.64 per cent, the women literacy rose more proportionately from 39.29 per cent to 54.03 per cent thus narrowing down the gulf between two ratios to some extent from 24.84 percentage points to 21.61 in 2001. The increase in female literacy by 14.87 per cent outpaced that of male literacy by 11.72 per cent. Despite the fact that literacy and school enrolment among both males and females has increased yet at least 60 million girls lack access to primary education in India. According to a recent National Sample Survey Organisation (NSSO) report, the literacy rate in India during 2004-05 was 64 per cent, with Kerala having 83 per cent of its rural population and 85 per cent of its urban residents as literate. Bihar's rural areas had the lowest literacy rate 44 per cent. While the urban literacy rate was lowest in Rajasthan at 64 per cent. The literacy rate (ages 5+) of India increased to 62 per cent in 1997 from 52.91 per cent in 1991, but in 1997 the female literacy rate was just 50 per cent and the rural female literacy rate was just 43 per cent. The adult rates (ages 15+) were 54 per cent total and 40.7 per cent for women. The total enrolment in secondary schools in 1997-98 was only 50 per cent. Of the eligible population of which 44 per cent were girls in primary school, 40 per cent in middle school and 37.1 per cent in secondary school. Literacy rate among rural Indian women was average around mere 30 per cent. Is it not true that the rate of enrolment in higher education is 10 per cent in India in which the rate of female's enrolment is only 3 per cent? Undoubtedly, the percentage of female education has steady increased since Independence but the overall picture is not so much heartening when we make a comparison with other developed countries. Although it has risen from 10.77 per cent in 1947 to 44.71 per cent in 2002 in case of general higher education whereas in case of professional and specialised education this has been raised from 9.21 per cent in 1947 to 32.83 per cent in 2002 but this growth appears to be largely with the upper and middle classes of the urban population. Amongst females belonging to poor rural section of the society the overall picture is gloomy yet now and the disparity between male and female education prevails in the society. One of the major reason for lack of education among women in India is high drop out rate among girls at the early stages of schooling as compared to boys. As per data, 45 per cent of girls and 41 per cent of boys drop out of school between class 1 and 5. The data on school attendance by age show the proportion of girls attending school decreases with age while for boys it remains somehow stable. The drop out rate of girls was 62.5 per cent in 1980-81 at primary level against 56.2 per cent drop out rate for boys, which came down to 39.9 per cent for girls and 38.4 per cent for boys. This figure for girls and boys at elementary level in 1980-81 was 79.4 per cent and 68.0 per cent respectively which came down to 56.9 per cent and 52.9 per cent respectively for girls and boys in 2001-02. At the secondary level the drop out rate for girls was 86.6 per cent in 1980-81 which came down to 68.6 per cent in 2001.02 per cent where the figure for boys was 79.8 per cent in 1980-81 and 64.2 per cent in 2001-02. What would be where spending on education, especially educating a girl child in rural areas is perceived as waste of money and resources. Before or after marriage, a girl's role in family is primarily linked to the household, thus expenditure on her formal education is seen as a waste of resources. Often a choice is made between sending either son or daughter to school and parents would rather spend scarce family resources educating a son as it is considered as a long-term and sure investment. It is commonly perceived that girl child would be married into another family and would take advantages she gains from education. It is also perceived that parents send their daughters to school with a view to keeping them engaged till their marriage and prevailing early marriage in most cases is the main reason for high drop out rate. No doubt, among various reasons poverty is one of the prime cause for lack of education and high drop out rate among girls especially in rural areas but unfortunately even girls themselves are not less responsible for their low literacy.

Most of girls do not take interest in studies as they think that there is no need for education in doing domestic work. They do not like to take extra load of doing some jobs after getting education. They think that it is pious duty of their life partners to maintain them and so there is no need for earning for them. Because many of most Indian women do accept their traditional role of dependence on their life partners. In most societies, women have been defined largely in terms of their functions as wives and mothers, and by cultural images of their sexuality. The rights of women to become educated and to hold jobs outside of the home have frequently been questioned; women who have to work have tended to be of low economic and social status (Dipti Singh, 2008). The Indian society has accorded differential status to women through out the history. The golden period for women was the Vedic period when girls were also welcome in a family; they were given equal education, their age of marriage was after maturation and they could select the mate of their own choice through the tradition of 'Swyamvar'. They had independence for decision taking and they have control over finances, agriculture and general welfare. They enjoyed power and participated in political, cultural and literacy activities. Then came to Brahmanic period. According to Tikoo (1985). "In Manu Samhita, ideas about womenhood are laid down, and morality is assigned in authoritarian codes which bring down women to the level of sub species." But there has been a significant change in the status of women in modern India and now it is established fact that education helps in improving income levels, thereby reducing the poverty and enabling the economic growth and our First Prime Minister Pandit Nehru has realised and declared "to awaken the people, it is women who must be awakened, once she is on the move, the family moves, the village moves and the nation moves." The beneficial interactions between education and such socio-economic variables as fertility, health and gender discrimination, on the one hand and heightened level of human articulation, including the urge to question and improve oneself-propelling norms of progress and play better citizenry, on the other, are now much better recognized (Knight, 1996). Despite such realizations gender inequalities are still dragging us much behind of many developed and even developing countries and carrying negative impact on human resources in the country.

Economic status paves the way of socio status and employment gives economic status to women. The United Nations declared 1975-85 as the Women's Decade but it is alarming to point out that even during this period, there has been global deterioration in the condition of women. A document in 1985, which reviewed the facts and studies, concerning women from all over the world, states "The almost uniform conclusion of the Decade's research is that with a few exception, Women's relative access to economic resources, incomes and employment has worsened, their burdens of work have increased, and their relative and even absolute health, nutritional and educational status has declined." Women constitute almost half of the population, perform two-third of its work hours, receive one-tenth of world's income and own less than one hundredth of the world prosperity. In India 56 per cent of the males and 33 per cent of the females in the rural sector are in the labour force and about 66 per cent of the female population in the rural sector is idle and unutilized due to existing social customs which do not allow young girls and women to work independently as earlier it is said-stay indoors to be safe but women have always faced violence within homes. Now it is being recognised. Overall, society also has become more violent. The corporate culture, which is very competitive, very aggressive, is creating a culture of violence and aggression that makes all disempowered section its victims. If there is violence in society, women are generally bound to get affected. So we have violence against women as well as sexual harassment in BOPs and in the corporate sector. Moreover, there is no denying that in traditional societies, a women learning the protection of her home in order to take employment is more likely to be perceived as a loose women and consequently willing for sexual activity. Undoubtedly, the group of women desperately in need of income constitute prime victims for sexual harassment. What may be; but it is true that women are seen working so much and so often, that their health is taken for granted. By the time a young girl particularly in the low income rural family, has reached the age of 5, she assumes adult responsibilities, both inside and outside the household. Sudha Deshpande (2002) has pointed out "In the context of child labour, the family is involved in two ways firstly, as an employer, when the child works as a helper in the family enterprise, especially in agriculture or at home in a home-based industry like handlooms and secondly, as a supplier of labour, whether the child works at home or outside." There could be two reasons why parents send their child to work: firstly, to supplement the meager family income, when the total income which all workers in the household earn is inadequate to make the two ends meet. Alternatively, a similar situation may arise when the head of the family loses his job or dies; in which cases children may be sent for work for ensuring family survival. Secondly, it is believed that certain skills or crafts are acquired better if children are initiated in these crafts at a young age and this helps them get gainful employment later when these children are adults. It is needless to say that child work has dire consequences on children as it prevents them from attending school and investing in human capital. Children who attended school participated in economic activity only marginally. Thus, school attendance ratios of girls would be negatively associated with economic participation of girls. Notably, because of gender discrimination, girls are likely to be sent to school and are readily available for work, however low paid it is. The level of economic participation of girls would be positively related to the incidence of poverty measured as a percentage share of population that lived in poverty. Naturally, there would be negative relationship between per capita income and level of economic participation rate of girls. Likewise, the women enter labour market if *(i)* there is no man to earn in the family *(ii)* men may not be able to earn income which will fulfill family requirements, and *(iii)* man may not be ready to share his whole income with other family member rationally, leaving women and children at a very low level. Thus, low levels of income compell women to join labour market. In the case of children the decision to work is taken not by the child who actually works whereas adult women take decision themselves to work. But generally women, having no required skills to join high yielding, secure and lucrative jobs, have to join inferior jobs and their low payment and insecure jobs keep them at subordination of their husbands. They usually behave as labour reserve to be pulled into or pushed out of the labour force at will. Reserve army of labour, as Karl Marx has referred, works in two ways. It helps in capital accumulation because women are paid less than their marginal physical productivity, stretching profit margin for employer and helping in creation of capital and secondly, women are forced to be subjugated by men in family. In the international context, it has been argued that the growing flexibility in the labour market had led to feminisation of the labour force. Of course, not long ago but last two decades, especially the 1980s, saw a phenomenal change in the labour market situation in both developed and developing countries and comparable data compiled by the international sources indicate that 9 out of every 10 industrialized, while 7 out of every 10 industrializing economies reported increase in female activity rates in the 1980s. In one third of the industrializing while two-thirds of the industrialized economies the male participation rate declined during the same period (ILO, 1980, 1988). This phenomenon of global feminization has increased female participation rates in the face of either decline or constancy in the male participation rates. This has not only increased their share in the total labour force but has resulted in feminization of certain jobs that were traditionally done by men (Standing, 1989). The process in all countries has weakened the bargaining capacity of the workers while threatening their employment security (U.N. 1992). With the new economic policies the structure of labour markets has become increasingly more flexible than in the past and firms prefer employing flexible labour that can be disposed off if necessary after a specific job. This has increased the use of casual, temporary, contract and female labour at firm level. Employment of this kind of cheap labour reduces not only the wage costs but also non-wage costs for the firm since this labour is non-permanent. The economic rationality of flexible labour practices fits in well in the strategy that preaches liberalization and cost effective production. Most countries that accepted the strategy have reported increase in employment. But this employment growth has been mostly of low cost flexible labour (Sudha Des Pandey, 1992). Feminization is one of the facets of this increase in the employment of low cost labour (UN; 1992). However, available macro statistics indicate that in India in a period of relative liberalization of the economy, the trends in women's employment pattern were, if anything, in the reverse direction. The share of women in the rural workforce had been increasing in the 1970s but in the late 1980s, it comes down from a high 36 per cent in 1983 to about 34.5 per cent and had remained there till 1993-94. There was a slight rise in women's share in the urban workforce, which, according to Visaria reflected mainly the growth in women's rate of urbanization (Visaria, 1996). The decline in the share of women workers was much sharper in the rural non-form sector, particularly in the 1990s. As we saw before, there are as yet no sings of feminization of the Indian workforce and there are no obvious reasons why this should take place in the coming years (Nirmala Banerjee, 1997). Of course, Indian women are not being subjected to the dangers of such international exploitation in one sense but it is not less worrying that women's economic empowerment for the last thirty years or more have brought little change in their economic status. Now the main question arises why women have the low supply price that employers are looking for. Condemning the employers alone does nothing to reduce the initial vulnerability of those women. Nor is the state, at least in India, capable or willing to challenge the patriarchal norms which treat women basically as a flexible family resource rather than as a person with independent rights and priorities. The supply price of women's labour is lower because they enter the labour market more handicapped by family responsibilities and their lack of assets. This is as true of the domestic servants of Calcutta as of the garment factory workers of Dhaka. It would be difficult to find instances where women are not as, or even more, exploited as in the MNC firms for export production. Hereby, it is worth noting that gender-based discrimination in employment, occupation and wages is often attributed to pre-entry discrimination against women in access to education. The question needs to be replied whether it is the subordination of women in the family that causes their subordination in the labour market or whether it is the latter that causes their subordination in the family. Providing women jobs may not radically after their subordinate status that has been reinforced over centuries, but by enhancing their self respect and economic independence, it can help to reduce the worst forms of deprivation and oppression but a job may only increase a women's drudgery and exploitation if it is in the informed sector and is characterised by low pay and poor working conditions. Irrespective of how unemployment was defined, it was higher among women than men resulting in compelling impact on women to accept low-paid, poor-conditioned-insecured-jobs in the informal sector. The ratio of causal labourers to regular employees is much more in the case of rural females compared to rural males. The shift to non-agricultural occupations is much less in the case of females, even when they shift to the low paid occupations. Boserup (1970) in her comprehensive analysis of participation of women in the labour force argues that the change from traditional to modern economic system hinders rather than helps women's participation in the labour force as modernisation widens the gap in the levels of knowledge and training between men and women and augments men's prestige at the cost of women. Scott (1986) mentions four visible dimensions on the basis of which female marginalisation can be ascertained i.e., *(i)* exclusion of women from productive employment either in the form of a decline in the overall work participation rates of women or a decline in their share in wages and salaried employment; *(ii)* a concentration of all working women in the informal sector or in the unpaid categories, *(iii)* a segregation of women in certain types of jobs which are low in the occupational hierarchy and are low paying and low status, commonly referred to as feminization or segregation in employment, and *(iv)* economic inequality reflected through wage differentials and casualization of female labour force. Still another manifestation is the lack of decision making power and economic independence (Karlekar, 1992). Women are treated as respectable life partners but not respectable work partners (G.K. Chandha, 2003). And so G. Parthsarathy and K.A. Nirmala (1997) have clear concept that unless women are empowered, they have to face both social and economic marginalisation. The bias against the girl child deprives them of general education, vocational training or skills which are necessary in a technologically advancing economy. It has hardly ever been recognized that failing to invest adequately in educating women reduces the potential benefits of educating men "(Giri, 1997) The failure to see through that man-women complementarily in education has been a costly failure in terms of lost opportunities to raise productivity, to increase family income and to improve quality of life"; without education, women in particular are condemned to inferior work, low social status and a life of perpetual dependence. Why discrimination against women right from the cradle stage continues. The question is addressed more to rural than to urban areas, more to parents than the state, and more to women's own attitude of resignation than to male chauvinism (G.K. Chandha, 2003).

CONCLUDING REMARKS

Since the inception of planning, the planner and policy makers in India, and all the world over, conceive and take rural development with the implicit assumption that their impact will be homogenous on both men and women and thus, women's development cannot be separated from or viewed in isolation from the development of the whole community. However, their presumption of equitable distribution of benefits to both the sexes is subject to examination. When any change introduces or increase inequality within a society and more so in a rural society, women of poor strata become doubly and badly affected, first, as members of the rural poor; and secondly, as women (S.P. Sinha, 1992). In 1991 the Government of India adopted as Structural Adjustment Programme (SAP) in response to a mounting burden of debt leading to a balance of payment crisis. The SAP has increased women's drudgery and hardship in the struggle for survival. The inflationary impart of the SAP reduces the purchasing power of a household which in turn increases unpaid labour of women. The SAP has forced working women into the unorganised sector, thus depriving them of their trade union rights. By doing this, the women fall outside protective labour laws (Vibhuti Patel, 2007). In recent years, momentum has been gathering not only in India but all over the World, demanding gender equality and push for equal representation of women in all sphere as of activity. But there is no denying the fact that even after 61 years independence women suffer from ignorance, family violence, wife battering, dowry death, ghunghat phenomenon, prostitution, burden of domestic labour etc. What have we achieved? Too little, whether it is the macro situation of the Nehruvian Model or Post reform Manmohan economics, there is a steady decline. The suppression of Women from participation in social, economic as well as political life hurts the people as a whole, not just women. Gender disparity is not only a social failure in itself; it also leads to other social failures. Any attempt to improve the status of Indian women, any weaning away from the Patriarchal bias, any attempt to undo the centuries of injustice meted out on the other half of the society, any aggressive movement towards women autonomy must necessarily carry an economic base. Short of this it would only be a political platitude. Our Ex-President A.P.J. Abdul Kalam has rightly observed that "Empowering women is a pre requisite for creating a good nation, when women are empowered, society with stability is assured. Empowerment of women is essential as their thoughts and their value systems lead the development of a good family, good society and ultimately a good nation." Thus, empowerment of women has been recognized as a central issue in determining the status of women and education is the milestone for women empowerment because it enables them to respond to opportunities and to face challenges created in the global era. Hereby it is worth noting that the Radha

Krishan University Education Commission says "There cannot be educated people without educated women, if general education had to be limited to men or to women, the opportunity should be given to women, for them it would more surely be passed on to the next generation." But unfortunately, the changes taking shape in the economy, modernisation and tradition all appear to be loaded against women. Nisha Srivastava (1997) is of the opinion that either women increase their skills and qualifications and make it to the top or they sink in the tidal wave of change. In this scenario, several factors militate against women. In the post reform period, women are trapped in a bind. On the one side, with the increasing pressure to effect cuts on higher education and on educational institutions to generate their own funds, professional and technical courses are becoming prohibitive. On the other, in a traditional society, where a girl is considered paraya dhan and marriage is her destiny, from the perspective of parents it makes little economic sense to spend large sums on her education. The question, Sen (1984) rightly avers in the last analysis is as much about tradition as it is about modernisation. It is tradition that restricts Women's mobility, their access to education and to skills, and it is tradition which ties women down the crushing burden of house work and child care. Technological changes may become threats to women's jobs because of legacies women have inherited from the past. Thus, it is inappropriate to chastise modernisation when the blame would seem to lie as much on tradition. Consequently, redemption would lie not only in the right type of strategies towards modernisation, but more importantly in correcting the asymmetries at home and in scociety.

"The world as Kapstein writes' may be moving inexorably towards one of those tragic moment, that will lead future historians to ask, why was nothing done in time?" (quoted by Sau). If gender inequalities harm people's well-being and a country's prospects of development, why do harmful gender disparity persists? Of course, to promote gender equality, policies for institutional change and economic development need to consider. Thus, how to deepen understanding of the links between gender equality and development and how to reflect these links in policy decisions is a key challenge for the present and the future. Good things happen when women govern. As per UNDP Report 2007-08 it is found that the percentage of women at ministerial level in Spain, Norway, Australia, Chile, Bahrain, India and Yemen having 50, 44.4, 20, 16.7, 8.7, 3.4 per cent and 2.9 per cent respectively witness 13, 2, 3, 40, 41, 128, and 153 HDI country ranking respectively. A 2007 Survey of OECD Countries by the women's Forum for the economy and society, and various studies by the World Bank find that women are more difficult to corrupt than men and that there is less corruption when there are more women in positions of responsibility. In the Indian context too, various researchers have shown that women representatives are not only less corrupt, they are also more responsive to community than men. Indeed, when women gain voice in decision making, they would be in a position to take decision for improving poor socio-economic status and begin to transform gender relation and call into question the deeply entrenched patriarchal system. And so women have to be treated as equal partners in decision making and implementation rather than as beneficiaries.

For various historic and socio-cultural reasons, women are a vulnerable section of our society and several macro indicators related to education, health, employment, economic participation etc. point towards an adverse status women *vis-a-vis* men. Development and empowerment of women has been a priority in successive plans and several public expenditure programmes are directed to this objective. However women face gender specific barriers and socio-economic status of women cannot be said satisfactory. And so improving socio-economic status of women what is highly desirable is good governance for implementing governmental policies and constitutional provisions effectively and honestly.

Last but not the least important is that women need to stand themselves to safe their interests. What can be expected in the men-dominated society when the court declared that 'Mathura was not raped by the men in uniform but Mathura being a woman of an easy virtue gave a willful consent for sexual intercourse? (quoted by Vibhuti Patel 2008) Edmund Burke was right enough in his observation, "Shed a few tears, you women, and you would have none, except your own lovely hands to wipe them off."

REFERENCES

Singh Dipti (2008) Education and its Impact on Women in 'Developing Countries in Education in Third World and India' (ed.) by Meenu Agrawal, Kanishka Publishers, New Delhi.

Standing Guy (1989) Global Feminization Through Flexible Labour World Development, Vol. 17, No. 7, pp. 1077-1095.

Deshpande Sudha (1992) Structural Adjustment and Feminization in Women and Work in India (ed.) by A.N. Sharma Ex. Seema Singh B.R. Publishers Corporation.

United Nations (1992) Economic and Social Survey of Asia and The Pacific, 1991, New York.

Baneerjee Nirmala (1997) How Real is The Bogey of Feminization in The Indian Journal of Labour Economics, Vol. 40, No. 3.

Srivastava Nisha (1997) Striving for Toe-Hold: Women in the Organised Sector in the ISLE Vol. 40 No. 3.

Sau R. (1996) Industry, Finance and Employment: A Disordant Trinity EPW No. 9-16.

Sen Amartya (1984) Women, Technology and Sexual Divisions Mimeo UNCTAD April

Visaria P. (1996) Level and Pattern of Women's Employment in India presented in Seminar.

Chadha G.K. (2003) What is Dominating the Indian Labour Market Peacock's Feathers or Feet. Presidential address ISLE 45th Annual Conf.

Patel Vibhuti (2008) Women's Struggle and Movement in Bhartiya Samajik Chintan Vol. VI, No. 4, January-March.

Patel Vibhuti (2007) Globalization and Women in Bhartiya Samajik Chintan, Vol. VI, No. 2, July-September.

Deshpande Sudha (2002) Girl Child Labour and Food Insecurity in India in Coming to Grips with Rural Child Work (ed.) by N. Rama Chandran L. Massun.

Scott A.M. (1986) Women and Industrialization: Examining The Female Marginalisation Thesis Journal of Development Studies, Vol. 22, No. 4.

Boserup (1970) Women's Role in Economic Development St. Martin's Press New York.

89th IEA Annual Conf. Vol. 2006.

Conference Issue IJLE, 2004.

Kurukshetra, Vol. XLIII, No. II August, 1995.

Kurukshetra, Vol. 56, No. 3, 2008.

Yojana August, 2007.

Yojana October, 2006.

Yojana February, 2008.

Frontline January, 2008.

7

Socio-Economic Condition of Rural Women in Rural India

Harender Kumar

INTRODUCTION

Women constitute almost one half of the population of the world. But their social, economic and political status is lower than that of men in many countries including India. The social status of women in a given society depends upon the role assigned to men and the social attitudes of the society towards that role. Though certain biological differences do exist between men and women, discriminations is made and enforced by men with a view to subjugate women. Of late, the biological myths about inferiority of women have been exploded and women are seen in almost all activities competing with men.[1]

Women, constituting half of the total population, are of vital importance for the production system and social processes connected with economy. Their contribution and role in the family as well as in economic development and social transformation are pivotal. They have been managing and supporting the survival system, particularly in the case of the poor households constituting 30 per cent of the total persons. However, the status of women till recent times leaves much to be desired. Inequality, illiteracy, sexual exploitation and gender bias in a male-dominated society are the bane of women's development programmes. In matters of health, nutrition and educational inputs, women and girls are, even today discriminated against.

The above inequalities severely constrain the ability of women to acquire good health and education and the women-implementation of centered development programmes. At the household level, these disparities translate into a lack of autonomy and control over household resources-both material and non-material. Few women, including working women, have any control over the household's economic resources while most have restrictions on their freedom of movement. Seclusion practices and other behavioural norms further reinforce women's lack of freedom of movement; lack of self-confidence and the acceptance of self-denial, including matters relating to seeking health and food intake.

Women's unequal and inequitable status, their physical and economic hardship becomes worse because neither the society nor the women themselves perceive their role in society as anything but marginal; they themselves fail to assign value to their work, which is highly significant for the very survival of their families, and even the society. This misperception occurs because the man is always regarded as the bread-winner and the woman goes out to earn only when the man's income is not enough. Value is attached only to such works, which earn women money. That is why when women earn half of what men do, their work is assessed as half-efficient or half-productive even if it is actually not so.[2]

STATUS OF WOMEN IN INDIA

Literacy and education are the most essential inputs for empowerment of women. In 1951, shortly after independence, the Census recorded that only 25 per cent of men and 7 per cent of women were literate. By the 1991 Census, female literacy had risen to 39 per cent. Census 2001 provisional figures indicate that 54.16 per cent of women are now able to read and write. Still, 245 million Indian women cannot read or write, comprising the world's largest number of unlettered women. National averages in literacy conceal wide disparities. The girls are enrolling in school at an increasing rate but smaller percentages are retained in the education system. The overall drop out rate for boys were 59 per cent whereas it is 68 per cent for girls. Life expectancy at birth for females has raised steadily from 31.7 years in 1951 to 62.1 in 1996. The mean age at marriage of girls has also increased from 15.6 years in 1951 to 19.4 years in 1995. But the sex ratio has been on declining trend, it was 946 in 1951 and has declined to 917 in 2001. The maternal mortality rate is 4.37 per 1000 live births. The reasons for maternal mortality are absence of maternal health services, early marriage, malnutrition, repeated pregnancies, anemia and ignorance. According to old studies. Indian women spend 16 years of their life in pregnancy or lactation, deliver 6 children out of which 4 survived. Maternal mortality accounts for 2.5 per cent of all female deaths in India, but 12.5 per cent of deaths of rural women is between the ages of 15.45.

DEFINING RURAL SOCIETY

India has been, and continues to be, a predominantly rural country. According to the 2001 census, 72.25 per cent of India's population of (total population 1027 million) lives in villages. Besides, the incidence of poverty in India is much more severe in the villages than in the towns. Nearly half of the rural population is estimated to live below the poverty line. So, the Government of India has been committed in evolving strategies that would improve majority of our population living in rural areas and several programmes for poverty alleviation directed towards selected target groups were launched. This initiative was in response to a consensus that the benefit of fast growth failed to percolate significantly to the lower income groups and weaker sections of society. Mostly both socially and economically disadvantaged groups are living in the rural areas and they are facing all kind of misery in leading their lives.[3] Rural society can be used interchangeably with terms like 'village', 'countryside', or 'folk society'; of these, the term most commonly used in sociological literature on rural society is the village.[4]

In rural society a maximum number of rural people are engaged in agriculture, which is the mainstay of their lives. In addition, a rural society has several other groups, engaged in various other occupations of arts and crafts, usually known as artisans and craftsmen, who regularly supply their services to agriculturalists in exchange of grains and cereals. These groups indulge in agricultural pursuits, especially during the monsoon and the agricultural produce of such specialists and small agriculturists is mainly for domestic consumption.[5]

In comparison with the urban society, rural society is a small society having a small population, and extends over a shorter physical area. The institutions/facilities such as police stations, hospitals, schools, post offices, clubs etc. may or may not be there, and if existent, they are not available in plenty. Density of the rural population is low, and it may be clustered according to the criteria of social status. In other words, people occupying the same status may share the same neighbourhood, and may observe considerable social and sometimes physical distance from others, especially those lower in hierarchy.

Rural society basically preserves traditional culture, and many of its values and virtues are carried forward to urban areas, of which they become a part after their refinement. The fundamental values of Indian society and civilization are preserved in villages, where from they are transmitted to towns and cities. A sizeable number of rural people are engaged in agriculture, which is the mainstay of their lives. In addition, a rural society has several other groups engaged in various other occupations of arts and crafts, usually known as artisans and craftsmen who regularly supply their services to agriculturalists in exchange for grains and cereals. The term 'rural society' includes a wide variety of people and villages of different sizes and compositions. Generally, a rural society is an agrarian society, which includes agriculturists, artisans, craftsmen, and other occupational groups, and they are all dependent, in one way or the other, upon agriculture.[6]

STATUS OF WOMEN IN AGRICULTURAL AND ALLIED ACTIVITIES

Agriculture is a family enterprise in which women and men share their work. Women's contribution to food production and processing is vital and crucial. In almost all the activities, women are involved right from land preparation till storage and marketing of harvested grains.

Women play significant, if not dominant, roles in supplying all ingredients necessary to achieve food security in developing countries. But women play these roles in the face of enormous social, cultural and economic constraints. This chapter brings together the evidences on the key roles that women play in maintaining the food security and examines the way to strengthen this through policies and programmes that enhance women's abilities and resources to fulfill their roles. A more equal distribution of existing resources between women and men can be achieved by addressing the specific constraints women face.

Most of the work that women do, such as collecting fuel, fodder and water, or growing vegetables, or keeping poultry for domestic consumption, goes unrecorded in the Census counts. Many women and girls who work on family land are not recorded as workers.

Women constitute 90 per cent of the total marginal workers of the country. Rural women engaged in agriculture form 78 per cent of all women in regular work. They are a third of all workers on the land. The traditional gender division of labour ensures that these women get on average 30 per cent lower wages than men. The total employment of women in organised sector is only 4 per cent. A recent study conducted by Women and Population Division of FAO revealed that in developing countries women provide 70 per cent of agricultural labour, 60-80 per cent labour for household food production, 100 per cent labour for processing the basic food stuffs, 80 per cent for food storage and transport from farm to village, 90 per cent for water and fuel wood collection for households.

Women produce between 60 and 80 per cent of the food in most developing countries and are responsible for half of the world's food production; therefore, women's role in food production ensures the survival of millions of people in all regions. Women's livelihood strategies, and their support and means of ensuring food security are diverse and complex, from cultivating field crops to livestock rearing, home gardening, gathering etc. They make these contributions despite unequal access to land, inputs and information. A growing body of evidence indicates that if male–female access to inputs were less unequal, substantial gains in agricultural output would occur, benefiting both women and men. Estimate from FAO of United Nations show that women account for more than half of labour required to produce the food consumed in the developing world.

In addition to working in the fields, women not only ensure fuel, fodder, water, and food, but also have to look after the emotional needs of their families-the children, elders and husbands. The nurturing, caring and reproductive responsibilities are the dimension that have never been computed economically, but are essential and significant aspects of women's workload. Women's role as food producers is related also to their role as mothers and nurturers and in sustaining their families and communities. Their work is integral to the quality of life of people.[7]

The major constrains for participation of women in agriculture are unequal land rights, limited access to use of resources, lack of equipment and appropriate technology, limited contact with agricultural extension, lack of access of credit and lower level of education. Population explosion, heavy pressure on land, leading to fragmentation, making the size of land holdings uneconomical for cultivation, indiscriminate use of chemical fertilizers and pesticides have also lead to the degradation of the quality of arable lands. On top of this, continuous failure of monsoon, occurrence of drought, degradation of soils and various other factors have also contributed to the decline in the economic status causing threat to food security of the resource poor families in fragile areas.

Under these circumstances, the men are forced to leave their homes for plains and urban areas in search of employment and the main burden of agriculture and animal husbandry has fallen on women. In addition to this due to the degradation of the forest, women have to undertake longer walks than before, scaling steep heights and descending deep valleys to collect water, fuel wood, fodder and other forest produces and this adds further hours to their already stretched working hours. While men migrate in search of livelihood women become heads of the households without adequate income support to absorb greater family responsibility, sometimes, determinant of their health.[8]

CONTRIBUTION OF WOMEN IN RURAL SOCIETY

The contribution of women farmers to the Indian agriculture is enormous. Women, who are almost half of our total population and contribute monetary and non-monetary inputs towards national income, however, occupy low position in the socio-economic index of India. Rural Indian women are extensively involved in agricultural activities. However, the nature and extent of their involvement differs with the variations in agro-production systems. The modes of female participation in agricultural production depend on the land owning status of farm households. Their roles range from managers to landless labourers. In overall farm production, women's average contribution is estimated at 55-66 per cent of the total labour with percentages much higher is certain regions. Numerous studies on participation of women in agriculture have clearly shown the intense involvement of rural women in farming in terms of volume of work performed and value of agricultural products produced.

Women share abundant responsibilities to perform wide spectrum of duties both in the home and outside but their participation is considered as normal by the society. Women are extensively involved in activities related to production, processing, preparation and marketing and selling of foodgrains, oilseeds, fruits, vegetables and fishes, dairy and other animal products.

In Indian agriculture women perform four different types of roles as worker (a source of power), as operator (a controller), as manager (a farmer), as entrepreneur (a business person). As workers the rural women are usually employed in arduous field operations like sowing behind the plough, transplanting, weeding, intercultural, harvesting and threshing, agro-processing involving cleaning/garding, drying, parboiling, milling, grinding, decortications and storage. These tasks not only demand considerable time and energy but also are source of drudgery for the farmwomen which are not yet precisely identified and quantified. The result is that women's needs for a comfortable work participation remain neglected.[9]

HEALTH ISSUES RELATED TO RURAL WOMEN

Rural communities at low levels of economic development usually have high levels of fertility. Young children can substitute for adults in many forms of agricultural and domestic work, including child care, animal husbandry, and gathering and transport of food and fuel wood. Therefore, children are likely to contribute more to family production of goods and services than they consume, at least if they are not sent to school.

Moreover, child mortality continuous to be high in rural areas of most third world countries in spite of the spread of modern medicine and improvements in sanitation. In the recent past, mortality was often so high that many families had few surviving children in spite of high fertility, and many women died before the end of their childbearing years. In regions with low levels of economic development, a sufficient reproduction of the population was a condition of survival both of the parents and of the community. The young generation had to support their elders, and in communities where the maintenance of law and order was left largely to members of the family or the village, adult sons had to defend family and village against enemies.

Until recent times, the need for defense against enemies motivated not only parents, but also governments, local and national, to be pronatalist. The social pressure on parents to maximize family size was bolstered by granting a high status to fathers and mothers of large families, and a low status to the unmarried and infertile, especially women. Under these circumstances, family organization was based on the institution of early and universal marriage for girls, with men tending to divorce or abandon infertile and subfecund women.

Families were organized as autocratic age-sex hierarchies. Younger family members owed obedience to older persons, and the oldest man in the family was the decision maker. In daily life men and women could dispose of the labour power of younger members of the their own sex according to the customary distribution of labour, but when a change in the distribution of labour, became necessary-because of changes in the method of production or in the availability of resources, for example-the family head decided on the new distribution of labour. By assigning as much work as possible to women and younger family members, he could increase family income while reducing his own work burden.

Either custom or the marriage contract stipulated that the wife must do the work that was needed to serve male family members and children. This obligation included not only child care and domestic duties, but also carrying water, gathering fuel, and often caring for domestic animals and processing crops. In most rural communities, women were obliged to work in the fields, and in some communities women and children did nearly all the agricultural work.

Frequent pregnancy and prolonged breastfeeding tax a woman's health. If a woman married early and spent the entire period between puberty and menopause being either pregnant or breastfeeding, and if she also worked hard at multiple tasks in the household and in agriculture, the strain on her health was heavy. Maternal and infant morbidity and mortality and the frequency of involuntary abortion were attributable to or aggravated by such patterns of childbearing and work. Thus, a conflict existed between the family's interest in a large number of surviving children and the family head's interest in obtaining as much work as possible from the adult women.

Rural societies have dealt with this problem in a variety of ways. One is spacing of births, another is polygyny, and a third is customary strictures on women's work in agriculture.

In communities where modern contraception is not practiced, a family can prolong the period in which the wife can recover strength between the end of breastfeeding and the onset of a new pregnancy by abstinence or other traditional means of fertility restriction. Traditionally most African societies had enforced periods of abstinence after each birth, and in many parts of India women moved back to their parent's household after child birth.

The custom of marital abstinence after child birth provides an inducement to polygyny. Moreover, the conflict between motherhood and work is attenuated when a number of wives share the burden of serving the husband and performing tasks related to domestic duties, child care, and agriculture labour. In sparsely populated regions with free access to cultivation of common land, polygyny is highly advantageous to the family head, because he can combine large family size with a negligible work burden, all the work being done by his wives and children. Where market access is available for surplus products, he can expand the area under cultivation in step with the increase in the family labour. In other words, polygyny is a means to create family wealth in regions without land shortage and without the availability of labour for hire. A likely outcome for the society as a whole is increased income inequality.

The sexual division of labour is different in rural areas where increasing population density has led to the replacement of long-fallow production on common land with more intensive systems of agriculture using animal draught power. The use of animals for land preparation and transport is always a male monopoly. Men perform the operations for which animals are employed, while women and children perform some or all of the tasks for which only human muscle power is used. In this system of agriculture, women and children contribute a smaller share of total agricultural work and animals and men a larger one. Moreover, since additional land can only be obtained by purchase, if at all, women's agricultural work is less of an economic asset than under common land tenure. There is less economic motivation for polygyny, which at most is practiced only by a small number of rich men.

In many rural communities, men exercise control over women to such an extent that they prevent them from working outside the home. women who do no work in the fields can devote all their time to child care, domestic work, and other activities that can be performed in or close by the home. With this type of family organization, as well, only a small minority of rich men can afford to be polygynuous.[10]

RURAL WOMEN AND LABOUR

In India, the female labour is a socio-economic problem and is very complex and complicated in nature. These women have to do all the household work along with their employment outside the home, which add immensely to their mental as well as physical burden. Moreover, the household work is usually not shared by the family members. Therefore, doubling quantum of work thus results in reduced efficiency in the work, unhappiness in the family and ill health of the family members.

Generally, the women engaged in the labour force belong to the weaker sections of the society. Their families are unable to provide the basic necessities of life such as food, clothing and shelter to their family members. In addition to this, there are multifarious factors which compel these women to join the labour force, viz. poor economic conditions of the family, too large a family size to support, illiteracy, rising prices of consumable goods, immature death of husband, chronic illness in the family, less male earning hands, unhealthy habits of the husband (drinking, drug addiction, fighting nature and gambling). All this add immensely to their mental as well as physical burden and results in stress.[11]

GOVERNMENT INITIATIVES FOR WOMEN WELFARE

Since Independence, government's policy on women's development has taken varying types of emphasis; from the initial welfare oriented approach to the current focus on development and empowerment.

The Planning Commission, with the aim of converging the benefits in the social and economic development sectors for women in the Ninth Plan, envisaged "inclusion of an identifiable women component plan in the programme of the respective ministries right from the planning process, and to monitoring and implementation of programmes to ensure the reach of benefits to women." The Ninth Plan Document (1997-2000) also laid emphasis on the participation of people in the planning process, and the promotion of self-help groups. Empowerment of women was one of the nine primary objectives of the Ninth Plan.

Successful working of SHGs in Andhra Pradesh, Tamil Nadu, Karnataka etc. and successful implementation of Social Development Programmes such as Mahila Samakhya, some part of DWCRA and programmes undertaken by NABARD and RMK for women's development and empowerment highlighted the need for a change in women's traditional roles and for organizing them into small, homogenous self-help groups; training them to increase their production skill and productivity; and equipping them through skill upgradation, entrepreneurship training, etc., to undertake more remunerative on-farm and off-farm activities.

Thinking and further deliberations in this direction resulted in the culmination of a pilot project viz. Swa-Shakti Project assisted by IFAD and World Bank in October, 1998. This project was originally approved as Rural Women's Development and Empowerment Project. Given the long-term nature of the issues which negatively impact on women, the overall objective of the project was to launch a programme which strengthens the process to promote the social and economic development of women and creates an environment for social change to improve their quality of life.[12]

CONCLUSION

Autocratic methods of family organization, with men as decisionmakers and women obliged to obey them, promote adaptation to population growth by labour-intensive methods, and they help small farms to survive the competition with large farms that must pay for their marginal labour supply. The exception is regions in which women are prevented from working in agriculture for status reasons. In these regions, the need to pay male wages for marginal labour provides a disincentive to agricultural intensification. The subsistence crops that are grown by women are likely to be neglected in efforts to improve productivity, with serious effects on nutrition and family welfare in many countries.

Because women in most underdeveloped rural settings are forbidden to use mechanized equipment and other modern inputs, low (or zero) female wages for labour-intensive operations compete with much higher wages for male use of modern inputs, and the resulting distortion of cost calculations is a deterrent to agricultural modernization. Under these conditions, agricultural work has even less attraction for female than for male school leavers, and the former are likely either to migrate to towns, to become housewives without agricultural work, or, in areas where there are such opportunities, to seek local employment in service or processing industries. The incentives to male migration are strongest in areas where women are secluded and where women produce the family food without male help.

The subordinate status of women is conducive to large family size. Women dependence upon the goodwill of their husbands and older family members makes them hesitant to practice contraception, and, because their opportunities for self-support in case of divorce and widowhood are limited by labour market restrictions and wage discrimination, they run a great risk of becoming dependent upon help from their children. However, when rural development raises men's interest in family limitation, the inferior status of women may actually serve to reduce fertility, because it is usually the husband who decides on family size.

REFERENCES

1. Guar, K.D., (1997), "Economic Development in India: Problem and Prospects," p. 325.
2. Behera, M.C., (2006), "Globalising Rural Development," p. 374.
3. Venkata Ravi, R., Siva Ram, P. and Sunder Raj, D. (2006), "Empowering Rural India," p. 1.
4. Kurukshetra, "A Journal of Rural Development," August-2007, p-19.
5. *Ibid.*, p. 20.
6. *Ibid.*
7. Raveendaran, N., Anita, S. and Anjugam, M., (2006), "Social and Institutional Framework of Female Participation in Agriculture," p. 93.
8. *Ibid.*, p. 95.
9. Indian Farming (Journal), Volume 56, No. 4, July-2006.
10. McNicoll, Geoffery and Cain, mean, (1990), "Rural Development and Population: Institutions and Policy," p. 45.
11. Sharma, S.L., Sharma, Satish K. and Pavda, Jayaram, (2005), "Ethic, Rural and Gender Issues in Contemporary North West," p. 250.
12. Yojana, a Development Monthly, March 2006, p. 73.

8

Social Condition of Rural Women from Ancient to Modern

Dr. Pravesh Kumari

India is a developing country of village there are more than 638596 villages (senses 2001) and about 1/3 of the total population of country lives in village. Women are almost 48 per cent of population. In Indian society the condition of women has been continuously changing in the course of time; the changes in social condition too has affected the position.

This chapter is an attempt to look into the condition of Indian women beginning from ancient period in the framework of social condition and in the concluding part of this chapter there is an attempt to emphasize the change in the social condition of women.

WOMEN IN ANCIENT INDIAN SOCIETY

Some scholars believe that in Ancient India the women enjoyed equal status with men in all fields of life. However, some others hold contrasting views. Work by Ancient Indian grammarians such as Patanjali and Katyayana suggest that women were educated in the early Vedic period.

In Rigvedic society the position of women was fairly satisfactory. The daughter in a Rigvedic family was not a shy and meek creature like her modern representative in the Hindu family. But she was bold, free and strong; and women enjoyed a very respectable position in the society. Women in Vedic age enjoyed complete equality with man in all fields of life. Daughter enjoyed as much freedom as son. Women capable of carrying religious discussions were admitted in assemblies and were encouraged to enhance their scholarships.

Education to all children and to help them in settling in life were the twin duties of the Vedic Parents and in this there was initially no discrimination between a boy and a girl. Since Rigvedic age education of women was given much importance. Upanayana or ceremonial initiation into the Vedic studies was a rule. As it was for boys, the marriage of a girl used to take place at a fairly advanced age. The position of the wife was an honored one in the family. During this period some girls even remained unmarried in their father's houses up to an advanced age. A well-known example of this was Ghasha.

Some famous kingdom in Ancient India had traditions such as Nagarvadhu (bride of the city), women competed to win the coveted title of the Nagarvadhu. Amarpali is the most famous example of a Nagarvadhu.

Women enjoyed equal position and right during the early Vedic period condition. However in later Vedic period approximately the conditions of women began to decline with Smritis (Manusmriti) and other religious texts curtailing women's freedom and rights.

Although reformatory movements such a Jainism allowed women to be admitted to the religious order, and the women in India faced confinement and restrictions.

WOMEN IN MEDIEVAL INDIAN SOCIETY

The Indian women's position in the society further deteriorated during the medieval period. Sati Pratha, Polygamy and ban on widow remarriages became part of social life in India. The system of Purdah become stricter, prostitution become more popular. In the medieval period was education was, by and large, ignored. During the Muslim conquest in the Indian Society, among the Rajputs of Rajasthan, the Jauhar was practiced. In some parts of Indian Society the Devadasis or the temple women were sexually exploited. Polygamy was widely practiced.

In spite of these conditions, some women excelled in the fields of politics, literature, education and religion. The only women who had occupied the throne of Delhi was Raziya Sultana who was known as a wise ruler.

The gond queen Durgavati ruled for fifteen years, before she lost her life in a battle with Mughal Emperor Akbar's general Asaf Khan in 1564. Chand Bibi defended Ahmednagar against the mighty mughal forces of Akbar in 1590s. Jehangir's wife Nurjahan effectively wielded imperial power and was recognized as the real force behind the mughal throne. Gulbadan Begum was a woman of exceptional poetic talent, she wrote the Humayun Namah, a work which has been recognized as the most valuable contemporary record of Humayun's reign. It is unfortunate that a good part of the work has been lost. Shivaji's mother, Jijabai was deputed as queen regent, because of her ability as a warrior and administrator. These ladies could learn and attain dominance by sheer strength of their personality. Thus, we may conclude the during Muslim period while the women from royal families enjoyed much respect and freedom and were interested in learning, the women of lower and middle strata of society were largely ignorant and illiterate.

All these evils caused deterioration in the conditions of women so much that the birth of a girl was regarded inauspicious in the family and the number of prostitutes also increased.

WOMEN IN BRITISH PERIOD

During the British period and position of women in India was vague as Sati system was evidently prevalent. Parda was strictly enforced on Muslim women. All most the Hindu temple openly or surreptitiously bounded Devadasis. The contacts with western culture, tradition, literature and education influenced very deeply the mind of the Indian leaders. The result of it was the social movements for reforms against these evils which were prevalent in the society. The leaders and the social reformers who were in the forefront of the struggle for women emancipation were Raja Ram Mohan Roy, Ishwar Chandra Vidyasagar, Swami Dayanand Saraswati, Swami Vivekanand, Mahatma Gandhi, Jawaharlal Nehru and many others.

Then come the period of religious and social reforms—the Brahma Samaj of 1828. Prarthna Samaj, Arya Samaj of 1875 and such other institutions advocated widow remarriage, emancipation of women and decried sati and child marriage; consequently sati system was abolished (1829), Widow Re-marriage Act (1856) was enacted. Raja Ram Mohan Roy's efforts led to abolition of sati. Ishwar Chandra Vidyasagar's crusade for the improvement in condition of widows led to the Widow Re-marriage Act, fourteen years as the minimum age of marriage for a girl was stipulated through the efforts of Mohamed Ali Jinnah. Many women reformers such as Pandit Ramabai also helped the cause of women upliftment.

An Act was passed in 1929 which gave the son's daughter and her son their natural places in the order of inheritance. In 1937 the

Indian legislature passed the Hindu Women's Rights to Property Act which conceded to the Hindu widow a share in her husband's property and the right to demand partition; and provision were also made for their education.

A regular system of female education was practically unknown at the beginning of the nineteenth century. Education of female was discouraged, it was regarded as being against the injunctions of Hindu scriptures and their was a wide spread belief that the education of girl leads to their withdrawal, it is significant to mention that the social reformers and the British Government made positive attempts to educate Indian girl.

So, pre-independence period marked the beginning of awareness of the sufferings of women due to oppressive social custom. During this phase a favourable climate was created to improve the condition of women through legal reforms. But their condition was not much improved.

Women played an important part in India's Independence struggle some of the famous freedom fighters include Bhikaji Cama, Dr. Annie Besant, Vijayalakshmi Pandit, Rajkumari Amrit Kaur, Anjali Ammal, Aruna Asaf Ali, Sucheta Kriplani and Kasturba Gandhi other notable names include Durgabai Deshmukh etc. Rani Lakshmi Bai, the queen of Jhansi, led the Indian Rebellion of 1857 against British.

She is now widely considered as a nationalist leader. Sarojini Naidu, a poet and a freedom fighter, was the first Indian women to become the President of the Indian National Congress and also the first women to become the Governor of a State in India.

WOMEN IN CONTEMPORARY INDIA

(i) Legal and Constitutional Provision

After independence the framers of Indian Constitution, keeping in view the importance of women education as well as their place and position in our society, have made clear provisions. In Part III of the constitution specifies the fundamental right of equality of men and women in all spheres.

The fundamental rights provides right to equality before the law and equal protection of law within the territory of India (Article 14).

Article 15 clause I of the says the state shall not discriminate against any citizen on grounds of religion, race, caste, sex or place of birth or any of them. Clause (3) of Article 15 enables the state to make special provisions for women and children.

Article 16 provides equal opportunities to all citizens in matters relating to employment or appointment to any office under the state.

Article 16(II) – No citizen shall on grounds only of religion, race, caste, sex descent, place of birth, residence or any of them be ineligible for or discriminated against in respect of any employment or office under the state.

Article 19 deals with Right to freedom of speech and expression, right to form association, right to assemble peacefully and without arms and to more freely through out the territory of India.

Part IV of the Constitution contains Directive Principles of State Policy. Article 39(a) says that the citizens-men and women equally have the right to an adequate means of livelihood. Clause (d) of Article 39 says that there is equal pay for equal work for both men and women and holds clause (e) that the health and strength of workers-men and women and the tender age of children are not abused and the citizens are not forced by economic necessity to enter an occupation unsuited to their age or strength.

Article 42 provisions for just and human condition of work and maternity relief.

Article 51(a)(e) imposes a fundamental duty on every citizen to renounce the practices derogatory to the dignity of women.

But the Directive Principles are of the non-justiceable nature and it depends on the will of the state to follow them or not.

For the purpose of social welfare and betterment of the Indian society and for betterment of the conditions of Indian women there are some laws and acts which the Government of India has enacted.

They include (1) Child Marriage Restraint Act 1929, Hindu Succession Act 1956, which provides that Indian women shall have an right to property they were formerly deprived of (2) Dowry Prohibition Act 1961, which provides for protection of Indian women against the oppressive demands of dowry (3) Hindu Marriage Act 1955 and (4) Special Marriage Act which provides for the maintenance of Indian married women in case of their divorce (5) Maternity Benefits Act 1961, (6) The recent introduction by the Union

Government of special reservation in services for the Indian women in the matter of recruitment in various government services, the Government of India declared 2001 as the year of women empowerment. The National Policy for the empowerment of women came in 2001 and the protection of women from Domestic Violence Act 2005 came into force on October 26, 2006 so that they may become aware of their position and participate in the development of the nation.

In present time women facing so many hurdles are entering all fields such as medical, engineering, journalism, politics, business, science, administration, sports and social work. Indira Gandhi, Kiran Bedi, Kalpana Chawla, Punita Arora, Indra Nui, Pratibha Patil and many more are very well known personalities.

(ii) Actual Condition of Indian Women

Indian rural women after 60 years of Independence, the actual condition of women is not satisfactory. The unfavourable condition of women is reflected in many social practices, ceremonies and beliefs which continue even today. The legal securities and educational facilities provided to women, however, have not been able to change the traditional way of thinking, the implementation of laws is tardy, dowry death, child marriages, discrimination, sexual abuse and atrocities in our society, the reasons are many the Indian society accepts a sharp distinction between men and women's spheres. We are now entering in the 21 century, but women have to face various types of violence; the condition of women has not still changed.

In family also there is a dominant role of a men and woman has to play a subordinate role. While economically dependent women are likely to be beaten, and economically dependent women are more likely to stay on in a violent home.

The concept that women are meant for home and man for fields is such widely accepted one that it is difficult for people to get over it. Many educated girls do not take up any career as it is regarded incompatible with smooth and peaceful family life. Even if women do other jobs due to certain pressure or her desires, they are expected to perform their home making duties without any concession.

The rigid distinction in men's and women's society resulted in women's economic subjugation and dependent position in society. Society in the past has looked down upon women opting for a career. Moreover, there were fewer job openings for them, and discrimination has been evident in matters of wages where women are paid less than men for similar type of work. This economic situation has largely been the cause of the lower condition of women in Indian rural society.

Moreover, since most of Indian rural women remain confined to home and there sphere is strictly limited. They have no interaction with the other world and remain unexposed to the influence of progressive societies. Consequently, they develop a narrow outlook and depend on men for security and decision making.

The condition of women in modern Indian society is still inferior, oppressed and one of degradation although Indian women of today are acquiring higher education, becoming employed in various kinds of jobs and professions, thereby becoming economically self-sufficient while in rural India of today they are still struggling for survival from acute poverty. Position of rural Indian women is inferior and sub-servient to men. One of the prominent feature of Indian society of today is that the Indian women of the rural areas are put to such inferior and subordinate condition that they haplessly depend on the mercy of their male counterparts for their survival and sub-sistence having no dignity of their own in the society. Consequently, they develop a narrow outlook and depend on men for security and decision making. Such a situation withholds the women from protesting against their sub-servient conditions in the society.

The general outlook of men in our society, particularly their attitude towards the Indian women, has not undergone any substantial changes. Their attitude still remains conservative, rigid, static and outdated towards the Indian women who are faced with hindrances in their way to the healthy development in the society.

But one very encouraging development which has occurred during the last ten years is the emergence of women's movements wherein women have started raising their voice against inequality and patriarchal values in favour of an egalitarian social structure.

Therefore, mere introduction of legal and social reforms is not at all adequate, our society urgently requires a dynamic change in the outlook and attitude of the Indian men towards women as well as a humane understanding by the men of the problem of Indian women and also a proper appreciation by the men of the aims and aspirations of Indian women as individuals and as citizens of a modern republic and democratic polity.

Lastly, the responsibility is a joint one. There is need for a change in the attitude of men. Parents can change the attitudes to their children and bring them up in a way that may reflect equality and that then may improve the social conditions of Indian rural women.

REFERENCES

Mishra, R.C. Towards Gender Equality (2006). https://www.vedamsbooks.com/no43902.htm). Authorspress. ISBN 81-7273-306-2.

Comments to Ashtadhyayi 3.3.21 and 4.1.14 by Patanjali.

Upadya, B.S. Women in Rig Veda. Nand Kishore and Bros., Banaras 1941.

Majumdar Maya. Social Status of Women in India, Dominant Publishers and Distributors, New Delhi, 2004.

Jain, Shashi Prabha; Singh, Mamta. Violent against Women. Radha Publications, New Delhi, 2001

Sharma Anuradha. Encyclopedia of Indian Women, Vol. I, Common Wealth, New Delhi, 1998.

Agrawal, C.M. Nari Facets of Indian Womenhood, Vol. III, Publishers, Indian Distributors, Delhi.

Mishra, S.N.; Sweta, Anil. Public Governance and Decentralization, Vol. 2, Mittal Publishers, New Delhi, 2003.

Nand, J.E. Women and Politics in India, Deep & Deep Publications, New Delhi, 1996.

Sarkar's Munir, J.S. The Constitution of India, Publication Alia, Law Agency Allahabad, 2007.

Majumdar, R.C. & Pusolbar, A.D. (editor). The History and Culture of Indian People. Vol. I, the Vedic age Bombay, Bharatiya Vidya Bhawan, 1951.

S. Ram, Women Socio-economic Problem, Common Wealth Publishers, New Delhi, 2004.

Lal Sundar. Social Status of Women Dominant Publishers, New Delhi, 2005.

Ghadially Rehana. Women in Indian Society, Sage Publication, New Delhi, 1998.

De'Souza, Agred. Women in Contemporary India Traditional Image and Cleaning Role. Manohar Publications, New Delhi.

Singh, Parmanand. Equality Reservation and Discrimination in India. Deep & Deep Publication, New Delhi, 1985.

Roy, Kalpana. Women and their Environment. Vol. I, Rajat Publication, New Delhi, 1999.

9

Changing Occupational Pattern of Rural Women

Dr. Rupesh Tyagi & Bhawna

INTRODUCTION

The status of women in a society is the true index of its socio-economic, cultural, religious and spiritual level. The status of women in a society is directly linked with its economic position and the level of participation in economic life which in its own turn, depends on rights, roles and opportunities for participation in economic activities. The economic status of women now accepted as an indication of the stage of development of an economy.

As historical records show the position of women has been culture specific, in that it varied from society to society and time to time. The position of women during the Vedic Period was almost equal to men but during the time of Upanishads the overall status of women was not similar to that of Vedic times. The status of women in the age of smritis declined further and the position of women in the age of Purans was not much different from the age of smritis. The status of women in the Epic age was very much similar to age of Upanishads and Puranas. The age of Jainism and Buddhism is considered little progressive and women status was little satisfactory as compared to previous times. During medieval period the status of women started to decline and reached its all time low under the Islamic rule when economy and the status of women stagnated for long time. It started to change for the better very slowly with the advent of British education system but, women are still victims of the basically exploitative system operating against them. In fact, like the resulting development pattern of the Indian economy, Indian women has suffered a dualism in her status on her way to play effectively her economic and social role in the economic development.

SOCIO-ECONOMIC STATUS OF RURAL WOMEN

Women are the vital human infrastructure and their empowerment (economic social and political) would hasten the pace of social development. Investing in women's "capabilities" and empowering them to achieve their "choices" and "opportunities" is the surest way to contribute to economic growth and overall development. In this regard, it can be high lighted that separate economic planning system can be advocated.

Rural women's contribution acquires more importance, because they are assigned triple role in the society, and therefore contribute more then men. In the agrarian society the family is the unit of production. The place of work being close to the home, men, women and children all participate in the production process. As a society moves from the traditional agricultural and household industry to organized industry and services from rural to urban areas, the traditional division of labour ceases to operate and the complementary relationship of the family is substituted by the competitive one between individual units of labour. The scarcer the jobs, the sharper are the competition. Technical changes in the process of production call for acquisition of new skills and specializations which are very different from the traditional division of labour. Women, handicapped by lack of opportunities for acquisition of these new skills, find their traditional productive skills unwanted by the new economy.

The traditional village community in India consisted of the cultivators the artisans and those performing menial services. In each of these, women played a distinctive and accepted role in the process of earning a living for the family. By and large this pattern is still prevalent in the traditional forms of the economy. Among the agricultural classes in most part of the country earning a livelihood is still a family endeavour with or without the division of labour between women and men. The patterns of women participation vary according to regional and cultural norms. Throughout the Himalayan region, the major role in agricultural production is played by women. Among the Khasis of Meghalaya, women dominate economic process and even educated women holding high positions in offices do not hesitate to do manual work in agriculture.

OCCUPATIONAL PATTERN OF RURAL WOMEN

Women play more pronounced and crucial role in agriculture sector in our economy. According to M.M. Srinivas rural women can be classified in four classes normally:

1. Women belonging to big land owner families who engage labour to cultivate their lands assumes supervisory jobs.
2. Women belonging to small landholding households who personally cultivate their land with or without the services of labourer.
3. Women belonging to tenant, share cropper, artisans households and;
4. Agricultural labourers who subsist entirely on hiring them selves for labour work. The first category of women are always not in labour work outside their own homes, while category four women are always in labour work in addition to burden of their home work. In our country in spite of more than three decades of planned development, organized sector provides only about 12-15 per cent employment to women so they mostly find jobs in agriculture and allied activities. The rural female cultivators and agricultural labourers comprised 37 per cent and 50 per cent respectively in female work force in recent years.

The contribution of women in economic development is gauged by their work participation rate. "Participation rate is usually measured in terms of the proportion of workers to total population." The National Committee on the status of women revealed that female work participation rate declined from 33.7 per cent in 1911 census to 28 per cent in the 1961 census. Thereafter it hovered around that percentage level. But there was a sharp decline over the 1961-1971. One of the reasons which is attributed for this decline in the female participation rate is the definitional changes adopted in different census reports. But again during 1971-1981 there was some improvement in the work participation rates. This trend also followed in recent years.

In most of the rural areas work participation rates of female workers increased more rapidly because of spread effect of modern technology, education, health programmes and the rural development programmes launched by the government.

Data regarding main workers and marginal worker show that about 33 per cent females are cultivators and more than 46 per cent are agricultural labourers and nearly 5 per cent are engaged in household industries. It is logically follows from this that women work mainly in primary sector as cultivators and agricultural workers.

In the category of marginal workers we see that out of every 100 females nearly 48 and 41 as cultivators and agricultural labourers respectively. In household industry about 4 per cent of them is engaged. In factory, trade, transport etc. their number is very low. Thus they contribute more to agricultural development of the other sectors in the economy. About 80 per cent of female workers are engaged in agriculture as labourers or cultivator. It should also be born in mind that the participation data for women do not include the majority of rural women who spend their time and effcort in the collection of fuel, fodder and vegetables which are either for direct consumption by family or are sold to meet the family's other needs. Similarly women who help in family occupations like dairying poultry farming, raising and maintenance of kitchen gardens, sewing, weaving and similar subsistence level of occupations are not counted.

Changing Nature of Rural Women's Work

It is important to note that women's participation in the agricultural production was strongly encouraged since the liberation. The socialist state was ideologically committed to women's liberation and considered their participation in the social production as a necessary condition. During agricultural collectivization, the management of land was in the hands of the collectives which had disrupted the patriarchal control over women's labour in significant ways. Various functions of the present households such as childcare and domestic responsibilities were largely taken over by the collectives. This certainly gave women the freedom to get involved in the remunerative work outside home.

The agrarian changes that are taking place here are illustrative of similar processes set in motion by the rural reforms. The increasing commercialization has changed the occupational structure which has prevalent in this region until recent times. The study conducted has brought to light the changes in the occupational profiles of women in the village. For this limited purpose, the main survey results are enumerated here. There are mainly three kinds of women's works that can be seen in the villages. Women in nearly 70 per cent of the households are still engaged in agricultural work, mainly vegetable and flower cultivation. Needless to state here that household work is not regarded as a work to be mentioned separately. Only elderly women who form just 10 per cent of the total, said they were engaged in only housework. This category mainly includes women who are too old to work on the land, and have given it to their sons for cultivation. They stay at home to take care of their grandchildren and do other household chores. This kind of labour arrangement is quite prevailed in the villages. And category is of those who stay in the village and do not participate in farm work as they are preoccupied with child rearing. Women who were able to expand their income-earning work in way of becoming small-scale entrepreneurs constitute the third category. They are mainly engaged in marketing vegetables, flowers, fruits and fisheries.

However, the nature of women's work within a household is determined by a number of factors. In this village, women's labour within the household tend to vary according to the size and nature of commercial production they are engaged in. This study uses these two variables to differentiate village households and women's labour participation in various stages of production activities. On an average, large landholding households engaged in cash crop production are few. In some cases, they have taken additional land on lease to increase production so as to have surplus capital to invest in farmland. In village parlance such households are referred to as "hard working section" or rich farmers implying that sufficient economic resources will also help them to earn the right political connection. In these households, generally men make all major decisions regarding production as well as management activities and women's role tends to be limited to assistance in farm labour.

Women entrepreneurs in the village have no doubt emerged as significant factors in the new commercial economy. The new market forces in the agrarian economy have certainly enabled them to emerge as income-earners. This has seriously weakened earlier dichotomy that existed in the division of labour where women worked in subsistence agriculture and men in wage earning jobs. However, these women entrepreneurs and face a range of constraints when they attempt to start, sustain and expand their ventures. These constraints can be understood largely in terms of inadequate institutional support that make them vulnerable and limit their potions to compete equally with men in the highly competitive market economy.

Policy Implications and Conclusions

The changing occupational distribution of women has far reaching policy implications and indicates the need for several changes in implementing these programmes for progressive participation of women in economic development.

The Policy implications can be stated in relation to employment and labour policy. The concentrated legislative and development efforts to rectify the long standing imbalances with the Indian society have accorded considerable opportunities and advantages to women in some sections of society. The promise of equality has not been realized for the large masses of Indian women. Implementation of the Equal Remuneration Act has to be strengthened. Areas where women's employment is low has to be identified and special agencies may be set up for extending credit facilities for self-employment may be made by making suitable changes in recruitment policy of the public sector and government services. Age-relaxation and extending part-time jobs for women may be considered. Wage differencials and discrimination still prevailing in several sectors which may be altered with suitable legislative measures. There is need for institutional support for women to take any enterprise and the present stress on voluntary agencies may be replace with a suitable institutional voluntary agencies. The programmes for women under the social welfare sector are be strengthened which have been found useful in skill formation and creation of gainful employment among women. There must be close coordination between educational programmes for women and developmented programmes of the Central and State Government. The proliferation of inter-changeable roles and dynamic occupational distribution of women work force within the changing pace of economic development has given rise to new problems, often of a serious nature. Each policy has to work out for a balance between the varying demands of occupation. The central conclusion that can be drawn from this chapter is clear. In the post independence era the number of women working in India has increase. As women entered the labour force, the labour market has not fully responded yet on variety of new opportunities was created. The occupational choices seem to be driven not only by expectations regarding life time hours of work but also by trade-off among the characteristics of different occupations. However the imperfections in labour market is reflected in extending equal opportunities for women and men. The regulations enacted with best of intentions, restricted the flexibility and inhibited the abilities of the markets to adapt. In contrast, free and flexible labour markets provide employment opportunities for new workers, even in the face of rapid structural change.

From the discussions above it is clear that women play vital role in socio-economic development of our country. Their contribution to agricultural development is greater than to the development of other sectors. Due to limitations and apparent handicaps and constraints such as lack of education, skill, health, nutrition, information, transportation etc. most of the women are engaged in lowly paying jobs. This situation needs to be changed if we want to utilize their potentialities to the fullest extent. Women can play even more positive and active role if they are imparted education, training, and are enabled to use improved/new technology. This will improve their efficiency and productivity and they can become more active partners in economic development. Women need educational opportunities that would enable to undertake economically and psychologically rewarding work. Fast changing scenario and emerging conditions they are expected to play more prominent role in the years to comc.

REFERENCES

Manohar, K.M. (ed.) (1983): "Socio-economic Status of Indian Women," Seema Publications.

Saran, A.B. and Sandhwar, A.N., (1990): "Problems of Women Workers in Unorganized Sector (Brick Klins, Quarries and Mines of Bihar and West Bengal)" Northern Book Center.

Seshila (1982) "Revolution and the Status of Women in India." Publishes Metro Politen-book Co. New Delhi, p. 166.

Sayed Afzal (2005) "Empowerment of Women: A Study of Kurukshetra, Vol. 54, No. 1, p. 7.

10

Economic and Social Reforms: Violence and Increasing Insecurities Against Women

Juhi Gupta

Economic reforms are the new edition of the old charter of capitalism. It has become the new testament of world. Economic reforms are driving through economic policy and due to this policy the direction of world economy has almost changed.

Economic reforms are one of the factors that have changed the entire scenario of social and cultural environment within the country, especially for the women.

Economic reforms are often projected as a panacea for economic progression and economic invigoration which according to the advocates of globalisation will lead to reduction in poverty levels, squalor and regression. These global reforms though are discernible option, can itself be lopsided in. Increasing the trauma of the poor and thus bring down the status of women if the communities in the developing world are not empowered on the effects of such reforms. As one observes the direction of globalisation, it is quite skeptical as to what changes the globalisation can do to ameliorate poverty or in altering the status of children and women in the developing world.

It is of course well-known that violence against women has deeply systemic roots, and that there is a "normalisation" of such violence where the economic and social status of women is already low. It is also increasingly recognised that such violence takes many forms. In addition to the overt physical violence there are what could be called "structural" forms of violence through economic, social and cultural processes.

Economic violence ranges from the denial of property to women, the use of their unpaid labour as a norm in households, the denial of equal access to education and discrimination in labour markets, unequal access to credit and other markets to practices such as dowry payments.

Social violence include not only various forms of discrimination and curbs on women's mobility and freedom, but also practices such as early marriage, pressure to bear male children, disparities in access to nutrition and health, as well as to education.

Social violence also includes primarily gender disparity. Varying levels of male domination exists in most societies. Indian society is highly patriarchical. We continue to practice gender discrimination in all spheres of life. Indeed, the UNDP Human Development Report had come up with comparative figures to establish that gender discrimination in South Asian Countries including India is more acute than even in Arab countries.

Gender discrimination is evident even in the demographic indicators of the country. While most of the major countries have a sex ratio favourable to women, our sex ratio continues to remain favourable to men. Not only that, child sex-ratio has been moving inexorably against the girl child in the recent decades.

Of course, this is not a biological phenomenon. It is the result of sex-selective abortions and the blatent violation of PNDT Act, 1994. The 2001 census figures indicate that illegal sex-selection is more prevalent in some of the most prosperous parts of the country, like Punjab, Haryana and Delhi. Studies based on hospital statistics in South Delhi indicate that sex-ratio at birth is as low as 500 females per 1000 males. This truly reflects the frightening gender discrimination of the middle class and elites in Delhi.

Though the gender gap in literacy has been declining over the decades, still there exists considerable difference. According to 2001 census while male literacy is 76 per cent, female literacy is as low as 54 per cent at the national level. In States like Bihar, UP, Rajasthan, MP and Orissa, the gender gap in literacy is even more. Indeed, this gap could be taken as an indicator of the level of gender discrimination in these societies. Low level of female literacy is often associated with poor access to health and family planning facilities, poor awareness of proper child care and other hygienic practices which adversely affect the welfare of the whole family. Lower literacy and educational attainments result in lower earning capacity. The ratio of estimated female to male earned income in India at 31 per cent is one of lowest in the World. Though women constitute a third of the labour force in India, they account for less than one-fifth of the employees in the organized sector. Further, often they are engaged in activities of a repetitive nature which can be characterized as drudgery.

With globalization there is a trend of feminization of certain activities especially in textile and garment industries, electronics and agro – processing industries. These are often repetitive in nature and low-paying.

Women earners often have to bear the double burden of work in the sense that they are expected to carry on their traditional role as home makers also. Many of their socially highly valued activities like caring the children are not assigned any economic value in national income accounting.

Cultural norms that oppress women and girls often have a strong psychological element to them, as patterns of objectification and subjugation can lead to self-oppression and low self-esteem.

In addition, of course, the many forms of direct physical violence against women also tend to have strong links with economic, social and material processes. This operates throughout the life-cycle of women. Thus, pre-natal sex selection and female infanticide are much more common where female progeny are seen as an economic or social burden. Sexual abuse, including in its worst form of rape, can reflect not only patriarchal desires for control and punishment but also the lack of economic protection of the victims.

Violence associated with practices such as dowry, as in dowry deaths, has a very obvious material link. But even domestic and marital abuse is made more possible when women have fewer options for escape out of such oppressive relationships because of lack of assets or economic security in the form of gainful occupations. So lack of economic security becomes a deterrent to complaint or resistance by women victims. Even apparently non-economic atrocities such as "honour killings" have often been found to have underlying economic motivations, such as the desire to ensure control of land and other assets within particular communities, and prevent inheritance by children of "mixed" marriages.

Trafficking of women and girl children in turn has strong material underpinnings. The association of trafficking with poverty is obvious and well-known. But there needs to be more appreciation of the fact that in many cases, as Radhika Coomaraswamy has pointed out, "trafficking is really abuse of the desire to migrate", which essentially reflects poor material conditions and oppressive social constraints in the place of origin.

Even violence against older women, and particularly widows, often has a strong economic basis—either in the need of the perpetrators to control the family property or to avoid expenditure on the consumption of someone who is less able to provide unpaid labour for the household.

So there is a strong though complex relationship between violence against women and economic processes. This means that the evidence of increasing violence against women in India in the past decade must have something to do with the very rapid economic changes that have also been so apparent over this period.

Over the past two decades, the Indian economy has been thrown more open to market processes than ever before, and these market processes have been regional, national and international. This period has been associated with a tendency towards privatisation of state assets, reduction in crucial government investment, especially in infrastructure areas, reduced per capita public spending on health, reduced public expenditure in the rural areas generally, deregulation of and a number of tax benefits and other sops provided to large domestic and multinational capital, trade liberalisation which has affected the viability of small scale manufacturing units and agriculturalists, even as it has created more export possibilities for textiles and IT-enabled services.

All this in turn has created both very rapid growth in some sectors, and stagnation or worse in other sectors and regions. Economic inequalities have increased quite substantially, both spatially and within regions, and material insecurities have increased, not only for the poor but even for more prosperous groups.

The most significant feature that affects the lives of people is employment and the conditions of livelihood. This is where the past decade has created growing insecurity. The difficulty of finding remunerative work opportunities has become the single most important problem for large sections of the population. Wage employment of all kinds has fallen as a share of total employment, and self-employment has emerged as the fastest growing form even in non-agriculture, now accounting for around half of the workforce. But self-employed, especially those engaged in relatively less skilled and less productive occupations, face daily problems of survival, creating additional tensions.

Agriculturalists continue to face huge problems of viability as cultivators because of the combination of threats from highly subsidised imports which are keeping prices down, and rising costs because of withdrawal of subsidies. It is striking to note that the crisis in agriculture, which is especially marked in some pockets of rain-fed cultivation, has continued even as international prices of crops have increased in the past few years, suggesting that domestic policy and institutional failures have been significant in this.

In the urban areas, the rate of overall employment generation has been slightly better, but not in the formal sector, where employment has barely grown at all. There has been some growth in services employment, and especially in IT-enabled services that has reduced the rate of educated unemployment. But even in the urban areas, the problem of lack of sufficient employment for all those who need to work, remains significant. For less skilled workers, and especially women, the problem of access to productive work is especially acute.

Women are being drawn into the paid labour force in some more regressive ways, in the form of home-based work as part of large chains of production organised by large capitalists, or as low-paid and exploited service sector workers. The largest increase in regular employment of urban women (amounting to around 3 million new workers) between 1999-2000 and 2004-05 was as domestic servants.

In addition, there is the problem of reduced security of work and of incomes generally. Of course this is most marked for wage workers in less skilled and more unstable occupations. That is why the National Sample Survey of 2004-05 could find that 80 per cent of workers in India earn less than Rs. 20 per day. But it is ironically true that even in the higher ends of the job spectrum, employment has become more volatile and fragile, and the earlier security that was implicit in formal sector employment has all but disappeared in the new contracts.

In addition, even non-wage incomes are now less secure and more volatile, simply because many markets, and the income accruing from them, fluctuate much more wildly than they did in the past.

Material insecurity has been increasingly expressed in other negative features, most notably food consumption. Food insecurity has once again become an important national issue, not only for traditionally deprived groups, but in the aggregate. Foodgrain availability per head of population for the economy as a whole has been lower on average in the past few years, than even thirty years ago. Per capita calorie consumption, even for the poorest forty per cent of the population, has also declined.

There have also been evident declines in the availability of basic public services in the areas of health and sanitation. The decline in public expenditure investment has not only meant that the rate of expansion of much-needed health facilities has declines. The cuts in public expenditure have also meant that maintenance and repair of such facilities, as well as basic running expenditures, are not provided, so that the actual quality of and access to public health and sanitation facilities has declined.

This has affected both prevented preventive and curative health care in the public sector, which in turn means that even poor households are forced to undertake much more expenditure on private health care, even when this cuts into the incomes necessary for sheer physical survival. Naturally, this tends to affect women and girl children more adversely, and compounds the effects of gender discrimination in nutrition as well. There are even some states where the rates of child immunisation have actually worsened in recent years, and this includes apparently "fast-growing" states like Gujarat.

Along with this, the growing emphasis on markets has implied the commoditisation of many aspects of life that were earlier seen as either naturally provided by states and communities, or simply not subject to market transaction and property relations. Thus, the inability or refusal of the government to provide safe drinking water has led to the explosive growth of a bottled water industry. A whole range of previously services and utilities like power distribution and telecommunications have been privatised. Even the growing recognition accorded to intellectual property rights marks the entry of markets into ever newer spheres.

Of course, markets imply marketing and drawing more and more consumers into the web of purchase through advertising and attempts to manipulate peoples' tastes and choices. In this effort, advertising companies have notoriously used women as objects to purvey their products. The dual relationship with women, as objects to be used in selling goods, and as a huge potential market for goods, creates a peculiar process whereby women are encouraged and persuaded to participate actively in their own objectification. The huge media attention given to beauty contests, "successful" models, and the like, all feed into the rapidly expanding beauty industry, which includes not only cosmetics and beauty aids, but slimming agents, beauty parlours, weight loss clinics, and so on. Many of these contribute to the most undesirable and backward attitudes to both women and their appearance, such as the advertisements for fairness cream that emphasise that it is necessary to be fair to make a "good" marriage, which is in turn seen as the basic goal of a woman.

All this seems plausible enough, but many would argue that the link between all this and violence against women is not all that obvious. But there are identifiable mechanisms for this.

The most basic mechanism comes from the sheer fact of greater material insecurity. As ordinary life becomes more volatile, insecure and unpredictable in various ways, people search for security in whatever ways they can muster. Precisely because some degree of certainty is seen as a comfort, often the more rigid a system is (whether it is a set of intellectual and spiritual beliefs, or a religious order, or a relatively close grouping claiming a particular special social identity) the more attractive it perversely becomes. (This may explain why some of the more rigidly structured and sectarian religious and social groups that strongly emphasise patriarchy have attracted growing following in recent times).

And there is a strong undercurrent of violence in all this. The tendency towards violence of various sorts—towards other "communities" or caste groups, and especially towards women—can be seen as another reflection and result of the economic and social processes outlined earlier. The greater insecurity and sheer difficulty of ordinary life, the complications and worries involved in providing for basic needs, all make for much greater levels of everyday irritation in people. This can only rarely find an outlet in places of work, and requires other means of expression.

In addition, the massive increase in inequality, the growth of rampant consumerism, and the explosion of new media that brings all the lavish new lifestyles into open public view, all serve to add to the resentment and frustration of have-nots. The gap between aspiration and reality becomes ever wider, and this creates a strong urge to somehow get at those who are seen as "responsible." Of course, the real agents of these processes—the unresponsive government, the large companies and multinationals, the foreign investors—are all too large, too distant and too powerful to be touched. How much easier, then, to direct one's ire against those who are seen as more easily attacked—minority communities or lower caste groups, women within and outside the household, and so on. The substantial increase in violence against women is not just because of higher reporting of incidents, but because of this process which results in an actual increase in the number of such crimes.

The other philosophy that is invoked and sought to be spread is that which lies at the heart of the reliance on markets—individualism. The "competitive spirit" is unleashed and used to make people feel that it is each man or woman for himself or herself, and that individuals can succeed in making gains at the expense of others in their own social group. This has two significant effects that further aggravate problems of violence: it makes each act that of an individual, and it reduces the possibility of solidarity among victims and possibilities of collective action.

CONCLUSION

It is so important to recognise and trace the economic, social , cultural roots of violence against women. It is essential not only to mobilise for policies that shape the state and societal response to individual acts of violence, but also to change the processes of liberalisation and corporate globalisation that have indirectly aided such violence in general.

REFERENCES

N.J. Kurian, Indian J Med Res 126, October 2007, pp. 374-380.

Jayati Ghosh, Macroscan, January 29th 2008.

Dr. Meenu Agrawal.

Nagesh Kumar (2000) "Economic Reforms and their Micro Economic Impact" Economic and Political Weekly, Vol., XXXV. No. 10 March, 4-10.

Shridhar Pandey and Jay Shanker Tiwari (2003), "Economic Liberalization and Employment in India: Economic Liberalization and its Implications for Employment, Deep and Deep Publications.

www.google.co.in

11

Rural Women and Development of Entrepreneurship with Special Reference of Punjab

Dr. Prabha Singh

INTRODUCTION

Development of the society is directly related with the income generation capacity of its Members. With agriculture as the key income generation activity the entrepreneurship based on farm and home can directly affect the income of a major chunk of our population. The growth of modernization processes such as industrialization, technical change; urbanization and migration further encourage it. Entrepreneurship on small scale is the only solution to the problems of unemployment and proper utilization of both human and non-human resources and improving the living conditions of the poor masses.

Kuratko and Richard (2001) in their book on entrepreneurship stated that it is the dynamic process of creating incremental wealth. This wealth is created by individuals who take the major risks in terms of equity, time and career commitment of providing value to some product or services the product or service itself may or may not be new or unique but value must somehow be infused by the entrepreneur by securing and allocating the necessary skill and resources. In other words it is the application of energy for initiating and building an enterprise. Rural women's participation in agro based activities is much more than what statistics reveal. This is mainly due to the fact that most of the work done by the women at farm and home is disguised as daily chores. Mechanization and easy availability of labour provide more time to energetic women to engage themselves in self-employment or entrepreneurial ventures. Rural women having a pool of human and non-human resources to take up an enterprise need only an innovative mind and motivation.

Entrepreneurship is the only solution to the growing employment among rural youth. It helps to generate employment for number of people within their own social system. This is more beneficial for women in rural areas as it enable them to add to the family income while taking care of their farm, home and livestock centered tasks. Rural women possess abundant resources to take up an enterprise. She has the benefit of easy availability of farm and livestock based raw material and other resources. Hence she can effectively undertake both production and processing oriented enterprises. But to be a successful entrepreneur, women should process certain fundamental qualities beside the support of the family and government organizations. Entrepreneurial development among rural women helps to enhance their person capabilities but also decision making status in the family and society as a whole. But a successful entrepreneur requires some essential pre requisites.

Objective

To develop entrepreneurial empowerment strategies based upon the participation of rural women in farm and home system.

METHODOLOGY

In order to capture the contribution of women in varied area of her work the data was generated through case studies representing the five agro-climatic zones of Punjab. The participatory approach was used to study each case. Ten cases each of five distinct landholding categories namely landless, marginal, small, medium and large from each zone were studied. The qualitative data was thus generated from 250 rural families represented by the female decision maker of the family.

FINDINGS

Rural women play a vital role in farm and home system. She contributes substantially in the physical aspect of farming, livestock management, post harvest and allied activities. Her direct and indirect contribution at the farm and home level along with livestock management operations has.

KIRANJOT SIDHU AND SUKHJEET KAUR

Not only helped to save but has also led to Increase in family income. She performs various Farm, livestock, post harvest and allied activities and possesses skills and indigenous knowledge in these areas. This is in spite of her being the socially suppressed, educationally at a disadvantageous position and having a little say in the decision making process due to lack of independent income source in hand. Present era of mechanization, easy and cheap availability of labour in Punjab has led to availability of free time. Hence it becomes imperative to empower them technically so as to cope with the changing times and productively use her free time and existing skills for setting and sustaining enterprises. This will not only generate income for the family but also improve the decision making capabilities of the rural women leading to overall empowerment.

Areas for Micro-Enterprise Development

Variations in role performance and direct and indirect contribution varied within the state. Depending on number of factors ranging from landholdings, subsidiary occupations, agro climatic conditions and socio-personal characteristics of the rural women and her family members. Based upon the results of the case studies the following areas for micro enterprises development are suggested:

Micro-Enterprise Development Related to Agriculture and Allied Agricultural Activities

Women have been performing agricultural operations and have been very actively participating in seed selection, seed treatment and vegetable growing. They can be trained and motivated to adopt micro-enterprises in which her skill and patience can be exploited. Ali (1997) in his paper on post harvest processing of agricultural produce stated that value addition includes processes like sorting, grading, cutting, seeding, shelling and quality packaging etc. Growing of organic vegetables, flowers, oilseeds and seed production are some of the areas beside taking up mushroom growing and bee-keeping. Some more areas can be like dehydration of fruits and vegetables, canning or bottling of pickles, chutneys, jams, squashes, dairy and other products which are ready to eat.

Micro-Enterprise Development Related to Livestock Management Activities

The major share of work is being handled by women in performance of livestock management operations. Hence this area needs to be exploited for micro enterprise development. Empowerment of women through formation of self-help groups and all women dairy and poultry cooperatives can help women to control the decision making and the financial aspects of livestock management. Livestock feed production and production of vermicompost using the animal waste can be an important area in which women can utilize both her technical skills and raw material from the farm and livestock to earn substantial income. Value addition to livestock based raw material and establishment of small scale agro-processing units can benefit the women.

Micro-Enterprise Development Related to Household Based Operations

Women perform many household tasks besides looking after the needs of the family. This involves taking care of the children, cooking cleaning the house etc. but at the same time she is equipped with skills such as knitting, stitching, weaving, embroidery etc. Bakery and flour milling are some more examples of the enterprises that can be taken up by women in this area of her activity.

Personal and Environmental Prerequisites for Entrepreneurial Development Extension Strategies to Promote Entrepreneurship

Creating Awareness

Awakening of rural women to the possibilities of the easily accessible micro-enterprises is the foremost task. The government, semi-government and non-government organizations should create awareness among the most productive age group of rural women. The printed media can be effectively put to use for the purpose.

Motivating Entrepreneurs

Psychological stimulation is the prerequisite for putting any idea virtually into action. For proper motivation of rural women, the economic, social and health benefits of various possible enterprises should be highlighted. The use of farm visits, video film shows, dramas, puppet shows, group meeting etc. will help in motivating the potential group.

Expertise Development

After awakening and motivating the next step in development and success of an enterprise is the acquisition of knowledge and skill up-gradation and polishing of existing knowledge and skills in production.

ENTREPRENEURIAL DEVELOPMENT

Processing, packaging and marketing techniques are the basic requirements. Saha (1999) also emphasized the need of value addition as it ensures high premium to the producer. He stated that India ranks second in food production but only two per cent of the produce is processed. In addition to this, knowledge regarding accessibility to loans, various funding agencies, procedures Regarding certification etc. should be provided. Lectures, printed material, discussions, institutional and non-institutional skill trainings for imparting first hand technical knowledge in production, processing, procurement and management should be provided to rural women Who are interested or already engaged in various enterprises? Education in direct and indirect marketing of the produce and finance management should been-built component of future training programmers for women.

Continuous Follow-Up

Constant follow-up should be ensured for the sustainability of emicro-enterprises. During this phase various constraints such as personal, social, economic, marketing etc. faced by entrepreneurs should be addressed. Possible help in the form of knowledge, Technical skills and inputs should be provided to enable them to solve their problems.

Benefits of Entrepreneurship to Rural Women

Empowering women particularly rural women is a challenge. Micro-enterprises in rural area can help to meet this challenge. Micro-enterprises not only enhance national productivity, generate employment but also help to develop economic independence, personal and social capabilities among rural women. Following are some of the personal and social capabilities which are developed as a result of taking up enterprise among rural women.

- Economic empowerment.
- Improved standard of living.
- Self confidence.
- Enhanced awareness.
- Improvement in decision making status.
- Sense of achievement.
- Increased social interaction.
- Improvement in leadership quality.

CONCLUSION

Rural women perform variety of operations infirm and home system and have basic indigenous knowledge, skill, potential and resources which can prove helpful to establish and manage enterprises. What they need is awareness, motivation, technical skill and support from family, government and other organization. With the right assistance they can strengthen their capacities besides adding to the family income and national productivity.

REFERENCES

Ali, N.1997. Post Harvest Processing of Agriculture Produce for High Quality and Export. Theme Paper published in Souvenir of XXXI Annual convention of Society of Agricultural Engineers, Agricultural Engineering, PAU, Ludhiana.

Kuratko, Donald, F. and Richard, M. Hodgetts. 2001. *Entrepreneurship A Contemporary Approach.* New York, U.S.A.: Harecourt College Publishers Saha, 1999.Value Addition A USP for Processed Food." *Agriculture Today,* 2(5): pp. 46-47.

Kiranjot Sidhu and Sukhjeet Kaur, Development of Entrepreneurship Among Rural Women, Punjab University Ludhiana.

12

Socio-Condition of Rural Women in Rural India

Dr. Babita Agrawal & Aditi Tyagi

In India, rural women constitute nearly 80 per cent of the female population. They contribute largely to the country's economy which is mainly agriculture based. Although distributive justice has been categorically underlined in all the development plans, the needs of women have not been adequately addressed. Rural development programmes for women have only in recent decades recognized the crucial role of organization and mobilization as strategies for women's empowerment and development.

The Constitution of India provides for equal rights and privileges for men and women make special provisions for women to help them to improve their status in society. A number of social enactments have been introduced for removing various constraints which hindered the progress of rural women. No doubt that the constitution contemplates a social resolution brought out through the use of law as an instrument of directed social change. But inspite of these, there has been staggering process in ameliorating the working conditions and socio-economic status of rural women.

Traditional India has seen a women only as a member of the family or a group-as daughters, wives and mother and not as an individual with an identity or right of her own. The radicalism of the constitution and its deliberate departure from the social position or accomplishments, will allow women to function an a equal citizen and an individual partner in the task of nation building.

While motherhood is an important social and biological function, the constitution implied that this could no longer he regarded as the only significant role for women. A gap between traditional social attitudes and institution, and the new roles that women are expected to play in the political, social and economic spheres, creates problems and imposes constraints on women's ability to perform such roles.

The women of India have been exposed to greater insecurity, to poverty, illiteracy, casteism, orthodoxy unhealthy living conditions traditionalism, backwardness, corruption, criminalization and male dominance in most of the fields. They have been affected by lack of opportunities and facilities owing to the innate discrimination prevalent in the society. In the last 20 years, there has been a global effort with a strong support from the United Nations to understand the discrimination and restore a status to women of the world. The slogan has been equality, development and peace.

The United Nations General Assembly declared the International year of women in 1975 followed by the International women's decade and organized three world conference-Mexico in 1975 copenhagen in 1980 and Nairobi in 1985. The world has consciously marched forward with various instruments for eliminating discrimination against women during 20 years. The fourth world conference an on. Women held in Beijing in 1995, focused on the structural changes that are necessary in the society. It emphasized that no enduring solution to society's most threatening social, economic and political problem can be found without the full participation and full empowerment of the women. India's strategies and action plans are to eliminate all discrimination against women, remove the chasm between legal status and defect status, create an environment of harmony and partnership of men and women.

The status of women social and political can be defined as the degree of equality and freedom enjoyed by women in the shaping and sharing of power and in the value given by society to this role of women.

The Indian Constitution guarantees political equality through the institution of adult franchise which prohibits discrimination inter-alia on grounds of sex. It should be kept in mind that this recognition of political equality of women was a radical departure not only from the socio-cultural norms prevailing in traditional India but also in the context of the political evolution of even most advanced countries at that date. With the exception of the socialist countries, no other state in the world had accepted women's equality as a matter of course.

The 19th century reform movement and the spread of education among the women had definitely initiated the process of improving the status of women. However, this process was essentially limited to improving the position of women with in the traditional family structure. Prevalent social attitudes, particularly among the upper and middle classes, continued to regard domestic life as women's sole occupation.

Nevertheless there was a minority of women who voluntarily participated in both social welfare and revolutionary movements. They were active in the cause of women's education, welfare of weaker sections in society and relief to distressed persons during emergencies like floods, droughts, famines etc. A still smaller group became involved in the revolutionary movement, actively participating as countries, distributing literature, looking after various institution and risking police repressions, imprisonment and even capital punishment.

In both these cases the women received a certain degree of support from their families in such activities, either overt or covert. Most of them came from the affluent or middle class families in urban areas. The social attitude to this first awakening was one of reserved acceptance, extending sometimes to admiration and pride in the heroism displayed by some of these women. But it by no means amounted to accepting this as a norm for women's role and behaviour in society.

The 19th century reformers professed concern for the low status of women, but their efforts were concentrated towards improving women's position with in the family, for the purpose of strengthening the family as the basic unit of social organization Raising the status of women was seen only as granting her the right to property, re-marriage after widowhood, abolition of child marriage and the right to education.

A characteristics of this movement was its elitist approach. Most of the demands were relevant only for a limited section of women i.e, the upper and middle classes. They did not represent the problem affecting the majority of women. The social change envisaged was a limited one of transformation with in the system, rather than that of the system.

Majority of the third world women are involved in the informal sector of economic activities in which they are disproportionately represented among the poorest of the poor. With limited education, skills and few formal employment opportunities, poor rural women in developing countries often turn to sell-employment as the means of supporting themselves and their families Rural women's self-employment in the informal sector is based on various types of activities like: *(a)* Farm based activities and allied, *(b)* home based production using non-traditional and acquired skills, *(c)* retail trading and services like flower and vegetable selling, garment making catering, petty shop, retail business in paddy etc.

Yet most of these informal activities do not yield sufficient income to extricate women out of poverty. They lack capital technical and managerial know-how access to credit, market and materials as well as services necessary to expand or even to make marginal improvement in productivity and income. Though self-employment is seen as the panacea for rural poverty, initiating self-employment activity is not easy, either for men or for women in the informal sector. It is made doubly so for women by high rate of illiteracy, lack of access to resource along with socio-cultural taboos. The lack of funds and lack of staying power. Limit self-employment and the scale of operation of self-employed women. As the majority of rural women do not own capital or tools and equipments of their trade, they remain vulnerable in the clutches of the private money lenders. Indebtedness puts them in a weak bargaining position with the middleman and traders of their livelihood, thus perpetuating state of high interest payment, low income, insecurity of work opportunities and completing the vicious circle of indebtedness. Out of the variety of ameliorative strategies proposed, to improve the income earning activities of women provision of finance at reasonable rates on regular basis for women in the informal sector is the crucial one.

The Economic status of women in now accepted as an indicator of a society's stage of development. This does not, however, mean that all development results in improving women economic status.

Patterns of women's activity are greatly affected by social attitude and institutions, which stem from the social ideology concerning basic components of status in any given period. These may differ according to the stage of economic development. For cx, at certain stages of development, capacity for work may provide the higher claim to status. At other stages, when society becomes inegalitarian, leisure may substitute work as a basic indicator of status.

The debate regarding women economic role and the need for equality of rights and opportunities for economic participation has centred round three basic arguments.

Women's economic subjugation, or dependent position is the result of a rigid destination men's and women's roles in society and leads to exploitation.

According to *Karl Marx and Freidrich Engels:* The emancipation of women and their equality with men are impossible and must remain so as long as women are excluded from socially productive work and restricted to house work, which is private.

M.K. Gandhi had stated in young India, 26.2.1918 that: Today the sole occupation of a women amongst us is supposed to be to bear children, to look after her husband and otherwise to drudge for the household not only is the women condemned to domestic slavery, hut when she goes out as a labourer to earn wages, though she works harder than man she is paid less.

13

Social Economic Condition of Women in India

Meenakshi Sharma

The women who participate in and lead ecology movements in countries like India are not speaking merely as victims. Their voices are the voices of liberation and transformation... The women's and ecology movements are therefore one, and are primarily counter-trends to a patriarchal maldevelopment.

—Vandana Shiva

The Indian Constitution grants women equal rights with men, but strong patriarchal traditions persist, with women's lives shaped by customs that are centuries old. In most Indian families, a daughter is viewed as a liability, and she is conditioned to believe that she is inferior and subordinate to men. Sons are idolized and celebrated. *May you be the mother of a hundred sons is a common Hindu wedding blessing.*

The persistence of hunger and abject poverty in India and other parts of the world is due in large measure to the subjugation, marginalization and disempowerment of women. Women suffer from hunger and poverty in greater numbers and to a great degree then men. At the same time, it is women who bear the primary responsibility for actions needed to end hunger: education, nutrition, health and family income.

There are the following seven major areas of discrimination against women in India:

Malnutrition

India has exceptionally high rates of child malnutrition, because tradition in India requires that women eat last and least throughout their lives, even when pregnant and lactating. Malnourished women give birth to malnourished children, perpetuating the cycle.

Poor Health

Females receive less health care than males. Many women die in childbirth of easily prevented complications. Working conditions and environmental pollution further impairs women's health.

Lack of Education

Families are far less likely to educate girls than boys, and far more likely to pull them out of school, either to help out at home or from fear of violence.

Overwork

Women work longer hours and their work is more arduous than men's, yet their work is unrecognized. Men report that "women, like children, eat and do nothing." Technological progress in agriculture has had a negative impact on women.

Unskilled

In women's primary employment sector—agriculture—extension services overlook women.

Mistreatment

In recent years, there has been an alarming rise in atrocities against women in India, in terms of rapes, assaults and dowry-related murders. Fear of violence suppresses the aspirations of all women. Female infanticide and sex-selective abortions are additional forms of violence that reflect the devaluing of females in Indian society.

Powerlessness

While women are guaranteed equality under the constitution, legal protection has little effect in the face of prevailing patriarchal traditions. Women lack power to decide who they will marry, and are often married off as children. Legal loopholes are used to deny women inheritance rights.

India has a long history of activism for women's welfare and rights, which has increasingly focused on women's economic rights. A range of government programmes have been launched to increase economic opportunity for women, although there appear to be no existing programmes to address the cultural and traditional discrimination against women that leads to her abject conditions.

The origin of the Indian idea of appropriate female behaviour can be traced to the rules laid down by Manu in 200 B.C.: "by a young girl, by a young woman, or even by an aged one, nothing must be done independently, even in her own house." "In childhood a female must be subject to her father, in youth to her husband, when her lord is dead to her sons; a woman must never be independent."

A study of women in the Swayam Shikshan Prayog (SSP), based in 20 villages in four districts in Maharashtra state was introduced in this way:

The primary issue all women in the SSP were struggling with was that of everyday survival. Insufficient incomes and the lack of employment were reported to be their most pressing concerns. Survival is a constant preoccupation and at its most basic, survival means food (Chambers 1983). The most common problems were the lack of basic amenities such as food, water, fuel, fodder and health facilities. In addition, the deterioration of the natural environment and the fact that many of their traditional occupations were no longer viable were conditions that were making it increasingly hard for women to continue sustaining their families, as they had done in the past.

SSP is a loose, informal network of women's collectives, voluntary organizations, action groups and unions.

IMPACT OF POLLUTION ON WOMEN

Women's Health is Further Harmed by Air and Water Pollution and Lack of Sanitation

The impact of pollution and industrial wastes on health is considerable. In Environment, Development and the Gender Gap, Sandhya Venkateswaran asserts that "the high incidence of malnutrition present amongst women and their low metabolism and other health problems affect their capacity to deal with chemical stress. The smoke from household biomass (made up of wood, dung and crop residues) stoves within a three-hour period is equivalent to smoking 20 packs of cigarettes. For women who spend at least three hours per day cooking, often in a poorly ventilated area, the impact includes eye problems, respiratory problems, chronic bronchitis and lung cancer. One study quoted by WHO in 1991 found that pregnant women cooking over open biomass stoves had almost a 50 per cent higher chance of stillbirth."

Anaemia makes a person more susceptible to carbon monoxide toxicity, which is one of the main pollutants in the biomass smoke. Given the number of Indian women who are anaemic—25 to 30 per cent in the reproductive age group and almost 50 per cent in the third trimester—this adds to their vulnerability to carbon monoxide toxicity.

Additionally, with an increasing population, diseases caused by waste disposal, such as hookworm, are rampant. People who work barefooted are particularly susceptible, and it has been found that hookworm is directly responsible for the high percentage of anaemia among rural women.

THE INVISIBILITY OF WOMEN'S WORK

Women's Work is Rarely Recognized

Many maintain that women's economic dependence on men impacts their power within the family. With increased participation in income-earning activities, not only will there be more income for the family, but gender inequality should be reduced. This issue is particularly salient in India because studies show a very low level of female participation in the labour force. This under-reporting is attributed to the frequently held view that women's work is not economically productive.

In a report of the National Commission on Self-Employed Women and Women in the Informal Sector, the director of social welfare in one state said, "There are no women in any unorganized sector in our state." When the Commission probed and asked, "Are there any women who go to the forest to collect firewood? Do any of the women in rural areas have cattle?" the director responded with, "Of course, there are many women doing that type of work." Working women are invisible to most of the population.

If all activities—including maintenance of kitchen gardens and poultry, grinding food grains, collecting water and firewood, etc.—are taken into account, then 88 per cent of rural housewives and 66 per cent of urban housewives can be considered as economically productive.

Women's employment in family farms or businesses is rarely recognized as economically productive, either by men or women. And, any income generated from this work is generally controlled by the men. Such work is unlikely to increase women's participation in allocating family finances. In a 1992 study of family-based textile workers, male children who helped in a home-based handloom mill were given pocket money, but the adult women and girls were not.

THE IMPACT OF TECHNOLOGY ON WOMEN

The Shift from Subsistence to a Market Economy has a Dramatic Negative Impact on Women

According to Sandhya Venkateswaran, citing Shiva, the Green Revolution, which focused on increasing yields of rice and wheat, entailed a shift in inputs from human to technical. Women's participation, knowledge and inputs were marginalized, and their role shift from being "primary producers to subsidiary workers."

Where technology has been introduced in areas where women worked, women labourers have often been displaced by men. Threshing of grain was almost exclusively a female task, and with the introduction of automatic grain threshers—which are only operated by men—women have lost an important source of income.

Combine harvesters leave virtually no residue. This means that this source of fodder is no longer available to women, which has a dramatic impact on women's workload. So too, as cattle dung is being used as fertilizer, there is less available for fuel for cooking.

"Commercialization and the consequent focus on cash crops has led to a situation where food is lifted straight from the farm to the market. The income accrued is controlled by men. Earlier, most of the produce was brought home and stored, and the women exchanged it for other commodities. Such a system vested more control with the women."

LEGAL PROTECTION OF WOMEN'S RIGHTS HAVE LITTLE EFFECT IN THE FACE OF PREVAILING PATRIARCHAL TRADITIONS

Marriage

Women are Subordinate in Most Marriages

Exposure to and interactions with the outside world are instrumental in determining the possibilities available to women in their daily lives. The situation of women is affected by the degree of their autonomy or capacity to make decisions both inside and outside their own household.

"The position of women in northern India is notably poor. Traditional Hindu Society in northern rural areas is hierarchical and dominated by men, as evidenced by marriage customs. North

Indian Hindus are expected to marry within prescribed boundaries: the bride and groom must not be related, they have no say in the matter, and the man must live outside the woman's natal village.

"Wife givers" are socially and ritually inferior to "wife takers", thus necessitating the provision of a dowry. After marriage, the bride moves in with her husband's family. Such a bride is "a stranger in a strange place." They are controlled by the older females in the household, and their behaviour reflects on the honor of their husbands. Because emotional ties between spouses are considered a potential threat to the solidarity of the patrilineal group, the northern system tends to segregate the sexes and limit communication between spouses—a circumstance that has direct consequences for family planning and similar "modern" behaviours that affect health. A young Indian bride is brought up to believe that her own wishes and interests are subordinate to those of her husband and his family. The primary duty of a newly married young woman, and virtually her only means of improving her position in the hierarchy of her husband's household, is to bear sons.

Sonalde Desai points out that the perception that sons are the major source of economic security in old age is so strong in the north that "many parents, while visiting their married daughters, do not accept food or other hospitality from them. However, given women's low independent incomes and lack of control over their earnings, few can provide economic support to their parents even if parents were willing to accept it."

In the south, in contrast, a daughter traditionally marries her mother's brother or her mother's brother's son (her first cousin). Such an arrangement has a dramatic impact on women. "In southern India, men are likely to marry women to whom they are related, so that the strict distinction found in the north between patrilineal and marital relatives is absent. Women are likely to be married into family households near their natal homes, and are more likely to retain close relationships with their natal kin."

"Over the past several decades, however, marriage patterns have changed markedly. Social, economic, and demographic developments have made marriages between close relatives less common, and the bride price has given way to a dowry system akin to that in the north. Nevertheless, as long as the underlying ethic of marriage in the south remains the reinforcement of existing kinship ties, the relatively favourable situation of Southern Indian women is unlikely to be threatened."

Child Marriages

Child Marriages Keep Women Subjugated

A 1976 Amendment to the Child Marriage Restraint Act raised the minimum legal age for marriage from 15 to 18 for young women and from 18 to 21 for young men. However, in many rural communities, illegal child marriages are still common. In some rural areas, nearly half the girls between 10 and 14 are married. Because there is pressure on women to prove their fertility by conceiving as soon as possible after marriage, adolescent marriage is synonymous with adolescent childbearing: roughly 10-15 per cent of all births take place to women in their teens.

Child marriages contribute to virtually every social malaise that keeps India behind in women's rights. The problems include soaring birth rates, grinding poverty and malnutrition, high illiteracy and infant mortality and low life expectancy, especially among rural women.

A 1993 survey of more than 5,000 women in Rajasthan, which showed that 56 per cent of them had married before they were 15. Barely 18 per cent of them were literate and only 3 per cent used any form of birth control other than sterilization. Sixty-three per cent of the children under age 4 of these women were severely undernourished.

"Each year, formal warnings are posted outside State Government Offices stating that child marriages are illegal, but they have little impact."

One man interviewed has seven daughters. He borrowed some 60,000 rupees to pay for the dowries for six of his daughters, ranging in age from 4-14. He reported that "the weddings mean that he can now look forward to growing old without being trapped in the penury by the need to support his daughters." (NYT)

Dowries

Women are Kept Subordinate, and are Even Murdered, by the Practice of Dowry

In India, 6,000 dowry murders are committed each year. This reality exists even though the Dowry Prohibition Act has been in existence for 33 years, and there are virtually no arrests under the Act. Since those giving as well as those accepting dowry are punishable under the existing law, no one is willing to complain. It is only after a "dowry death" that the complaints become public. It is estimated that the average dowry today is equivalent to five times the family's annual income and that the high cost of weddings and dowries is a major cause of indebtedness among India's poor.

A December 1997 Article in *India Today,* entitled, Victims of Sudden Affluence states, "A woman on fire has made dowry deaths the most vicious of social crimes; it is an evil endemic to the subcontinent but despite every attempt at justice the numbers have continued to climb. With get-rich-quick becoming the new mantra, dowry became the perfect instrument for upward material mobility." A study done by a policy think-tank, the Institute of Development and Communication, states, "the quantum of dowry exchange may still be greater among the upper classes, but 80 per cent of dowry deaths and 80 per cent of dowry harassment occurs in the middle and lower stratas."

The article goes on to state, "So complete is the discrimination among women that the gender bias is extended even toward the guilty. In a bizarre trend, the onus of murder is often put on the women to protect the men. Sometimes it is by consent. Often, old mothers-in-law embrace all the blame to bail out their sons and husbands."

Despite every stigma, dowry continues to be the signature of marriage. Says *Rainuka Dagar,* "It is taken as a normative custom and dowry harassment as a part of family life."

Divorce

Divorce is not a Viable Option

Divorce is rare—it is a considered a shameful admission of a woman's failure as a wife and daughter-in-law. In 1990, divorced women made up a miniscule 0.08 per cent of the total female population.

Maintenance rights of women in the case of divorce are weak. Although both Hindu and Muslim Law recognize the rights of women and children to maintenance, in practice, maintenance is rarely set at a sufficient amount and is frequently violated.

Both Hindu and Muslim Personal Laws fail to recognize matrimonial property. Upon divorce, women have no rights to their home or to other property accumulated during marriage; in effect, their contributions to the maintenance of the family and accumulation of family assets go unrecognized and unrewarded.

Inheritance

Women's Rights to Inheritance are Limited and Frequently Violated

In the mid-1950s the Hindu Personal Laws, which apply to all Hindus, Buddhists, Sikhs and Jains, were overhauled, banning polygamy and giving women rights to inheritance, adoption and divorce. The Muslim personal laws differ considerably from that of the Hindus, and permit polygamy. Despite various laws protecting women's rights, traditional patriarchal attitudes still prevail and are strengthened and perpetuated in the home.

Under Hindu Law, sons have an independent share in the ancestral property. However, daughters' shares are based on the share received by their father. Hence, a father can effectively disinherit a daughter by renouncing his share of the ancestral property, but the son will continue to have a share in his own right. Additionally, married daughters, even those facing marital harassment, have no residential rights in the ancestral home.

Even the weak laws protecting women have not been adequately enforced. As a result, in practice, women continue to have little access to land and property, a major source of income and long-term economic security. Under the pretext of preventing fragmentation of agricultural holdings, several states have successfully excluded widows and daughters from inheriting agricultural land.

Panchayat Raj Institutions have been taken some Staps for Women

Through the experience of the Indian *Panchayat Raj Institutions* (PRI) 1 million women have actively entered political life in India. The 73rd and 74th Constitutional Amendment Acts, which guarantee that all local elected bodies reserve one-third of their seats for women, have spearheaded an unprecedented social experiment which is playing itself out in more than 5,00,000 villages that are home to more than 600 million people. Since the creation of the quota system, local women–the vast majority of them illiterate and poor–have come to occupy as much as 43 per cent of the seats, spurring the election of increasing numbers of women at the district, provincial and national levels. Since the onset of PRI, the percentages of women in various levels of political activity have risen from 4-5 per cent to 25-40 per cent.

According to Indian writer and activist *Devaki Jain*, "the positive discrimination of PRI has initiated a momentum of change. Women's entry into local government in such large numbers, often more than the required 33.3 per cent, and their success in campaigning, including the defeat of male candidates, has shattered the myth that women are not interested in politics, and have no time to go to meetings or to undertake all the other work that is required in political party processes...PRI reminds us of a central truth: power is not something people give away. It has to be negotiated, and sometimes wrested from the powerful."

Contrary to fears that the elected women would be rubber stamp leaders, the success stories that have arisen from PRI are impressive. A government-financed study, based on field work in 180 villages in the states of Uttar Pradesh, Rajasthan and Madhya Pradesh, and coordinated by the Centre for Women's Development Studies in New Delhi, has found that a full two-thirds of elected women leaders are actively engaged in learning the ropes and exercising power. Says *Noeleen Heyzer*, Executive Director of UNIFEM, "This is one of the best innovations in grassroots democracy in the world."

Women Leaders in the Panchayati Raj are transforming local governance by sensitizing the State to issues of poverty, inequality and gender injustice. Through the PRI, they are tackling issues that had previously gone virtually unacknowledged, including water, alcohol abuse, education, health and domestic violence. According to *Sudha Murali*, UNICEF Communications Officer in Andhra Pradesh, women are seeing this power as a chance for a real change for them and for their children and are using it to demand basic facilities like primary schools and health care centers.

The PRI has also brought about significant transformations in the lives of women themselves, who have become empowered, and have gained self-confidence, political awareness and affirmation of their own identity. The panchayat villages have become political training grounds to women, many of them illiterate, who are now leaders in the village panchayats. Says *Sudha Pillai*, Joint Secretary in India's Ministry for Rural Development, "It has given something to people who were absolute nobodies and had no way of making it on their own. Power has become the source of their growth."

By asserting control over resources and officials and by challenging men, women are discovering a personal and collective power that was previously unimaginable. This includes women who are not themselves panchayat leaders, but who have been inspired by the work of their sisters; "We will not bear it," says one woman. Once we acquire some position and power, we will fight it out... "The fact that the Panchayats will have a minimum number of women [will be used] for mobilizing women at large." It is this critical mass of unified and empowered women which will push forward policies that enforce gender equity into the future.

An observation by *Deepak Tiwari* India's No.1 Weekly News Magazine, displays the promising future made possible by the PRI. He notes, "'Learning politics' is the latest fad for young village girls, who dream of joining the growing band of women panchayat representatives, 164,060 at last count, in the state."

Statistical Summary

Social Indicator	*India*	*World*	*Developing World*	*Kerala*	*Sri Lanka*
Infant Mortality Rate, per 1000 live births	73	60	66	16	17
Maternal Mortality Rate, per 100,000 live births	570	430	470		140
Female Literacy, %	58	77.6	70.4	86.93	90.2
Female School Enrollment	47	62	57	63	67
Earned Income by females, %	26	58.0	53.0	49.8	35.5
Underweight Children, %	53	30	30		38
Total Fertility Rate	3.2	2.9	3.2	1.9	2.1
Women in Government, %	6	7	5		9
Contraception usage, %	44	56	54	56	66
Low birth weight babies, %	33	17	7		25

Kerala and *Sri Lanka* are added for comparison as they are recognized as having made exceptional efforts in the field of female education.

CONCLUSION

As UN Secretary General *Kofi Annan* has stated, "Gender equality is more than a goal in itself. It is a precondition for meeting the challenge of reducing poverty, promoting sustainable development and building good governance."

This recognition is currently missing in India. Transforming the prevailing social discrimination against women must become the top priority, and must happen concurrently with increased direct action to rapidly improve the social and economic status of women. In this way, a synergy of progress can be achieved.

- As women receive greater education and training, they will earn more money.
- As women earn more money—as has been repeatedly shown—they spend it in the further education and health of their children, as opposed to men, who often spend it on drink, tobacco or other women.
- As women rise in economic status, they will gain greater social standing in the household and the village, and will have greater voice.
- As women gain influence and consciousness, they will make stronger claims to their entitlements—gaining further training, better access to credit and higher incomes—and command attention of police and courts when attacked.
- As women's economic power grows, it will be easier to overcome the tradition of "son preference" and thus put an end to the evil of dowry.
- As son preference declines and acceptance of violence declines, families will be more likely to educate their daughters, and age of marriage will rise.
- For every year beyond 4th grade that girls go to school, family size shrinks 20 per cent, child deaths drop 10 per cent and wages rise 20 per cent.
- As women are better nourished and marry later, they will be healthier, more productive, and will give birth to healthier babies.

Only through action to remedy discrimination against women can the vision of India's Independence—an India where all people have the chance to live health and productive lives—be realized.

BIBLIOGRAPHY

Abzug, Bella., and Davis, Susan. 1998. "India." Mapping Progress: Assessing Implementation of the Beijing Platform.

Bunch, Charlotte. "The Intolerable Status Quo: Violence Against Women and Girls." The Progress of Nations 1997 New York: UNICEF

Burns, John F. "Though Illegal, Child Marriage is Popular in Part of India." The New York Times. May 11, 1998.

Carr, Marilyn., and Chen, Martha., and Jhabvala, Renana. 1996. Speaking Out: Women's Economic Empowerment in South Asia. Southampton Row, London: Intermediate Technology Publications, Ltd.

Desai, Sonalde. 1994. Gender Inequalities and Demographic Behaviour: India. New York: The Population Council, Inc.

Neft, Naomi., and Levine, Ann D. 1997. Where Women Stand: An International Report on the Status of Women in 140 Countries. New York: Random House.

Omvedt, Gail. 1990. "Violence Against Women: New Movements and New Theories in India." Kali Primaries.

Purushothaman, Sangeetha. 1998. The Empowerment of Women in India: Grassroots Women's Networks and the State. New Delhi: Sage Publications.

Rajan. "Will India's Ban on Prenatal Sex Determination Slow Abortion of Girls?" Internet.

Ramalingaswami, Vulimiri., and Jonsson, Urban., and Rohde, Jon. "The Asian Enigma." The Progress of Nations. 1996 New York: UNICEF.

Reardon, Geraldine. 1995. Power and Process. Oxford: Oxfam.

Times of India. "Protest Against Atrocities in Women." Internet, p. 3.

Tinker, Anne. 1996. Improving Women's Health in India. Development in Practice Series. The World Bank.

Venkateswaran, Sandhya. 1995. Environment, Development and the Gender Gap. Sage Publications, New Delhi.

Vinayak, Ramesh "Victims of Sudden Affluence." India Today. December 15, 1997.

14

Gender Equality: Present Status of Indian Women

Harsh Awasthi & Dr. Neeraja Sharma

INTRODUCTION

Gender equality and gender development's question moves around the 'power' women held. Indian women regardless of their caste, religion or class, have never enjoyed equal status in the society even in their families. Although constitutional and legal safeguards and several empowerment programmes and policies of their development have improved the status of women, yet they lack power in many fields and hence they are subordinate to men. The meaning of gender equality in true sense is to provide equal or same opportunities for men and women in every walk of life. One should not take wrong meaning to compare gender equality with sex equality, while the sex equality means the number of males and females. Gender equality depicts the level of development among men and women.

India is committed towards millennium development goals and special efforts have been taken by Government to attain these goals. This chapter is based on the analysis of the outcome of the developmental programmes regarding women's upliftment. In this chapter we tried to explore all the factors which determine the gender equality, present status, causes behind their poor performance in the field literacy, health, self–reliance etc.

FUTURE FEASIBILITY FOR GENDER EQUALITY

Government has introduced a number of programmes and initiatives for 360 degree societal and economic development of Indian women along with the minority classes. The success of these programmes duly depends on the strategic scanning of environment, to formulate the rational policies and their successful implementation.

At present India the growth rate for the female population for the 1991-2001 decade is 21.79 per cent, which is 0.86 per cent points higher than that of males and 0.45 per cent points more than that of total population, yet the demographic imbalance between men and women continue to exist till date (Government of India-2002, pp. 237).

In Indian society the inequality between men and women is one of the most crucial disparities, which reflects right from the birth of the girl child up to death of women. Apart from this there exists a strong desire for the son child, often leads towards big family size and hence the increased population. Daughters are accepted reluctantly considered a liability for the family. Technological advancement in the field of gender identification has increased the tendency of female foeticide.

The sex ratio in India, which represents the survival scene of women, has been exceptionally unfavourable to women that are 933 female per thousand male while at world level it is 937 females per thousand males. The present maternal mortality rate is 301 per one lac live birth according to the population census 2001-03. The present infant mortality rate is 57 per thousand live births. The child mortality rate (0-4 years), according to 2004 is 17.0 years per thousand children. Life expectancy at the time of birth is 63.2 years.

Table-1
Selected Indicators of Human Development for Major States

Sl.No.	*Major States*	*Life Expectancy* at Birth (2001-05)*			*Infant Mortality Rate (per 1000 live birth) (2006)*			*Birth Rate (per 1000)*	*Death Rate (per 1000)*
		Male	*Female*	*Total*	*Male*	*Female*	*Total*	*2006*	*2006*
1	*2*	*3*	*4*	*5*	*6*	*7*	*8*	*9*	*10*
1.	A.P.	62.7	65.2	64.1	55	58	56	18.9	7.3
2.	Assam	58.3	59	58.7	67	68	67	24.6	8.7
3.	Bihar	62	60.1	61.4	68	63	60	29.9	7.7
4.	Gujarat	62.8	65	63.9	52	54	53	23.5	7.3
5.	Haryana	65.6	66	65.9	57	58	57	23.9	6.5
6.	Karnataka	63.4	66.9	65.1	46	50	48	20.1	7.1
7.	Kerala	71.3	76.3	73.9	14	16	15	14.9	6.7

Contd...

1	2	3	4	5	6	7	8	9	10
8.	M.P.	57.8	57.5	57.7	72	77	74	29.1	8.9
9.	Maharashtra	65.8	68.1	66.9	35	36	35	18.5	6.7
10.	Orissa	59.2	59.2	59.2	73	74	73	21.9	9.3
11.	Punjab	68.1	70.1	69.2	39	50	44	17.8	6.8
12.	Rajasthan	61.2	62.2	61.7	65	69	67	28.3	6.9
13.	Tamil Nadu	64.8	67.1	66	36	37	37	16.2	7.5
14.	U.P.	60.1	59.3	59.8	70	73	71	30.1	8.6
15.	W.B.	63.9	65.5	64.6	37	40	38	18.4	6.2
	India	**62.3**	**63.9**	**63.2**	**56**	**59**	**57**	**23.5**	**7.5**

Source: Office of the Registrar General of India, Ministry of Home Affairs.
*Bihar M.P. and U.P. include Jharkhand, Chattisgarh and Uttarakhand respectively.

CONTRIBUTION OF INDIAN WOMEN IN NATIONAL INCOME

Women's work still continues to be the most invisible in the national accounts, despite their high level of contribution to national income. In low income economies like India more than 75 per cent of women's work is in unpaid activities because much of the non market work performed remains statistically invisible. As a result women who prefer unpaid task neither economically rewarded nor socially valued or recognized as productive members of the society. The 2001 census shows only 25.7 per cent as female workforce. The reason being that women's work could never get recorded either in the population census or their contribution in the national accounts due to the problem of definitions (Government of India, 2001, p. 252). The census of India (2001) has registered 25.60 per cent of female population as workers numbering 127.22 million in absolute terms out of a total female population of 496 million. The majority of women workers is working in rural areas. Another dimension of women's well being is related to the unequal distribution of work and leisure according to gender. Women work longer hours than men and often they get a disproportionate share of wages. Usually women spend on an average 20 per cent more time than men in rural areas and 6 per cent more in the urban areas as of their reproductive role, their responsibilities relating to rearing of children and serving the old age persons in the family, their greater responsibility for agricultural work in family owned farms and barriers to their entry in urban labour market (UNDP 1995). Total work time in India is

391 minutes per day for men and 457 minutes per day for women. Thus the female work time, as percentage of male work time is 117 per cent on an average woman spend about 35 per cent of total work time on market related activities against 92 per cent by men.

Table-2
Allocation and Average Total Work Time of Men and Women in India, 2000 *(Percentage)*

	Total Work Time Spent by		
Activities	*Women*	*Men*	*All Persons*
Market Activities	35	92	61
Non-Market Activities	65	8	39
Total	100	100	100

Source: UNDP (2005), Human Development Report, 2005. Oxford University Press, p. 315.

Men spent only 8 per cent in non-market activities while women spent 65 per cent in the same (Table 2). Thus even after doing more work than men women's is not recorded in estimation of national accounts.

While the female work participation rate increased from 14.22 per cent in 1971 to 25.7 per cent in 2001, still it is much lower than the male work participation rate in both rural and urban areas, (Table 3).

Table-3
Sex Wise Work Participation Rates (1971-2001)
(in per cent)

Census	*T/R/U*	*Female*	*Male*	*Persons*
1971	Total	14.2	52.7	34.2
	Rural	5.9	53.8	35.3
	Urban	7.2	48.9	29.6
1981	Total	19.7	52.6	36.7
	Rural	23.1	53.8	38.8
	Urban	8.3	49.1	30.0
1991	Total	22.3	51.6	37.5
	Rural	26.8	52.6	40.1
	Urban	9.2	48.9	30.2
2001	Total	25.7	51.9	39.3
	Rural	31.0	52.4	42.0
	Urban	11.6	50.9	32.3

Source: Census of India, 1991, Series I & Census of India, 2001: Final Population Totals, Registrar General and Census Commissioner, Government of India, New Delhi.

LEVEL OF EDUCATION IN MALES AND FEMALES

The most glaring example of discrimination against women in India is literacy rate, in Bihar, which is as low as 33.1 per cent in women to 54.16 per cent for the nation as a whole according to census 2001. Nearly fifty crores of women do not know the reading and writing at all. According to the census 2001 female literacy rate is 54.16.

Table-4
Sex Wise Literacy Rates in India

		Literacy Rate in India		
Census Year	*Males*	*Females*	*Literacy Rate Gap*	*Total Persons*
1951	27.16	8.86	18.3	18.33
1961	40.4	15.35	25.05	28.3
1971	45.96	21.97	23.98	34.45
1981	56.38	29.76	26.62	43.57
1991	64.13	39.29	24.84	52.21
2001	75.26	53.67	21.59	64.84

Source: Census of India of respective years, Office of the Registrar General of India, Government of India, New Delhi.

Per cent as against 75.85 per cent for males. In female literacy rate it shows an increase from 29.76 per cent in 1981 to 54.16 per cent in 2001 (Table 4).

OTHER CONCERNED AREAS

The traditional perspective in India is followed the dominance of the males which has been supported by the females every single moment, but there is no light on their contribution for the success. Regarding gender equality some other areas of concern are as follows:

- Women workers are malnourished and the victim of over work and they have nutritional inadequacy.
- Women who are working in cities often face the problem of safe and comfortable accommodation.
- Working women are highly involved in non-market activities leaves limited scope for their development.
- Indian women have limited ownership rights and control over economic resources such as land, cattle, looms, plants and machinery.
- Due to wrong beliefs women are considered less efficient and less productive than men.

- Almost working women in unorganized sector and at least half of women in the formal labour force are excluded from social security benefits available to permanent workers.
- Women's role in the home and family and higher level of involvement in domestic activities is an obstacle in their development.
- Self-employed women have to depend on money lenders or middlemen who charge high rates of interest.
- Working women's sexual exploitation by employers, contracters, middleman, co-worker and senior boss's etc. is another serious issue it requires quick redressal.

CONCLUSIONS AND SUGGESTIONS

Gender equality and gender development are the key issues for the planners and policy makers. Every issue of gender development viz., Education, health and nutrition, growth and physical development, fair representation in urban local bodies and PRI's etc. have given due care in various five year plans. However their efforts neither could break the old traditions nor could reduce poverty level among women to a desired level.

Following are the issue which still requires some concrete measures for the upliftment of women.

- There should be compulsory primary education for the girls.
- Organization of women through Self-Help Groups with active support of NGO's.
- Pregnancy test and termination of pregnancy laws more strict and effective.
- There should be the involvement of corporate world for gender sensitization and draw upon their infrastructure and resources for the implementation of women's development programmes.
- Create an enabling environment for women to exercise their reproductive rights and choices freely.
- Effective enforcement of the Pre-natal Diagnostic techniques (Regulation and Prevention of Misuse) Act, 1994 with stringent punishment to pregnant women as well as to doctor.
- Government should create a gender sensitive educational system and promote gender sensitization of teachers on a regular basis.

- There should be effective and quick and quick implementation of schemes like 'SWADHAR'-an innovative intervention for *women in difficult circumstances* with a special focus on the *rehabilitation of sex workers, bar dancers, jogins, women*/ girls in social and moral danger, destitute etc.
- Ensure minimum and equal wages to women workers.

As a commitment towards Millennium Development Goals special efforts should be taken like *(a)* removal of the gender gap in education at all levels *(b)* increase the proportion of seats held by women in parliament and in state legislations either by reserving more seats for women through constitutional amendment or by consensus among the political parties *(c)* for the alleviation of poverty and unemployment among women steps are needed like expansion and diversification of the economy, specially the rural economy and areas of unemployed women' concentration *(d)* enforcement on removal of gender bias in the labour market, the work place and in skill development.

REFERENCES

UNDP (1995) Human Development Report, Oxford University Press.

UNDP (2006) Human Development Report 2005, Oxford University Press, New York.

IEA Annual Conference, Volume, 2006.

Jain Mahendra Indian Economy (special issue) Pratiyogita Darpan 2008.

Government of India (1997), Ninth Five Year Plan 1997-2002, Planning Commission, Vol. I, New Delhi, pp. 662-670.

Government of India (2007), Tenth Five Year Plan, 2002-07, Planning Commission, Vol. II, New Delhi, pp. 225-252.

Government of India (2000), National Family Health Survey-II, Ministry of Health and Family Welfare, New Delhi.

Government of India (1990), Report of the Task Force Projections of Minimum Needs and Effective Consumption Demand, Planning Commission, New Delhi.

15

Socio-Economic Condition of Rural Women in India

Meenakshi Madan

You can tell the condition of a nation by looking at the status of its women.

—Jawaharlal Nehru

INTRODUCTION

The persistence of hunger and abject poverty in rural India and other parts of the world is due in large measure to the subjugation, marginalization and disempowerment of women. Women suffer from hunger and poverty in greater numbers and to a great degree then men. At the same time, it is women who bear the primary responsibility for actions needed to end hunger: education, nutrition, health and family income.

Looking through the lens of hunger and poverty, there are seven major areas of discrimination against women in India:

- *Malnutrition:* India has exceptionally high rates of child malnutrition, because tradition in India requires that women eat last and least throughout their lives, even when pregnant and lactating. Malnourished women give birth to malnourished children, perpetuating the cycle.
- *Poor Health:* Females receive less health care than males. Many women die in childbirth of easily prevented complications. Working conditions and environmental pollution further impairs women's health.
- *Lack of Education:* Families are far less likely to educate girls than boys, and far more likely to pull them out of school, either to help out at home or from fear of violence.

- *Overwork:* Women work longer hours and their work is more arduous than men's, yet their work is unrecognized. Technological progress in agriculture has had a negative impact on women.
- *Unskilled:* In women's primary employment sector—agriculture-extension services overlook women.
- *Mistreatment:* Female infanticide and sex-selective abortions are additional forms of violence that reflect the devaluing of females in especially in rural Indian society.
- *Powerlessness:* While women are guaranteed equality under the constitution, legal protection has little effect in the face of prevailing patriarchal traditions. Women lack power to decide who they will marry, and are often married off as children. Legal loopholes are used to deny women inheritance rights.

Realizing the need for development of rural women and ensuring and improving their participation in the developmental activities, a new project entitled, "Development of Women and Children in Rural Areas" was started.

The primary objective of DWCRA is to cause socio-economic upliftment of the poor rural women by providing income generating skills and activities. It also seeks to encourage the habit of thrift and credit among poor rural women, and to make them self-reliant.

Women constitute half of our population and play a vital role in the development of the family, the community and the nation. It has been widely recognized that unless women's potential is properly developed, no transformation and economic development is possible. Therefore, to accelerate the growth and prosperity of the nation, it is very important to create opportunities for socio-economic development of women in rural India. In fact, since independence, it has been felt that women experience poverty to a greater extent than men do. The benefits of poverty eradication intervention programmes targeted towards the head of the household, have failed to trickle down and reach the women. Since then, the Government of India (GOI) has been emphasizing the need for designing separate development programmes for women and to earmark a specific percentage for women beneficiaries in other rural development programmes. However, it was only in the year 1975, the year declared by the UN as International Women's Year that the situation began to improve significantly.

India has a long history of activism for women's welfare and rights, which has increasingly focused on women's economic rights. A range of government programmes have been launched to increase economic opportunity for rural women, although there appear to be no existing programmes to address the cultural and traditional discrimination against women that leads to her abject conditions.

WOMEN ARE IN POOR HEALTH

As adults, women get less health care than men. They tend to be less likely to admit that they are sick and they'll wait until their sickness has progressed before they seek help or help is sought for them. Studies on attendance at rural primary health centers reveal that more males than females are treated in almost all parts of the country, with differences greater in northern hospitals than southern ones, pointing to regional differences in the value placed on women. Women's socialization to tolerate suffering and their reluctance to be examined by male personnel are additional constraints in their getting adequate health care.

WOMEN ARE UNEDUCATED

Women and girls receive far less education than men, due both to social norms and fears of violence. India has the largest population of non-school-going working girls. India's constitution guarantees free primary school education for both boys and girls up to age 14. This goal has been repeatedly reconfirmed, but primary education in India is not universal. Overall, the literacy rate for women is 39 per cent versus 64 per cent for men. The rate for women in the four large northern states – Bihar, Uttar Pradesh, Rajasthan and Madhya Pradesh – is lower than the national average: It was 25 per cent in 1991. Attendance rates from the 1981 census suggest that no more than 1/3 of all girls (and a lower proportion of rural girls) aged 5-14 are attending school.

WOMEN ARE OVERWORKED

Women work double then men.Women's contribution to agriculture – whether it be subsistence farming or commercial agriculture – when measured in terms of the number of tasks performed and time spent, is greater than men. "The extent of women's contribution is aptly highlighted by a micro study conducted in the Indian Himalayas which found that on a one-hectare farm, a pair of bullocks works 1,064 hours, a man 1,212 hours and a woman 3,485 hours in a year."

WOMEN'S WORK IS RARELY RECOGNISED.

In a report of the National Commission on Self-Employed Women and Women in the Informal Sector, the director of social welfare in one state said, "There are no women in any unorganized sector in our state." When the Commission probed and asked, "Are there any women who go to the forest to collect firewood? Do any of the women in rural areas have cattle?" the director responded with, "Of course, there are many women doing that type of work." Working women are invisible to most of the population.

WOMEN ARE MISTREATED

Male violence against women is a worldwide phenomenon. Although not every woman has experienced it, and many expect not to, fear of violence is an important factor in the lives of most women. It determines what they do, when they do it, where they do it, and with whom. Fear of violence is a cause of women's lack of participation in activities beyond the home, as well as inside it. Within the home, women and girls may be subjected to physical and sexual abuse as punishment or as culturally justified assaults. These acts shape their attitude to life, and their expectations of themselves.

INTEGRATED RURAL DEVELOPMENT PROGRAMME (IRDP)

Under the Integrated Rural Development Programme (introduced in 1978-79), the gender dimension was introduced on 2nd October 1980, so that women would not be deprived of the development benefits and could participate on equal footing with men. The broad objective of IRDP was to enable the identified rural poor families to augment their income and cross the poverty line through the acquisition of credit-based productive assets, which would provide self-employment on a sustained basis. It was further stipulated that, in the identified target group, at least 30.0 per cent of the assisted beneficiaries (now increased to 40.0%) would be women.

DEVELOPMENT OF WOMEN AND CHILDREN IN RURAL AREAS (DWCRA)

A separate chapter on Women in Development was introduced for the first time to the draft of the Sixth Five Year Plan (1980-85). Realizing the need for development of rural women and ensuring and improving their participation in the developmental activities, a new project entitled, "Development of Women and Children in Rural Areas" was started in the year 1982-83 as a sub-scheme of IRDP, on a pilot basis in 50 districts. As a justification for initiating a new programme exclusively for women, the Manual of IRDP and allied programmes of TRYSEM and DWCRA, published by the Ministry of Rural Development GOI in 1991, observed as follows: "The need for a special programme, designed exclusively for women, was felt as it was noticed that members of IRDP families were not availing benefits of that programme in adequate measure. However DWCRA and IRDP are not mutually exclusive."

The primary objective of DWCRA is to cause socio-economic upliftment of the poor rural women by providing income generating skills and activities. It also seeks to encourage the habit of thrift and credit among poor rural women, and to make them self-reliant. In addition, this programme also aims at enhancing the welfare and quality of life of the family as well as the community by improving rural women's access to health, education, safe drinking water, sanitation, and nutrition. In the words of GOI guidelines (1982), the DWCRA scheme intended to assist women of the target groups in the following manners:

(a) Providing assistance to individual women to take advantage of the facilities already available under IRDP;
(b) Organizing women in homogenous groups to adopt economically viable activities on a group basis;
(c) Providing women of the target group with necessary supportive services in terms of provision of day care facilities for children with working mothers, provision of working conveniences, suitable appliances etc. so that they could improve their efficiency and reduce the drudgery; and
(d) Organizing childcare facilities to provide for the security, health care and nursing of the children.

Administrative Set Up of DWCRA

Proper staffing at various levels is an important pre-requisite for successful implementation of programme. At the state level, there is one Deputy Secretary, who is solely incharge of DWCRA. She/he reviews the progress of implementation of DWCRA with particular reference to the achievements of physical and financial targets and ensures that all sanctioned staff at the block and district level is in position.

At the district level, there is one post of Assistant Project Officer-APO (Women's Development) belonging to a woman. She monitors the progress of the programme and sends periodical reports to the State Government. At the block level, there are three officers i.e., Block Development Officer (BDO), an Extension Officer (EO) and a Child Development Project Officer (CDPO).

BDOs are incharge of rural development activities. The Extension Officers are responsible for the implementation of the scheme (project). They also supervise the Gram Sevikas at the block level and gather information on repayment of bank loans by the groups.

CDPOs look after the organization of the groups and also look into the welfare of children. They have a supporting staff of one Mukhiya Sevika and two Gram Sevikas. Their job is to visit the group frequently and educate the group members about childcare. The group organizer works at the village level and the group leader (member of the group) helps the group with the selection of the activity, procurement of raw material, and marketing of products.

Selection of Activity

The selection of an income generating activity is left to the group so that they do not get the impression that the activity is being imposed upon them against their wishes. However, the activity selected should be viable i.e. it should have forward and backward linkages (skill training, raw materials and marketing) and be available locally.

Credit Pattern for DWCRA Groups

Each group is entitled to a revolving fund amount at the rate of Rs. 1,000 per member, subject to a maximum of Rs. 15,000 per group. The revolving fund is meant for following uses:

- *(a)* Purchase of raw materials and marketing.
- *(b)* Honorarium to group organizer Rs. 50 per month for a period of one year.
- *(c)* Infrastructure support for income generating and other group activities.
- *(d)* One time expenditure on child-care activities.
- *(e)* One time expenditure not exceeding Rs. 500 to meet travel allowance of group members for visit to bank etc.

In addition, the group organizer is entitled to Rs. 200 to be used as a travelling allowance for a period of one year. The programme strategy of DWCRA is unique in the sense that it has adopted a group approach instead of a family oriented approach as seen in IRDP. In DWCRA a group of women is the unit of assistance. Women members form groups of 10-15 women each for taking up economic activities suited to their skill, aptitude, and local conditions.

The basic differences between DWCRA and other development schemes are:

Other Development Schemes	*DWCRA*
■ Concerned with the whole population	■ Intended especially for poor women and children in rural areas
■ Emphasis on outside support	■ Emphasis on self reliance
■ Based on Institutional support	■ Based on awareness and stimulation for self-help
■ Individual or family oriented	■ Voluntary group oriented

The Seventh Five Year Plan revamped the scheme and recommended that it should be continued with the objective to "organize women in socio-economic activity groups" with the dual objective of providing them with self-employment opportunities and social strength. In this process, voluntary agencies and people's action groups would be involved to the maximum extent possible. It was also mentioned that due emphasis would continue to be given to direct maximum quantum of benefits towards women, who admittedly constitute a substantially deprived section of the society.

By the end of the Eighth Five Year Plan, with the goal that the programme is to cover the entire country, the GOI decided that DWCRA should be extended to 50 additional districts every year from 1991-92 onwards. It was also decided to reduce the group size so as to make the group cohesive. From the year 1995-96 Child Care Activities (CCA) have been incorporated under DWCRA with the objective of providing crèche services for children (below six years) and with specific emphasis on young female dropouts. It is also responsible for filling in critical gaps in the areas of immunization and nutrition for the children. Information, education and communication components have also been incorporated since 1995-96, for generating awareness among rural women about DWCRA and other development programmes.

Though DWCRA has specified objectives, it suffers due to many implementation problems. The comprehensive evaluation work, undertaken by UNICEF in 1990, highlighted the following problems in the programme's design and its field level implementation:

(a) Low priority was given to the DWCRA programme by the DRDA and block offices, particularly with respect to the non-economic objectives of the programme;

(b) Little effort was devoted to the programme by BDO, who is expected to be the effective controller of group level functionaries of DWCRA;

(c) Field functionaries (Mukhiya Sevika and Gram Sevikas) under the Community Development pattern were not available to provide support for DWCRA;

(d) Failure of the State Government to appoint Assistant Project Officer (WD) in many DRDAs for controlling the management and implementation of the programme; and

(e) Failure of the State Government to appoint additional Gram Sevikas for working in DWCRA.

The report of the National Commission on Self Employed Women and Women in Informal Sector also made similar remarks with respect to the implementation of DWCRA that mentions as follows: "DWCRA has had limited success, as in most cases it has not resulted in the growth of women's organizing capabilities and leadership qualities.... The planning of the programmes also does not take adequate care of the different components of self-employment like *(i)* the programme does not provide for adequate training for skill formation and *(ii)* for adequate qualitative and quantitative training in the areas of management including financial, marketing, and overall management."

The report also mentioned that, "it is observed by most of the DWCRA studies that the poorest of the poor women are usually left out from DWCRA groups and thus the programme was to serve the better off among the poor or sometimes non poor groups of women."

As for the benefits, women felt that the participation has helped them gain confidence and better status in their families.

The findings, on the whole, reflect that the implementation of DWCRA has resulted in the generation of additional employment. At the same time, looking at the meager contribution of women to the total family income, it is felt that the programme has not been able to make a significant improvement in the socio-economic status of the beneficiaries. Therefore, concentrated efforts such as providing them infrastructural facilities like regular supply of raw material, establishing linkages with marketing institutions for immediate disposal (distribution) of their produce as well as and a common work place, are required to strengthen the benefits of DWCRA.This is a holistic programme covering all aspects of self-employment such as: organization of poor into self-help groups, training, credit, technology, infrastructure and marketing.

SWARNAJAYANTI GRAM SWAROJGAR YOJANA (SGSY)

In April 1999, The Government of India gave a new direction to its poverty alleviation programme by integrating all the rural self-employment schemes (projects) into one single scheme called "Swarnajayanti Gram Swarojgar Yojana" (SGSY), with the following objective: To bring every assisted family above the poverty line within 3 years by establishing a large number of micro enterprises in the rural areas, building upon the potential of rural poor.

Selection of Swarojgaris

Under SGSY, the beneficiaries, who can either be individuals or groups, are known as Swarojgaris. The SGSY lays emphasis on the group approach, under which the rural people are organized into self-help groups. The basis for identification of families for assistance is formed by a list of BPL (Below Poverty Line) households identified through BPL census and duly approved by the Gram Sabha (Village Committee). Each Self-Help Group (SHG) consists of approximately10-20 people.

Selection of Key Activities

The SGSY lays emphasis on cluster approach, meaning instead of funding diverse activities, 4-5 key activities will be identified for each block. The activities will be based on the resources, occupational skills of the people and availability of markets. Selection of key activities will be under the approval of the Panchayat Samitis at the block level, and the DRDA/ZP at the district level.

Preparation of Projects

SGSY will adopt a project approach for each key activity, indicating the various elements such as training, credit, technology, infrastructure and marketing. The project report should indicate how many people in a block should be covered economically according to a key activity. Banks and other financial institutions will be closely associated and involved in preparing these project reports to help avoid a delay in the sanctioning of loans and to ensure adequacy of finance.

Funding Pattern

Central and State Government will share funds under SGSY using a ratio of 75:25.

Financial Assistance to Selected Families

Financial assistance to Swarojgaris is comprised of two components loan and subsidy. SGSY is a credit-oriented project. The subsidy is only a minor and enabling component. The size of the loan (both for fixed and working capital) depends on the nature of project. The bank will not take more than 15 days to sanction the loan. Subsidy will be uniform at 30 per cent of the project cost and be subject to a maximum of Rs. 7,500, whereas in case of SC/STs (scheduled castes/scheduled tribes), these will be 50 per cent and Rs. 10,000 respectively.

Main Features of SGSY

- *(a)* It is conceived as a holistic programme, of micro-enterprises covering all aspects of self-employment, organization of rural people into self-groups and their capacity building, planning of activity clusters, infrastructure build up, technology, credit and marketing;
- *(b)* SGSY will seek to promote multiple credits rather than a one-time credit injection;
- *(c)* Skill of the Swarojgaris will be developed through well-designed training courses. Two types of trainings are available under the basic orientation programme. Skill development training may be organized for them. The design, duration and curriculum of the training will be tailored to meet the need of the identified activities; and
- *(d)* SGSY will provide for the promotion of the marketing of goods produced by the Swarojgaris.

This Yojana aims at focusing on the vulnerable groups among the rural poor. Accordingly, the SC/STs will account for at least 50 per cent of the Swarojgaris, women for 40 per cent and the disabled for 3 per cent.

CONCLUSION

As UN Secretary General Kofi Annan has stated, "Gender equality is more than a goal in itself. It is a precondition for meeting the challenge of reducing poverty, promoting sustainable development and building good governance."

This recognition is currently missing in India. Transforming the prevailing social discrimination against women in rural India must become the top priority, and must happen concurrently with increased direct action to rapidly improve the social and economic status of rural women. In this way, a synergy of progress can be achieved.

- As women receive greater education and training, they will earn more money.
- As women earn more money—as has been repeatedly shown—they spend it in the further education and health of their children, as opposed to men, who often spend it on drink, tobacco or other women.
- As women rise in economic status, they will gain greater social standing in the household and the village, and will have greater voice.
- As women gain influence and consciousness, they will make stronger claims to their entitlements—gaining further training, better access to credit and higher incomes—and command attention of police and courts when attacked.
- As women's economic power grows, it will be easier to overcome the tradition of "son preference" and thus put an end to the evil of dowry.
- As son preference declines and acceptance of violence declines, families will be more likely to educate their daughters, and age of marriage will rise.
- For every year beyond 4th grade that girls go to school, family size shrinks 20 per cent, child deaths drop 10 per cent and wages rise 20 per cent.
- As women are better nourished and marry later, they will be healthier, more productive, and will give birth to healthier babies.
- GOI is making every effort to help women in every sphere of life. It is also taking steps to ensure proper planning, implementation and monitoring of development programmes, enabling the benefits of these programmes reach the deserving beneficiaries.

Only through action to remedy discrimination against women can the vision of India's Independence—an India where all people have the chance to live health and productive lives—be realized.

Therefore, convergence of various development schemes (projects) under SGSY, including its links and interactions with other agencies, may enhance the progress of rural development in general. Women in particular may benefit from this progress, as this convergence of programmes will help to reduce unnecessary dispersion and underutilization of resources. Considering the concern regarding women, positive changes are expected to take place in the lives of Indian women in future. However, we are yet to see what the situation of Indian women will be in 21st century.

REFERENCES

Abzug, Bella, and Davis, Susan. 1998. "India" Mapping Progress: Assessing Implementation of the Beijing Platform.

Bunch, Charlotte. "The Intolerable Status Quo: Violence Against Women and Girls." The Progress of Nations 1997 New York: UNICEF.

Burns, John F. "Though Illegal, Child Marriage is Popular in Part of India." The New York Times. May 11, 1998.

Carr, Marilyn, and Chen, Martha, and Jhabvala, Renana. 1996. Speaking Out: Women's Economic Empowerment in South Asia. Southampton Row, London: Intermediate Technology Publications Ltd.

Desai, Sonalde. 1994. Gender Inequalities and Demographic Behaviour: India. New York: The Population Council, Inc.

Neft, Naomi., and Levine, Ann D. 1997. Where Women Stand: An International Report on the Status of Women in 140 Countries. New York: Random House.

Omvedt, Gail. 1990. "Violence Against Women: New Movements and New Theories in India." Kali Primaries.

Purushothaman, Sangeetha. 1998. The Empowerment of Women in India: Grassroots Women's Networks and the State. New Delhi: Sage Publications.

Rajan. "Will India's Ban on Prenatal Sex Determination Slow Abortion of Girls?" Internet.

Ramalingaswami, Vulimiri., and Jonsson, Urban, and Rohde, Jon. "The Asian Enigma." The Progress of Nations. 1996 New York: UNICEF.

Reardon, Geraldine. 1995. Power and Process. Oxford: Oxfam.

Times of India. "Protest Against Atrocities in Women." Internet, p. 3.

Tinker, Anne. 1996. Improving Women's Health in India. Development in Practice Series. The World Bank.

Venkateswaran, Sandhya. 1995. Environment, Development and the Gender Gap. New Delhi: Sage Publications.

Vinayak, Ramesh "Victims of Sudden Affluence." India Today. December 15 GOI-Department of Women and Child Development, 1988. Report of the National Commission on Self-employed women and Women in Informal Sector June 1988.

GOI-Department of Rural Development, 1992. DWCRA programme Guidelines and Administrative Orders (1982-92), August 1992.

GOI-Department of Rural Development, 1990. Concurrent Evaluation of IRDP (January-December) 1989-1990.

GOI-Department of Rural Development. Annual Reports of 1990-91, and 1995-96.

Tripathi, R.S. and Tiwari, R.P., 1999. Perspective on Indian Women. A.P.H. Publishing Corporation, New Delhi, pp. 1-75.

World Bank, 1994. Enhancing Women's Participation in Economic Development.

16

Women—In Rural Area in India

Dr. Nadia Yusuf

"You can tell the condition of a nation by looking at the status of its women."

—Jawaharlal Nehru

The persistence of hunger and abject poverty in India and other parts of the world is due in large measure to the subjugation, marginalization and disempowerment of women. Women suffer from hunger and poverty in greater numbers and to a great degree then men. At the same time, it is women who bear the primary responsibility for actions needed to end hunger: education, nutrition, health and family income.

"Empowerment of women has emerged as an important issue in our society in recent times. The economic empowerment of women is being regarded these days as a sine-qua-non of progress for a country, hence the issue of economic empowerment of women is of paramount importance to political thinkers, social scientists and reformers, women activists, politicians, academicians and administrators."

Poverty hits hardest at the female half of humankind. If you are a woman living in a rural area of a developing country, you are likely to be poorer than a man, more vulnerable, own no land, be less educated and in poorer health. And you are unlikely to live as long.

Struggling to combine a 'double day' of low-paid work with care for the home, rural women often have to cope with frequent pregnancies and child mortality. For women, perhaps the cruelest reality of all is that they have less chance than men to escape from poverty. A rural woman is likely to have little or no say in the way the family spends its income.

Discrimination in education is the start of the vicious spiral of poverty. A girl may be deprived of schooling and literacy for no other reason than that she is female. Seventy per cent of poor women in India cannot read or write. Illiteracy often excludes people from written knowledge and decision-making.

"The type of work they do is limited by their low education levels", states the Rural Poverty Report 2001 on the subject of rural women. Cultural norms mean that in many countries women are excluded from participating in decisions affecting both their households and communities.

Looking through the lens of hunger and poverty, there are seven major areas of discrimination against women in India:

- **Malnutrition:** India has exceptionally high rates of child malnutrition, because tradition in India requires that women eat last and least throughout their lives, even when pregnant and lactating. Malnourished women give birth to malnourished children, perpetuating the cycle.
- **Poor Health:** Females receive less health care than males. Many women die in childbirth of easily prevented complications. Working conditions and environmental pollution further impairs women's health.
- **Lack of Education:** Families are far less likely to educate girls than boys, and far more likely to pull them out of school, either to help out at home or from fear of violence.
- **Overwork:** Women work longer hours and their work is more arduous than men's, yet their work is unrecognized. Men report that "women, like children, eat and do nothing." Technological progress in agriculture has had a negative impact on women.
- **Unskilled:** In women's primary employment sector – agriculture – extension services overlook women.
- **Mistreatment:** In recent years, there has been an alarming rise in atrocities against women in India, in terms of rapes, assaults and dowry-related murders. Fear of violence suppresses the aspirations of all women. Female infanticide and sex-selective abortions are additional forms of violence that reflect the devaluing of females in Indian society.

- **Powerlessness:** While women are guaranteed equality under the constitution, legal protection has little effect in the face of prevailing patriarchal traditions. Women lack power to decide who they will marry, and are often married off as children. Legal loopholes are used to deny women inheritance rights.

India has a long history of activism for women's welfare and rights, which has increasingly focused on women's economic rights. A range of government programmes have been launched to increase economic opportunity for women, although there appear to be no existing programmes to address the cultural and traditional discrimination against women that leads to her abject conditions.

People living with chronic hunger exist in conditions of severe poverty. What they lack is the chance to change their situation, to develop their own self-sufficiency. The most potent confirmation of this fact can be seen in the lives of women. They, along with their children, are the main victims of hunger, and they are also most lacking in opportunities to end their own and their families' hunger.

The Hunger Project has come to the recognition that the persistence of hunger in India—and elsewhere in the world where hunger is still an overriding social issue—is, to a large degree, due to the subjugation, marginalization and disempowerment of women. Furthermore, women's suppression is rooted in the very fabric of Indian society—in traditions, in religious doctrine and practices, within the educational and legal systems, and within families.

Ironically, much of the essential work of ending hunger rests in women's hands.

Traditionally, women bear primary responsibility for the well-being of their families. Yet they are systematically denied access to the resources they need to fulfill their responsibility, which includes education, health care services, job training, and access and freedom to use family planning services.

In order to gain a shared understanding of the condition of the status of women in India and its impact on the persistence of hunger, this document surveys papers done by leading scholars in Indian development issues. It is organized in a framework of seven issues that characterize the plight of resource-poor women, with a focus on rural women, in India: malnutrition, poor health, and lack of education, overwork, lack of skills, mistreatment and powerlessness.

Women's employment in family farms or businesses is rarely recognized as economically productive, either by men or women. And, any income generated from this work is generally controlled by the men. Such work is unlikely to increase women's participation in allocating family finances. Where technology has been introduced in areas where women worked, women labourers have often been displaced by men. Threshing of grain was almost exclusively a female task, and with the introduction of automatic grain threshers – which are only operated by men – women have lost an important source of income.

A number of factors perpetuate women's limited job skills: if training women for economic activities requires them to leave their village, this is usually a problem for them. Unequal access to education restricts women's abilities to learn skills that require even functional levels of literacy. In terms of skill development, women are impeded by their lack of mobility, low literacy levels and prejudiced attitudes toward women. When women negotiate with banks and government officials, they are often ostracized by other men and women in their community for being 'too forward.' Government and bank officials have preconceived ideas of what women are capable of, and stereotypes of what is considered women's work.

Some rural women have been affected by trade liberalization. They are unable to participate in the marketing of export crops as they lack land rights and access to essential farm inputs. On the other hand, some women have gained by securing jobs in new export activities.

Investment in rural women pays off. Female schooling can lead to a reduction in poverty by giving women the literacy skills and confidence they need to have a say about how things are run. A mother's education often leads to better health and nutrition for her children.

More investment in improving the lot of rural women could create a 'virtuous circle' of better education, improved health and higher income. And women need to be given the right to have more control over productive assets – land, water and credit, for example. Removing gender inequalities is not only morally right; it is good for economic growth and development.

REFERENCES

http://www.thp.org/reports/indiawom.htm

Economic Empowerment of Rural Women in India/edited by Rita Bakshi, M.S. Rathore, Meenu Agrawal and Manjula Tyagi. Jaipur, RBSA, 2003, 166 p., $20. ISBN 81–7611-184-8.

Conference on Gender Issues in Agriculture, ADB and UNIFEM. (Manila, 5-6 December, 1990).

UNDP, 1997. *Human Development Report,* Oxford University Press, New York.

Venkateswaran, S. 1992. *Living on the Edge: Women, Environment and Development,* Friedrich Ebert Stiftung, New Delhi.

17

Social and Health Status of Rural Indian Women

Preeti Chhabra & Priya Mittal

"You can tell the condition of a nation by looking at the status of its women."

—J.L. Nehru

Introduction

Poverty is an acute problem in India. Even though Government is taking a lot steps, poverty is getting entrenched in more backward areas especially rural areas.

Poverty hit hardest at the female half of humankind. If women living in a rural area of a developing country, they are likely to be poorer than a man, more vulnerable, own no land, be less educated and in poorer health. Struggling to combine a 'double day' of low—paid work with care for the home, rural women often have to cope with frequent pregnancies and child mortality. For women, perhaps the cruelest reality of all is that they have less chance than men to escape for poverty.

Rural women comprise more than one quarter of the total world population. 500 million women live below the poverty line in rural areas. Women perform 30 per cent of the agricultural work in industrialized countries.

Rural women fulfill multiple functions on a daily basis: They are mothers providing for their family's well-being, farmers producing food for the family, shopkeepers supplying indispensable additional income. They are also in charge of natural resources management which ensures future food security for their families. Traditionally the role of wife and mother has been seen as a woman's destiny. Although rural women represent a fundamental pillar for survival and management of the family unit but she remained totally dependent but on her husband financially and choose to remain unaware of the world outside her home.

Throughout the developing world, rural women engage in multiple economic activities that are critical to the survival of poor households. Rural poor women play an essential role in crop production and livestock care, and they provide the food, water and fuel their families need. This particularly the case in some of the poorest and most marginal areas characterized by extensive and increasing male migration.

Despite the essential economic and caregiving roles they perform, women have significantly less access to financial physical and social assets than men do; fewer opportunities to improve their knowledge skills; and voice in public decision-making.

The HIV/AIDS crisis, which is already reversing the economic gains achieved in some developing countries, affects women disproportionately, both as individuals and in their roles as mothers and caregivers. Over the next decade, the epidemic is expected to spread even further in developing countries. This epidemic is fuelled by cultural stereotypes, according to which men are expected to dominate and women to be passive in taking decisions about relationships. The need for women to care for sick family members, coupled with cuts in social spending, limits women's ability to engage in productive and income-earning activities that determine not only their families well being but also their own social and economic status. Thus HIV/AIDS is driven by gender inequality, and it also entrenches gender inequalities.

Overall, the neglect of women's needs and rights undermines the potential of entire communities to grow and develop. Poverty is therefore deeply rooted in the glaring imbalance between what women do and what they have—in terms of both assets and rights. As women's status increases, so do the benefits to society. Studies have shown, for instance, that the major contributing factor to improved child nutrition is women's socio-economic status, particularly their educational levels. In addition the countries that have closed the gender gap in education the fastest have experienced the fastest economic growth.

The persistence of hunger and object property in India and other parts of the world is due in large measure to the subjugation, marginalization and disempowerment of women. Women suffer from hunger and poverty in greater numbers and to a great degree than men. At the same time, it is women who bear the primary responsibility for actions needed to end huger: Education, nutrition, health and family income.

Looking through the lens of hunger and poverty, there are several areas of discrimination against women in india.

Lack of Education

Families are far less likely to educate girls than boys, and far more likely to pull them out of school, either to help out at home or from fear of violence.

Poor Health

Females receive less health care than males. Many women die in childbirth of easily prevented complications. Working conditions and environmental pollution further impairs women's health.

Malnutrition

India has exceptionally high rates of child malnutrition, because tradition in India requires that women est last and least throughout their lives.

Overwork

Women work longer hours and their work in more arduous than men's yet their work is unrecognized. Men report that "women, like children eat and do nothing." Technological progress in agriculture has had a negative impace on women.

Mistreatment

In recent years, there has been an alarming rise in atrocities against women in India, in terms of rapes, assaults and dowry—related murders. Fear of violence suppresses the aspirations of all women. Female infanticide and sex-selective abortions are additional forms of violence that reflect the devaluing of females in Indian society.

Women are Uneducated

Immediately after India overthrew the British rule in1948-49, the Government of India appointed the University. Education Commission Headed by Dr. S. Radhakrishnan, scholar, philosopher, and a President of India the Commission focused on higher education. The Commission report, prepared by Dr. Radhakrishnan, opens with an angry statement damning the British Government for their lax approach towards women's education. A large portion of the report is dedicated to women's education and it reiterates the importance and relevance of the same, along with a mention of the government's obligation to provide equal educational opportunities for married as well as unmarried women.

> *"India has the largest population of nom-school-going working girls."*
>
> *"Women and girls receive far less education than men, due both to social norms and fear of violence."*

Sonalde Desai in Gender Inequalities and Demographic Behaviour asserts that 'parents' reluctance to educated daughters has its roots in the situation of women. Parents have several incentives for not educating their daughters. Foremost is the view that education of girls brings no returns to parents and that their future roles, being mainly reproductive and perhaps including agricultural labour, require no formal education. As more and more boys are engaged in education, there is a growing reliance on the labour of girls. Girls are increasingly replacing their brothers on the farm while carrying on their usual responsibilities in housework. A large proportion of the roughly 40 million "nonworking" girls who are not in school are kept at home because of responsibilities in housework."

Educated mothers make a huge difference to the thinking of the entire family. Infact, it has been proven that in communities where the literacy rate of women is higher, instances of dowry deaths and female infanticide are far fewer.

(Kavita N.)

Education are powerful sources that can dissuade violence against women but *"We still have a long road to travel when it comes to the education of women in India,"* says Ajanana Nagabhushana.

Women are Malnourished

Gender disparities in nutrition are evident from infancy to adulthood. In fact, gender has been the most statistically significant determinant of malnutrition among young children and malnutrition is a frequent direct or underlying cause of death among girls below age 5 girls are breast-fed less frequently and for short durations in infancy; in childhood and adulthood, males are fed first and better.

Based on demographic projects made by United Nations Population Division for the year 2025, WHO issued estimates of adults with diabetes in all countries and reported that there will be more women with diabetes than men and we may anticipate a considerable increase in the burden of Gestational Diabetes Mellitus (GDM) especially in less prosperous countries. During last two decades there has been a marked increase in the prevalence of diabetes among urban Indian. Similar, though slower trend in also shown amongest peri-urban and rural population due to changes in life style, ageing and low birth weight leading to diabetes during adulthood.

(A.K. Verma, *et al.*, 2008)

A study on Andhra Pradesh a southern Indian state revealed that total of 4032 ever-married women aged 15-49 from 3872 households that rual women have higher prevalence of anemia compared to urban women, particularly among the lower income groups, and that women with low body mass index (BMI; <18.5 Kg/m^2) would have a higher risk compared to normal or overweight women. Prevalence of anemia was high among all women. In all 32.4 per cent of women had mild (100-109. 99g/l for pregnant women, 100-119.99 for non-pregnant women), 14.19 per cent had moderate (70-99.99 g/l) and 2.2 per cent had severe anemia (<70g/l).

(Bentely and Griffiths, 2003)

In populations where the average height at reproductive age female is ≤150cm (India, Bangladesh, Indonesia and Colombia) and pre-pregnancy weight <40 kg, poor pregnancy outcome (incidence of Low Birth Weight (LBW) and neonatal mortality rate) is usually documented. Garn and Pesick have shown that pre-pregnancy weight was a better predictor of LBW, and birth weight variability than various other height and weight indices. In general, higher the pre-pregnancy weight, the lower is the incidence of prematurity, (≤ 38 wk gestation) and there is decrease in incidence of very low birth weight <<2300g. If weight gain in pregnancy is high enough, the effect of lower pre-pregnancy weight can be partially compensated. If, however, the weight gain is also low then pre-pregnancy weight is of primary importance. Rural Women in India, often have low pre-pregnancy weight and low weight gain in pregnancy. In them, the former alone will be able to guide for selection of high risk women or those needing special nutrition and health care. In the present study, for evaluating pregnancy outcome including birth weight, and perinatal mortality, women's weight/height ratio <90 centile was a good predictor while BMI in the short statured women was non-discriminatory.

Undernourished women of non-pregnant, non-lactating group are not covered under any national nutrition or health programme. They represent pre-pregnancy status and constitute an important vulnerable group.

M. Srivastava *et. al.*, concluded in 6130 rural women of Varanasi (non-pregnant and non-lactating) in the reproductive age, 13.5 per cent were below 145 cm. 27.1 per cent were below 40 kg. BMI was below 18.5 (thinness) in 40 per cent and weight for height below 90 per cent of 90th centile was documented in 53.2 per cent. The present anthropometric data on rural women of Uttar Pradesh have thus clearly demonstrated that majority of women are not only underweight but also short statured.

Women are in Poor Health and are Overworked

"..... The poor care that is afforded of girls and women by their husbands and by elders is the first major reason for levels of child malnutrition that are markedly higher in South Asia than anywhere else in the world."

"The practice of breast-feeding female children for shorter periods of time reflects the strong desire for sons. If women are particularly anxious to have a male child, they may deliberately try to become pregnant again as soon as possible after a female is born. Conversely, women may consciously seek to avoid another pregnancy after the birth of a male child in order to give maximum attention to the new son."

> *"Women work longer hours and their work is more arduous than men's. Still, men report that "women, like children, eat and do nothing."*
>
> *"Women work roughly twice as many hours as men and women's work is rarely recognized."*

The tasks performed by women are usually those that require them to be in one position for long periods of time, which can adversely affect their reproductive health. A study in a rice–

growing belt of coastal Maharashtra found that 40 per cent of all infant deaths occurred in the months of July of October. The study also found that a majority of births were either premature of stillbirths. The study attributed this to the squatting position that had to be assumed during July and August, the rice transplanting months.

According to Mohapatra PC and Pattanaik B., "The economic role played by women is difficult to quantitate because of their lifestyle that combines domestic work and unpaid family or low-paid outside farm or cottage industry labour. Besides these tasks, women usually care for dairy animals, and carry water and fire-wood. Discrimination against women in this system is evident, however, from some available statistics. 46 per cent of women, as opposed to 20 per cent of men, work as agricultural labourers. Women are denied education because they are not expected to do responsible work, then they are denied employment because they are not educated. Their work is counted as worth only half that of men, and based on this assumption, they are paid less than men. Female literacy has risen to 14.3 per cent from 1 per cent 10 years before. Women usually worked in transplantation, weeding, harvesting and threshing, but also in heavier farm labour, construction of roads and buildings, quarrying and forestry. In this poor, hilly region, the custom of purdah was not practiced to the extent of keeping women from doing day labour outside the home. The author' suggested strategy for women's development included appropriate technology such as the Gobar methane gas plant, provision of credit for women's industries, retention of girls in school and literacy programmes for girls and women' and higher wages for women."

Sonia Suri examined the influence of women's work patterns on women's and children's health and health—seeking behaviour in rural Rajasthan and revealed that Rajasthani women are a very heterogeneous group and any economic and health care interventions must understand how this heterogeneity influences rural women's health and social status. Thus, for some groups of women (for example, high jati and Nai women living in sanjhe or extended households), work outside their homes only increases their overall burden and does not lead them to have more power or influence within the family, including health care decisions for themselves and their children. For many other women work outside their homes does give them more deisions-making power within the household. However, despite high decision-making scores, many

Rajput, Dangi, Vaishnav and Bhil women fail to properly utilize available health care services. This is because many social and cultural factors inhibit them from seeking health care in a timely manner.

While women in India face many serious health concerns though both work status and socio-economic factors influence health status, the latter are more important; most of the gross effect of work status is due to socio-economic conditions rather than work participation. This calls for policy intervention in providing better health facilities, female education and supplementary nutrition programmes for poor women.

Women are Mistreated

> *"Violence against women and girls is the most pervasive human rights violation in the world today."*

Male violence against women is a worldwide phenomenon. Although not every women has experienced it, and many expect not to, fear of violence is an important factor in the lives of most women. It determines what they do, when they do it, where they do it, and with whom. Fear of violence is a cause of women's lack of participation in activities beyond the home, as well as inside it. Within the home, as well as inside it. Within the home, women and girls may be subjected to physical and sexual abuse as punishment or as culturally justified assaults. These acts shape their attitude to life, and their expectations of themselves.

Domestic spousal violence against women in developing countries like India, is now beginning to be recognized as a widespread health problem impeding development. A cross—sectional household survey was carried out in rural, urban and urban-slum areas across seven sites in India, among women aged 15-49 years, living with a child less than 18 years of age. The sample was selected using the probability proportionate to size method. Trained field workers administered a structured questionnaire to elicit information on spousal physical violence. The main hypothesized variables were social support, witnessed father beating mother and experience of harsh physical violence during childhood, alcohol abuse by spouse and socio-economic variables. The behaviours of hit, kick and beat. Odds ratios were calculated for risk and protective factors of violence using logistic regression. Of 9938 women surveyed, 26 per cent reported experiencing spousal physical violence during the lifetime of their marriage. Adjusted odds ratios calculated using multiple logistic regression analysis suggest that women whose husbands regularly consumed alcohol (OR 5.6; 95% CI 4.7-6.6); who experienced dowry harassment (OR 3.2; 95% CI 2.7-3.8); had reported experiencing harsh physical punishment during childhood (OR 1.6; 95% CI 1.4-1.8) and had witnessed their fathers beat their mothers (OR 1.9; 95% CI 1.6-2.1), were at increased risk of spousal physical violence (beat, hit and kick).

(Jeyasee Ian *et al.*, 2007)

The insecurity outside the household is today the greatest obstacle in the path of women. Conscious that, compared to the atrocities outside the house, atrocities within the house are endurable, women not only continued to accept their inferiority in the house and society, but even called it sweet.

Domestic spousal violence against women has far-reaching mental health implications. Kumar S. *et. al.*, studied on 9938 women and found out that 40 per cent reported poor mental health. Logistic regression showed that women reporting 'any violence'—'slap', 'hit', 'kick' or 'beat' (OR 2.2, 95% CI 2.0-2.5)—or 'all violence'—all of the four types of physically violent behaviour (OR 3.5, 95% CI 2.94-3.51)—were at increased risk of poor mental health.

Mental health sequelae to spousal violence are significant and have long-term health implications. Battered women were found to have more depressive symptoms than other women. Studies have shown that the more severe the abuse, the greater its impact on a women's physical and mental health. Recently attempts have been made in India to systematically record data on the prevalence, nature and consequence of domestic violence. Davar's insightful commentary on the rigidly defined roles of Indian women outlines the barriers to expressing their stresses and conflicts; these barriers ensure that their mental health needs remain neglected.

Conclusion

India has a long history of activism for women's welfare and rights, which has increasingly focused on women's economic rights. A range of government programmes have been launched to increase economic opportunity for women although there appear to be no existing programmes to address the cultural and traditional discrimination against women that leads to here object conditions.

Rural women have to be made aware of their potential beyond the house. In all this the media should be careful, street plays and other audio-visual media can also be leveraged effectively. Strategies for women development include appropriate technology such as the Gobar methane gas plant, provision of credit for women industries, retentions of girls in school and literacy programmes for girls and women and higher wages for women.

New programme strategies are needed, particularly those that improve the overall nutrition status of women of reproductive ages. This will require tailored programmes across socio-economic groups and within both rural and urban areas, but particularly among the urban and rural poor.

Perhaps the most difficult of obstacles to be cleared are those of a socio-cultural nature. It is particularly complex for rural women to address the social practices of their communities and is a long-term challenge. These include standards and social rules (including land rights and inheritance procedures), religious practices and cast systems, social taboos, prejudice against women and rural women in particular.

As former UN Secretary General Kofi Annan has stated, "Gender equality is more than a goal in itself. It is a precondition for meeting the challenge of reducing poverty, promoting sustainable development and building good governance."

A mother's education often leads to better health and nutrition for her children. More investment in improving the lot of rural women could create a 'virtuous circle' of better education, improved health and higher income. And women need to be given the right to have more control over productive asstes—land, water and credit, for example. Removing gender inequalities is not only morally right, it is good for economic growth and development.

REFERENCES

N. Kavitha, Rural Finance for Rural Women an Overview. www.google.com

M. Muthu Gopalkrishnan and Arun Kumar, A Study on the Socio-economic Conditions of the Members of Self-Help Groups in Krishnagiri District. www. google.com.

Carol. S. Coonod (1998). Chronic Hunger and the Status of Women in India. www. google.com.

Mohapatra P.C. and Pattanaik B.E. (1988). How Can we Improve Socio-Economic Condition of Women? Yojna 16-31(9): 13-7, 25.

Sonic Suri, Women, Work and Health in Rural Rajasthan, India European Journal of Clinical Nutrition.

A.K. Verma, Bhupinder Singh and Vijay Hengi (2008). Gestational Diabetes in Rural Women of Jammu. Eur J. Clin Nutr. 33:1; 57-55.

Bentley M.E. and Griffiths P.L. (2003). The Burden of Anemia Among Women in India Eur J. Clin Nutr. 57 (1); 52-60.

M. Srivastava, D.K. Agarwal, A. Agarwal, S. Agarwal and K.N. Agarwal. Nutritional Status of Rural Pregnant Non-Locating Women in Repordutive Age. www. pubmed.com.

Sharmistha Basu and Shiv Narayan Sidh (2008). Work Status and Health of Women: A Comparative Study of Northern and Southern States of Rural India. Work Health and Population, 10 (2).

Jeyaseelan L. Kumar S. Neelkantan N. Pedicoyit A. Pillai R. and Duvvery N. (2007) Physical Spousal Violence Against Women in India. Some Risk Factor. Equib. 39 (5).

Kumar S., Jeyaseelan L. Suresh S. Ahuja R.C. (2005) Domestic Violence and its Mental Health Correlates in Indian Women Brij Psychiatry. 187:578-8.

Desai Sonalde (1994). Gender Inequalities and Demographic Behaviour: India. New York: The Population Council, Inc.

18

Socio and Economic Status of Women in Agriculture

Rakhi Mittal & Dr. Meenu Agarwal

India is a developing which depends very much an its vast potential of human resources if there resources are properly tapped the country is bound to progress efficiently, effectively and rapidly. Women contribute the most important part of the human resources of the nation and they may contribute very substantially in building a strong powerful and affluent nation. They can, however, make their best contribution in the economic progress of the country.

Economic independence is considered as are of the main status indicator in the society in the existing socio-economic scenario. Women especially in rural areas are the deprived section of the society an account of their dependence on others for economic progress. This necessitates generation of opportunities so as to make them economically independent.

Poverty hits hardest at the female half of humankind. If woman living in a rural area of a developing country, they are likely to be poorer than a man, more vulnerable, own no land, be less educated and in poorer health. And you are unlikely to live as long. Struggling to combine a 'double day' of low-paid work with care for the home, rural women often have to cope with frequent pregnancies and child mortality. For women, perhaps the cruelest reality of all is that they have less chance than men to escape from poverty. A rural woman is likely to have little or no say in the way the family spends its income. Discrimination in education is the start of the vicious spiral of poverty. A girl may be deprived of schooling and literacy for no other reason than that she is female. Seventy per cent of poor women in India cannot read or write. Illiteracy often excludes people from written knowledge and decision-making. Some rural women have been affected by trade liberalization . They are unable to participate in the marketing of export crops as they lack land rights and access to essential farm inputs. On the other hand, some women have gained by securing jobs in new export activities. Investment in rural women pays off.

- Indian population is 48.1 per cent women and 51.9 per cent men
- Female illiteracy is 62 per cent whereas the male illiteracy rate is 34 per cent
- The labour force participation rate of women is 22.7 per cent, less than half of the men's rate of 51.6 per cent
- In rural India, agriculture and allied industrial sectors employ as much as 89.5 per cent of the total female labour
- Women have extensive work loads with dual responsibility for farm and household production
- Women's work is getting harder and more time-consuming due to ecological degradation and changing agricultural technologies and practices
- Women have an active role and extensive involvement in livestock production, forest resource use and fishery processing
- Women contribute considerably to household income through farm and non-farm activities as well as through work as landless agricultural labourers
- Women's work as family labour is underestimated
- There are high degrees of inter-state and intra-state variations in gender roles in agriculture, environment and rural production.

Rural women comprise more than one quarter of the total world population. 500 million women live below the poverty line in rural areas. Women perform 30 per cent of the agricultural work in industrialised countries. "Rural women the world over are an integral and vital force in the development processes that are the key to socio-economic progress. Rural women form the backbone of the agricultural labour force across much of the developing world and produce 35-45 per cent of Gross Domestic Product and well over 50 per cent of the developing world's food. Yet, half a billion rural women are poor and lack access to resources and markets."

WOMEN'S RESPONSIBILITY IN AGRICULTURAL ACTIVITIES

Food crops are the basis of most rural production as they provide the necessary daily food rations for rural families. Within this context, women have a fundamental role in farming production activities, in particular looking after crops, and ensuring good management of these activities.

Faced with depletion of natural resources, men are increasingly forced to migrate and/or carry out non-agricultural activities in order to secure their livelihood.

Rural women are therefore left to take on full responsibility for agricultural activities.

Savings/loan systems can therefore have considerable impact in such cases. For example, loans can enable the acquisition of a new technology or make it possible to hire labourers, thus allowing rural women to save time—hence reducing the fatigue of manual labour—in their agricultural activities. They can therefore retain their income-generating activities which they might otherwise have had to sacrifice in order to provide food.

Over and above their own economic interests, savings/loan facilities for rural women include much wider notions of political and social development such as time saving, family well-being and food security, improved finance management, personal autonomy and increased representation.

SOURCES OF FINANCE ARE AVAILABLE TO RURAL WOMEN

Women have several possible sources of finance at their disposal, each with its own advantages and disadvantages.

The unofficial sector has always played an important part in financing rural women's activities. The different players in this sector are families, relatives or friends, private lenders including loan sharks, rural shopkeepers, and rural solidarity arrangements. The loans are thus either in money or in kind (for example loans of inputs reimbursed by harvested agricultural produce). A new system of "semi-unofficial" micro-financing has also appeared during the last decade: the system set up by the non-government organisations which provide savings/loans to local rural and/or urban populations allowing populations who do not have access to the official sector to obtain loans at rates which are much better than in unofficial systems.

SAVINGS/ LOANS IN THE UNOFFICIAL FINANCE SECTOR

Small farmers have always set up unofficial micro-finance systems, even before experts in the field of development made this one of its favourite themes. To begin with, these were only bartering systems, before the unofficial finance system developed into proper loans which could be large sums of money.

Despite the constraints of this system, the unofficial sector is still today widely used and very useful for small producers and for rural women in particular.

Moreover, since there are numerous obstacles preventing access to the official credit system, many people retain the unofficial system as a source of savings and loans even if this alternative has a number of negative implications.

RURAL WOMEN USE THE UNOFFICIAL FINANCE SYSTEM

Rural women often use this system as they need small amounts of cash and the loans are granted according to social, relational and cultural conditions, and not according to purely economical conditions which would not allow women to benefit from them.

They also constitute personal savings funds which enable them to address their family's basic needs. These savings, if they are not hoarded or invested in material goods (herds, gold, or land etc.), can be invested in the unofficial sector (private loans, relatives; tontines) and are generally given in the form of loans to another person.

Thus the unofficial sector functions as real banks with their own savings and loan criteria depending on the socio-economic context of the region in which it develops, and it is successful because it is appropriate to the local situation.

Revolving loans and savings associations meet both economic and social needs are very common in developing countries. There have considerable impact for rural women who have their own funds and control the use of them. Through women's groups they are also empowered to manage, to be represented and to make claims and demands and are thereby no longer alone to face obstacles encountered in their daily lives.

This revolving system of savings/loans is a basic element in the life of rural women and allows numerous activities to emerge from these funds which can sometimes attain quite high levels.

VARIOUS OBSTACLES TO THE UNOFFICIAL FINANCE SYSTEM'S EFFICIENCY

Numerous studies, mainly carried out by universities and non-government organisations, have highlighted obstacles in the unofficial savings/loans systems. According to purely economic criteria, the impact of loans is limited, partly because unofficial systems imply limited capital and high costs which do not permit the development of large-scale activities.

Moreover the system usually lacks reliability through insecurity of deposits and the lender's more or less good management of his finance system. Although the loans are granted at high interest rates, there is virtually no remuneration for savings.

Apart from the development of community relationships, one of the possible negative points that can be noted is the social dependence which comes about due to the existing relationships with the person who has facilitated and/or made the loan.

Finally, by using the unofficial finance system, rural women are not integrated into the official finance system and their economic activities continue to be marginal. Therefore, their activities remain on a small scale and cannot develop in a satisfactory manner.

The unofficial finance system is interesting in that it constitutes a recourse in the event of sudden difficulties. Its impact remains limited also because of the essential role of the personal relationships played in granting loans.

OFFICIAL SYSTEM: FINANCE INSTITUTIONS

The official system (public or private national banks, rural banks, or development banks) can ensure more ambitious financial services than unofficial systems. However, using them may be difficult for rural women.

As rural women are increasingly incharge of the family farm's general management (rural exodus of men) and have to deal with the official finance system, facilitating access to loans could be a driving force in developing their production and processing activities, and in progressing towards agriculture for the local market.

OBSTACLES PREVENTING RURAL WOMEN'S ACCESS TO THE OFFICIAL FINANCE SYSTEM

Rural women have little access to information concerning official savings/loans institutions. In fact banks have a considerable communication problem with the rural environment in general, and with women in particular. The rare extension programmes concern their operating and financial services, targeting mainly farmers, without worrying about the specific nature of female problems. This means that rural women have a very limited idea of the nature of institutional savings/loans facilities.

Rural women are often considered as being insolvent because they are subsistence farmers, and are seen as a high-risk population for finance institutions.

Banks and financial institutions hesitate to grant loans to women, as they are usually small loans and do not provide a good enough return for the banks.

They are heavy institutional constraints such as administrative procedures and the necessity for guarantees (land ownership title deeds). With the problems of illiteracy and the lack of management knowledge, rural women are discouraged from accessing these financial services. Of course groups of women have a better chance of being provided with credit, but this necessitates organising women inside the community and this is not yet common practice.

Perhaps the most difficult of obstacles to be cleared are those of a socio-cultural nature. It is particularly complex for rural women to address the social practices of their communities and is a long-term challenge. These include standards and social rules (including land rights and inheritance procedures), religious practices and cast systems, social taboos, prejudice against women and rural women in particular.

Lastly is the classical difficulty of all rural populations, and not necessarily specific to rural women. Banks rarely have agencies in rural zones and women therefore have to go to towns which often mean walking for many hours. This is the case not only to open an account or ask for a loan, but also whenever they make a deposit, require information, or have a request. To add to the cost in time and in transport, one must also add the social cost as many prejudices exist concerning rural women going to the town and the economic cost of their absence from their families with regard to their daily domestic tasks and production.

Difficulties in accessing loans encountered by rural women reduce the scope of their initiatives; block their economic and social development, with the result that they are kept in a state of dependency and daily insecurity.

AGRICULTURAL ORGANISATIONS WHICH PROVIDE FINANCE SERVICES

Specialized in the rural sector's problems, agricultural organisations are characterized by the fact that they are set up, owned, managed and controlled by their members. As they are independent and democratically operated, they can set up credit policies and programmes which are better adapted to rural environments and to rural women when their voices are heard. They are consequently an extremely important element for implementing rural policies and defending the interests of all farmers, women and men. Agricultural organisations have multiple sectors of intervention and can set up genuine rural development programmes. Loans are one of the tools used in a general rural development policy, working towards solving the various economic, political, technical, social and cultural difficulties of this sector. However, setting up such a programme of associating savings/loans for the development of other income-generating activities or parallel activities (training, techniques, nutrition, health etc.) requires several conditions for success.

RURAL WOMEN'S PARTICIPATION AND REPRESENTATION IN AGRICULTURAL ORGANISATIONS

To ensure a better participation, it is important that borrowers – and women in particular – take part in the assessment of savings/loans programmes so that they are involved in their sound management and therefore of their sustainability. Moreover, as there is no typical finance model, this active participation enables actual local needs to be identified and the best-adapted savings/loans system to be provided.

This is particularly true when the target population are rural women whose specific needs are not yet clearly defined. As the members of these organisations are in control of the policies set up, it is absolutely essential that agricultural organizations facilitate greater representation of rural women as members, allowing them to be represented in decision-making processes and on management committees.

Equal opportunities for men and women in becoming members of and participating in farmers' organisations are a fundamental precondition for success. Rural women need to be active within decision-making structures to be able to draw up savings/loans policies which really meet their specific needs.

RURAL WOMEN'S ACCESS TO FACILITIES PROVIDED BY AGRICULTURAL ORGANIZATIONS

A rural development programme including financial services should associate these services with improved access to inputs, land, technologies and training. It is very important for rural women to have full and direct access to the different services as members in their own right and not as wives of member farmers. This would enable them to have real control over the use of these facilities, in particular with respect to finance granted to them.

TAKING THE FAMILY UNIT INTO ACCOUNT

In rural development programmes, efforts should be made to develop savings/loans facilities for the whole family unit, with lines of credit specifically for women. This will mean less divisions within the family, the community and society as a whole.

Also, implementing a rural finance programme for women should entail considerations on maintaining the right balance between food production and commercial production so as not to affect family food and nutritional security. Such programmes should allow all daily activities of the rural woman to be linked together without endangering family unit's working and living conditions.

TRAINING OF AND INFORMATION FOR RURAL WOMEN

As regards training, extension and information on credit facilities from agricultural organizations, these should be adapted to the differences in men and women's knowledge, to their different activities and to their daily planning (schedule and length of meetings are an important element in optimizing the presence and participation of rural woman).

Agricultural organizations must therefore take into consideration the issues of rural women when drawing up policies which are more in keeping with their needs and requirements and thereby reducing the existing inequalities between men and women's access to their various facilities.

Under these conditions, finance can have a considerable direct impact on the life of farming families and on women in particular.

CONCLUSION

Female labour-force participation also relates to educational attainment. Higher levels of education increase the opportunity cost of a woman's time, leading to greater workforce participation when suitable jobs are available, and to lower fertility. The study showed that not only have workforce participation rates increased, but there has been a movement among the younger cohort towards more skilled occupations in the urban areas and away from family agricultural work in the rural areas. These productive activities can conflict with women's reproductive role. In both areas, paid work which interfered with childbearing depressed fertility. Work in the service industries seems to have led to lower fertility, though this occurred more in some sectors than in others, whereas domestic work and home-based economic activity did not. However, contemporary occupational status did not appear to have a significant effect on fertility, suggesting that decisions about having children, once made, are not affected by employment. However, the number of children had a negative effect on the probability of female workforce participation.

Female schooling can lead to a reduction in poverty by giving women the literacy skills and confidence they need to have a say about how things are run. A mother's education often leads to better health and nutrition for her children. More investment in improving the lot of rural women could create a 'virtuous circle' of better education, improved health and higher income. And women need to be given the right to have more control over productive assets—land, water and credit, for example. Removing gender inequalities is not only morally right, it is good for economic growth and development.

It is only when women move forward, the family moves, the village moves and the nation moves. As rightly said by Late Smt. Indira Gandhi "Women liberation is not a luxury for India but an urgent necessity to enable the nation to move ahead to a life which is more than satisfying materially, intellectually and spiritually."

REFERENCES

International Federation of Agricultural Producers: http://www.ifap.org/

Women's World Summit Foundation: Information on the World Rural Women's Day, http://www.woman.ch/

The Associated Country Women of the World (ACWW): http://www.acww.org.uk/

FAO Website: http://www.fao.org/ : in ?gender and food security?, you can find information about the different activities of women.

IFAD Website: http://www.ifad.org/ : in ?publications?, complete information on rural women.

EIU, 1997. India Nepal: Country Profile, The Economist Intelligence Unit, London.

ESCAP, 1997. Women in India: A Country Profile. United Nations, New York.

FAO, 1991. Women's Role in Dynamic Forest-based Small Scale Enterprises: Case Studies on Uppage and Lacquerware from India. Food and Agriculture Organization of the United Nations, Bangkok.

FAO, 1997. Forest Dependent Survival Strategies of Tribal Women: Implications for Joint Forest Management in Andhra Pradesh, India. RAP Publication: 1997/24. Food and Agriculture Organization of the United Nations, Bangkok.

Meena, N.L. 1991 'National Policy and Programmes for Women in India' in Papers and Proceedings of the Regional Conference on Gender Issues in Agriculture, ADB and UNIFEM. (Manila, 5-6 December, 1990).

UNDP, 1997. Human Development Report, Oxford University Press, New York. Venkateswaran, S. 1992. Living on the Edge: Women, Environment and Development, Friedrich Ebert Stiftung, New Delhi.

World Bank, 1991. A World Bank Country Report: Gender and Poverty in India, World Bank, Washington D.C.S.

Swiss Federal Bureau of Statistics. 1989. Indicators of the Social Status of Women in Switzerland: Disparities and Perspectives. Paper submitted by the Swiss Federal Bureau of Statistics to the Second Economic Commission for Europe (ECE)/International Research and Training Institute for the Advancement of Women (INSTRAW) Joint Meeting on Statistics of Women, Geneva, 1989.

Population Crisis Committee. 1985. Country Rankings of the Status of Women: Poor, Powerless and Pregnant. Population Briefing Paper 20. Washington, D.C.

19

Women Empowerment: Globalisation and Opportunities

Lipi

Empowerment means playing greater active role in all sphere of life and simultaneously empowers the person to control and change the major works. In other words it's a process which is directly related to power and for to change of power when we talk specially about women empowerment, we mean providing women social, political, religious and economical rights, so that the status of women may be equal to the men in society. Empowerment of women has emerged an important issue in our society in recent times.

With the shift in approach for development oriented the society has started realizing the importance of women as active vibrant and inevitable partners to the process of socio-economic development. The under utilization of the potential of women is an another important issue, therefore, the need of hour is to explore and inculcate the latent talent of women and to harness the full potential of women by destroying all kinds of 'visible and invisible' barriers and by allowing them equal status and opportunity with a sense of dignity and pride.

Today it is well established fact that women are equally capable of performing their role as their male counterparts. Therefore, what is required most for the women empowerment of women is the change in the mind set not only for women, but also of men along with greater social acceptance of gender parity and women's rights.

Discrimination of women from womb to tomb is well known. As women oppressed in all spheres of life they need to be empowered in all walks of life. In order to fight against the socially constructed gender biases. Women have to swim against the stream that requires more strength. Such strength comes from the process of empowerment.

Empowering of women pre-supports a drastic, dynamic and democratic change in the perception of and expectation from women in our society. To help women in attain economic independence in first priority of such changes.

Empowerment is a process and is not, therefore, something their case be given to people. The process of empowerment in both individual and collective, since it is through involvement in groups that people most after begin to develop their awareness and the ability to organize to take action and bring about change.

The women empowerment can be done through providing proper education, health and nutrition facilities. The government should ensure the quality among the female group.

Government is making continued efforts to provide equitable growth opportunities for women who are increasingly being reflected among other in increased participation by women in local governments and decisions making programmes for women studies point out that expanding women's economic opportunities results in their social empowerment thus, leading to improved livelihood. Creating an environment through positive economic and social policies for full development of women to enable them to realize their full potential. The national policy of empowerment of women has set certain objectives in India. The goal of this policy is to bring about the advancement, development and empowerment of women.

Objectives of Women Empowerment

1. To create safe and proper environment for women's physical, mental and moral development.
2. To develop skills for taking self decision capability.
3. To create capability to present their position in society effectively.
4. To create awareness among women to be truly ambitious and to dream for betterment.
5. To develop independent identification of women. Her position should not be determined by her husband, father, brother etc.
6. To create feeling of self pride so that they should not feel week, helpless, powerless, comparatively to their counter part men.

Role and Status of Women

Women constitute the backbone of the nation. Prosperity of nation depend upon the prosperity of its women. Women have found their due place of importance in all the western countries, but the same is not true in all the major asian countries including India. These equal opportunities are not provided to women and therefore they are regarded and treated as second grade citizen's inspite of the role they play in the society in all fields.

The questions of rural women's contribution acquires more important because in the present day contact they are assigned triple role in the society and therefore contribute more than men. In most low income household women's work includes not only reproductive work (the child bearing and rearing responsibilities) but also productive work, often as secondary income earners in agriculture.

It is a fact that ignorance in the society about the values of women. It is necessary to open the doors of perception not only amongst men but women too. There is a general condition that there can be no meaningful development without strong equal participation of women. But in the competition for employment and economic growth are still treated as unwelcome rivals. But with the speed of time the rural women and urban becomes more powerful. Her social-economic condition becomes strong and effective. Their fate being tied with child bearing and baby care besides the household responsibilities, their freedom of participation at other much status oriented and remunerative areas can be assured by the resistance of helping hands in domestic front.

Review of Literature

Various macro as well as micro level studies on women empowerment have been conducted by different social scientists and economists. These main findings have been discussed in the following paragraphs:

Srinivasan (1990) Female work participation in non-agricultural sector and level of wage are also considered as determinants of empowerments.

Dixon Mueller (1993) Women's gainful employment outside home exposes her to the outsides world; delay age of marriage, provide a sense of financial independence and increase her bargaining power and autonomy within the household and society.

Batliwala (1995) Empowerment is a process by which.women gain greater central over material and intellectual resources which will assist them to increase their self reliance and enhance them to assert their independent rights and challenge the ideology of patriarchy and gender based discrimination against woman. This will also enable them to organize themselves to assent think autonomy to make decision and choices and ultimately eliminate their own subordinate in all the institution and structures of society.

Jejeebhoy and Kishor (1996) Education enhances a woman's position through decision making autonomy, knowledge, exposure to the modern world.

Jejeebhoy (1988) Non-egalitarian gender relations deny women an egalitarian decision making role during health care need and other family matters.

United Nations (1999) Women's paid employment could alter the perception of women's value and motivate investment in the girl child's education and health.

Malhotra, A. (2002) A fundamental shift in perception or "inner transformation" is essential to the formulation of development choices. The input of empowerment also has to enhance her intrinsically by changing her attitude into egalitarian ideas.

Sundari (2004) Lack of decision making power by a woman could result into lesser timely health seeking behaviour and leads to greater adverse health consequences.

Globalisation and Women Empowerment

The concept of globalization is one that has become widely used in debates, in politics, business and need a over the past few years. A decade ago, the term "Globalisation" was relatively unknown. Today it seem to be on the top of everyone's tongue. Globalisation refers to the fact that we are, all increasingly living in one world, so that individuals, groups and nations become more independent.

In context of woman the impact of globalisation will have to be assessed carefully, the will documented facts regarding gender inequalities that so far have affected women's capabilities negatively demand unequivocally that policy-makers pay careful attention to enhancing women's capabilities. It is a general perception that women tend to bear the brunt of globalisation. On the one hand the general deterioration of living conditions and traditional patriarchal attitudes meant that they have had to take care of their families while generating an income, on the other hand, women are often the victims of plant closure.

The complete backwardness of women in observed in that their direct and indirect interaction with the rest of the world's is limited. Most of the women have not gone beyond their village physically and mentally. They don't know how the world's looks like outside, what is happening in the socio-political scene of the country, who is ruling and what policies are being introduced or implemented. Their knowledge is limited to just their families and village situations. They have a very narrow perception of things.

But now the rural women has changed the world's become globalize and women empowerment takes place. One of the best example of women empowerment is that now the birth of a girl child also welcomes and she will be equally treated at par with her brother and ever after marriages she will contribute to economic inter-dependence, participation, decision-making and finally equal status will be given in the family.

Further, education can redefine women's role and status the educated women can fight for a just place for herself and for a just social order. Studies have again and again proved that women's education can also bring about changes in family size, fertility, decision-making and participation.

Higher education of women is also a most important variable of women empowerment and globalisation. There is an another example of impact of globalisation that now women's are working in various fields which are only reserved for men and such as Navy, Air Force, Army, BPO Sector, Call Centres, Sales and Marketing and High Grade Supervisory Jobs of the organized sector.

Now days that women are becoming more conscious of their rights as the society has began to respond. More and more women these days are adopting career and findings employment as individual, while contributing to the building of rural economy of India.

Women in search of better status, social dignity, self earned income and greater influence and party with these of male counterparts have shown impressive results of their performance in second decade.

They seem to miss no opportunity in proving their worthiness and capacity. The examination results often place them for superior to the male examinees. In training, courses, service selection and as well as informed and alert mother the women are tending to indicate their performance orientation.

In the wake of globalisation employment avenues for women have also changed drastically in the past few years. Employment for women almost becoming a compulsion they would be ready to work for larger hours even for a meagre pay. With large scale opportunities for women in call centres, BPO during evening and night hours, women will be overburdened with a dual responsibility of managing the domestic *vis-a-vis* service fronts efficiently. Social taboos and other restriction on the working women are slowly but surely fading away because of the constantly rising standard in life and the pressure to make both ends comfortably.

In context of globalisation, there has also been casualisation and informalisation of labour market both for males and females. However, this was comparatively more for females than that for males. It is 2.4 per cent for males and 3.3 per cent for females. Now Indian women took the challenges and proved their capabilities in every sphere of life. It is more impressive in the technological sphere and economic spheres. Reservation in political participation encourage them to come forward inspite of revengeful outlook of contesting male counterpart. Sonia Gandhi, Sheela Dixit, Indira Gandhi, are the bigger in the political field. The lady President Smt. Pratibha Patil proves the importance and need of better women empowerment. These ladies prove that women can do everything as can men do.

Thus we can say globalisation of worlds helps in women empowerment in some manner but there are also some implication of globalisation.

Implications of Globalisation in the Context of Women Empowerment

Indecent Exposure of Women in Media

The studies of women's and media during last two decades indicates that media image tended to define women with narrow confines of traditional, domestic roles and sexual appeal. A close took at the portrayals of women in both in print as well as visual media will show that women are being treated as commodities for sale and to sell other's products. Even the Censor Board which used to the vigilant earlier has now shut down its eyes in the wake of the winds of globalisation and liberalization, sweeping the country.

Position of Women in Films

The scenes of molestation and cruelty to women are screened in the most undesirable manner. This gives impetus to the youngster to follow same pattern of life. It makes them ill treat all other women folk as presented in films.

Position of Women in T.V. Serials

There is a great of diversity and conflicting messages generating through serials. The daily soaps present the women's image such as second women, pre marital affair, divorce and extra affair etc. This portrayal of women in media affects society considerably.

Open Minded Employment

As the world become more globalize the women's are becoming less safer as earlier. Jobs like in BPO sector, call centres are less safer for women. Their duties in night shifts for longer hours permeates many serious unaccepted incidents.

Thus on the one hand outdated cultural practices continue as a part of social structure, while on the other hand the sexual presentation of women reinforce the negative aspects of women's role and relationship Paradoxical even after the great achievements of women and media has failed to highlight their aspect and make concerted efforts to discuss serious issues of women empowerment and make them play equal and rightful role in society.

Opportunities

1. Increases in employment avenues.
2. Decreases in social restrictions and social taboos.
3. Casualisation and informalisation of both male and female. However, it is more in females.
4. Strong Panchayati Raj Institutions (PRIs) can be a possible source for women's empowerment and for implementation of such programmes.
5. Promotion of women's empowerment through S & T with the collaboration commercial set ups (through setting up of rural technology parks SHGs etc.).

REFERENCES

Batra, G.S. (2000), Globalisation and Liberalization -- New Development, Deep & Deep Publication, New Delhi.

N.C. Nath (2003), Decent Work and Empowerment of Women in Agriculture, Kurukshetra, Published by Ministry of Rural Development, Vol. 54, New Delhi.

Internet sites like:

http://www.google.com

http://www.globalenvision.org

20

PRI & Political Socialisation Among Rural Women-Mahila Samakhya Experience

Roona

Panchayati Raj Institutions are the grassroots units of self-government and have been proclaimed as the vehicles of socio-economic transformation in rural India.

The world *'panchayat'* is a traditional one, referring to the five elders in a village who mediated conflict and spoke on behalf of all the residents of a village in pre-modern times. Their functions bordered on local governance akin to what was developed in other countries during their agrarian phases like the Russian *'Mir'*, German *'Mark'* and the medieval *'Manor'* of England. However in most parts of India, the panchayat system was based on the age-old caste system, social status and family. In these traditional bodies, the lower castes and women had no representation. During British rule in India, in the latter part of 19th century the local self-government concept was introduced, first in the town areas and later in the villages. Since then, it took more than hundred years for the local self-government bodies to become a part of the Indian Constitution. Effective and meaningful functioning of these bodies would depend on active involvement, contribution and participation of its citizens both *female and male.* One of the important, reasons why marginalised sections—Scheduled Castes, Scheduled Tribes and Women could not fully enjoy the fruit of development for more than 50 years of planning and development in India was their inadequate, ineffective participation and involvement in decentralised governance, planning and development. The highest national priority must be the unleashing of womanpower in governance. That is the single most important source of societal energy that has kept corked for half a century.

WOMEN'S MOVEMENT AND THE ISSUES OF REPRESENTATION

Feminist economist Devki Jain said, "Political empowerment through affirmative action is essential for women to break this hard rock of patriarchy."

Indian society represents a system of patriarchy; therefore the male domination inhibits the participation of women in the political and development process. Women have a marginalised position in the social, economic and political spheres of the country. Representation of women in political structures and decision-making bodies in India has been extremely low. Women are considered as mere 'numbers' and not 'members'. Women must be visible politically as women and be empowered to act in the capacity, because there is the continual possibility that they may have a need and attitude on vital issues that differ from those of men. This claim that women must he present in representative institution in order to represent women's interests is part of what *Anne Phillips* has called a *'politics of presence.'* Presence then cannot be just opposite of absence. It must be seen as a qualitative and not merely quantitative notion. Her argument of the necessity for a political of presence forms the justification used by feminists for claiming women's equal qualitative representation in the politics. Only women can transform *'women's issues'* as *'societal issues'* and legitimize it with state support. The demand for greater representation of women in political institutions in India was not taken up in a systematic way until the ***Committee on the Status of Women in India*** (CSWI) published its report "Towards Equality" in 1974. It highlights the absence of a serious political and social motivation that has contributed to lack of political conscious and political participation among the Indian women. Before this the focus of the growing women's movement was on improving women's socio-economic position. The CSWI report suggested that women's representation in political institutions, especially at the grassroots level, needed to be increased through a policy of reservation of seats for women.

In 1985, after the Women's World Congress at Nairobi, the ***National Perspective Plan*** was prepared which put down the forward-looking strategies for women's development. In this document the question of their political participation was highlighted. In 1988, the National Perspective Plan for Women suggested that a 30 per cent quota for women should be introduced at all levels of elective bodies. Women's groups insisted that reservation should be restricted to the panchayat level to encourage grassroot participation in politics. The consensus around this demand resulted in the adoption of the *73rd and 74th Amendments* to the Indian Constitutions in 1993. So it can be said that the *"politicisation of gender"* in the Indian political system is due largely to the success of the women's movement.

MAIN FEATURES OF 73RD AMENDMENT ACT 1992

Good governance is promoting people's participation in decision-making, including the participation of women in governance.

Representation of women in the local level democratic institution in India is a revolutionary step. The Passage of the Constitution *73rd Amendment Act,* 1992 marks a new era in the federal democratic set up of the country and provides constitutional status to the *Panchayati Raj Institutions.* The Act that came into force from *24 April, 1993* stipulates that Panchayats shall be given powers and authority to function as institutions of self-government. India was considered as the only country that has enacted legislation in reserving 33 per cent seats for women. Women were suddenly brought into this system as one dimension of this complex process and it defines the context in which they have to function. The Constitution made provisions for reservation of these groups for the post of members and chairpersons at *three levels of Panchayats.* It reserved 30 per cent of seats in elected village councils (Panchayats) for women, which has brought more than *1 million* elected women into the political life at the grassroot level. This gender-based reservation, in favour of women is made applicable even to the number of seats otherwise reserved for *Scheduled Castes/Scheduled Tribes and other backward caste women.* The panchayats have a 5-year tenure, and they are given 29 subjects to look after ranging from agriculture, forestry, and fisheries to family planning, health and education. The 73rd Constitutional Amendment offers the opportunity for a large number of powerless rural women to enter active local governance at its basic level and become equal partners in the developmental process. It provided the much-needed opportunity for women to actively participate in the decision-making processes of their locality through the political right that was conferred on them through the Central Act. It can certainly improve the social status and strengthen the empowerment of elected women representatives of the village Panchayats. This was the best innovation in grassroots democracy in the world. In U.P. 30.4 per cent (2003) is the female participation rate in local government level. The percentage of women elected in different layers of gram panchayat in U.P. is 33.30 per cent that means 120,591 are women headed out of total 406,895 Gram Panchayat, 33 per cent in Kshetriya panchayat that is 18,880 are women headed out of total 52,417 Kshetriya panchayat and 37.40 per cent in zilla panchayat, that is 793 are women headed out of total 2,127 zilla panchayat. Experience over the last 10 years has demonstrated that the implementation of the 73rd Amendment has been plagued by many problems and shortcomings. Broadly speaking, there are three main concerns that have emerged from the field experience of working panchayats. These are, *the inadequate functions, functionaries and funds made available to panchayats due to bureaucratic resistance and lack of political will; second, the overt or covert capture of panchayat institutions by local elites and third, the lack of capacities of elected representatives and panchayat institutions to perform their constitutionally mandated tasks.* This 10-year voyage of the panchayats has been lonely in the shadow of resistance from the bureaucracy and the political class and while there has been some support from the few rare pro-panchayati raj politicians and bureaucrats. But for the most part, this process has gathered its key supporters from *NGOs, research and academic institutions, donor organisations and international agencies.* Consequent to these limitations, civil society support for Panchayati Raj largely came in the form of support for capacity building of elected representatives. Women are taking up the challenge and gearing up themselves to enter politics at the lower level in the spirit of self-governance as committed citizens. As they do so, they find the need to educate themselves and others, on the general and gender issues confronting the local government and the nation, on the functions and methodology of local government, the intricacies of planning and management and the resolution of public and private challenges and tension. The gaps need to be identified and a set of training aids and inputs specific to the need of *Panchayati Raj Institutions* built up. In short, the women and other weaker sections need to empower themselves. Towards this the governmental and quasi-governmental, non-governmental and grassroot groups are getting into action, by way of creating new infrastructure for political education and training so that they will be able to generate hope and optimism amongst women representatives for securing the space and freedom for using the panchayats, a symbol of state power, for their 'own' developmental needs and objectives. As politics is not a traditional field for women it will take time for them to understand and analyse the functioning of panchayat.

CONTRIBUTION OF MAHILA SAMAKHYA TOWARDS POLITICAL EMPOWERMENT

Mahila Samakhya (MS) is a programme, which was formulated in pursuance of the national policy of education (1986) initiated in 10 districts of Uttar Pradesh. *Mahila Samakhya* is implemented through an autonomous registered '*Mahila Samakhya Society*'. This apex body receives grants form the Central Government. The basic objectives behind the scheme which was formally launched in 1989, is to create a mechanism whereby women are given an opportunity to plan and monitor their own education, and thereby to reach out to a new body of knowledge. *Empowerment, collective decision making power and raised self-image* being the essential elements, *education and Panchayati Raj, women's role and functions, their capacity to participate in the decision-making*, can be central aspects of the objectives of MS. Among all these political empowerment assumes the greatest significance because it affects the role of women in decision-making process in most spheres.

Ninth Five Year Plan (1997-2002) Document, "*The MS approach is an effective means to mobilise and organised women, and enabling them to take charge of their lives. This has resulted in many other sectoral programmes seek in to link with MS strategies. A major goal of Mahila Samakhya is that all policy decision should have a gender perspective. For this purpose, political participation of women at every level in the process of decision-making has been encouraged.*"

Mahila Samakhya strategy has centered on training and activating Panchayat members, especially women and the village people. This helps in compiling all the issues which act as impediments in political empowerment of women. MS helps to groom women candidates for elections through education and training and gives panchayat representatives the opportunity to meet with their counterparts from other states. MS has initiated a number of interventions and activities leading to new and energised consciousness through various intermediary processes of *self-reflection, training and education.* These have created positive impact in different aspects of women's lives.

Women empowerment being the goal of MS; their contribution in political empowerment of women are:

MS encouraged women to actively participate in Panchayati Raj Elections at village and block level as contestant and as voter.

- During pre-election period in blocks, dynamic women were selected by MS to fight panchayat elections in order to take advantage of reservation for women and their effective participation in panchayat elections.
- After elections training programmes for elected women were organised on Panchayati Raj Act, functions of panchayat, role of office bearers, issues of women development and empowerment etc. which help them to make a greater impact on local decision making.
- MS organised awareness programmes for voters regarding the significance of using the right to franchise by women, about the election process, filling nominations etc. with the help of innovative methods such as pamphlets, wall writings, role play, nukkad natak, folklore etc.
- MS acts as a watchdog for the activities of panchayats. It insists on holding of regular meetings, and tries to ensure attendance and participation of women in Gaon Sabha meetings. It also works as a pressure group for maintaining transparency in the working of panchayat.

NEED FOR STUDY

Reservation of seats help to create a political space for women in the male dominated political system and lead to *social justice, equality of status, adult suffrage and finally to political empowerment.* It provides them the capacity to influence decision-making process, an opportunity to raise their grievances and other related social and economic problems in a formal way. Their knowledge about the functioning of the panchayats will increase if they get outside support in terms of NGO intervention, women's groups, or any other social or political movement so that women will become relatively more vocal and they will participate effectively. Political empowerment as a process of social change has its own radiation effect and it would be useful to evaluate this effect, to examine as to what extend the MS has influenced the overall functioning of women-headed panchayat. In this light, the present study has attempted to examine the various aspects related to the nature of participation of women pradhans and women members in different meetings and activities and various development programmes of the village panchayats, social reform and welfare activities. It seeks to find out the different social and political groups of these women representatives. It also studies their outlook, the extent of their awareness of-their significant role as women representatives and the actual degree of their participation in the local government bodies and in the rural community. It likewise identifies factors that might enhance or impede the effective participation of women representatives. Finally, such a study will able to find out as to what extent the environment built through MS intervention has sustained and has influenced the overall functioning of the panchayats.

OBJECTIVES

- The main objective of the present study is to examine the role of MS in the political empowerment of the elected representative and explore to what extent the MS Panchayats are taking up development and social issues related to women and vulnerable weaker section of the society and their felt needs.
- To examine the level of attendance and participation of women in the meetings of Gaon Sabha and panchayats.
- To study the functioning of various sub-committees of panchayat which have been constituted.
- To highlight the initiatives taken in planning and implementation of development schemes relating to improving health status of the community particularly of women, children and development of weaker section of society.
- To highlight how the welfare schemes such as widow pension, old age pension etc. are being implemented.
- To identify the constraints faced by panchayat members in organising panchayat functions of the panchayat.
- To draw attention on the efforts made for bringing transparency in the functioning smoothly.
- To suggest measures to make PRI's a real participatory democratic institution with increased, meaningful and sustained participation of women.

METHODOLOGY

This study is basically an empirical study. It is based on both secondary data as well as primary data. The secondary data, on various aspects, was collected from the official documents and records available in the district offices of the Panchayats of the sample districts. The primary data and required information was collected from the women Pradhans with the help of specially designed structured and semi-structured interview schedules and questionnaires. Some of the basic information was also obtained through personal discussions with the officials and the people of the sample Block Panchayats. The study was conducted in the development block *'Chakia'* of *Varanasi*. *Chakia* block included four Gram Panchayats. This block was selected because it is culturally different where the role of women has been quite different as a part of tradition and social milieu. A total of 11 members including pradhans were interviewed from the Panchayat, community members also participated in participatory discussions done in the Panchayat.

PARTICIPATION OF WOMEN IN PRI—A STUDY OF MAHILA SAMAKHYA PANCHAYAT AT CHAKIA BLOCK

The Ashok Mehta Committee endorsed the i-iced for village level women's organisations and felt that they are likely to influence both directional and implementation levels.

Political process is an important point of address in order to tackle the issue of women subordination but it recognised that the result would be diluted if women were to merely joint the existing structure, without critical understanding of the political process. Viable women's organisation helps women to develop confidence and to engage in collective action. It enables women to achieve full and equal partnership in development and to work for the construction of a more equitable, healthy and prosperous society. Organisations facilitate and promote leadership quality, where women's organisations are active, changes are introduced quickly and their momentum maintained easily. For all women to be part in the whole process of political decision making it is important to develop leadership qualities in them and bring awareness among them about surrounding social, economic, cultural and political functions. Once women's organisations are formed and become strong, they can influence their neighbourhoods and also function as powerful pressure groups for implementing the existing programmes and for introducing other needed ones.

The programme of MS aiming at the development and empowerment of women is operational in the sample Gram

Panchayats of *Varanasi* from 7 to 8 years. The programme intervention include *mobilizing women and forming them into effective groups to fight against discrimination and their low status, raising the level of awareness of women, acquainting them with their rights, involving women in decision-making process, creating women leadership, launching effective campaign against social practices, economic exploitation etc. preparing them into effective pressure group for development and empowerment of women* are the salient features of MS programmes. Since the programme has been operational for the last few years in selected villages of the sample district, it would be interesting to assess the spread effect of MS programme. Women groups are also oriented and trained on their respective duties, roles and rights. They provide necessary information. MS demystify complex official document of the state so that these could be accessed and understood by larger audience, especially elected women representative. Women are also encouraged to join the literacy camp and centers run by MS so that they can improve their negotiation skills and bargain power, which ultimately resulted in the ability to carry out their roles more effectively.

PROFILE OF THE GRAM PANCHAYATS

The total area of Varanasi is 1550.20 sq.km. The total population (Census 2001) was 3147927 with 1497786 women and 1650138 men. The sex ratio, women per 1,000 men was 908. The total literacy rate in Varanasi was 67.09 per cent, in which female literacy was 48.89 per cent and male literacy was 83.66 per cent. It has one municipal board, two tehsils-Sadar and Pindara, 8 development blocks and 703 Gram Panchayats. It has 1,336 numbers of villages. This district has 6 representatives in the Parliament. In the district of Varanasi, *Chakia* Block was associated with MS (Mahila Samakhya). It was selected for the study. *Chakia* block included 4 Panchayats: *Heenauti, Sikandarpur, Barunjhi* and *Rampur*. Women pradhans associated with MS, which will be referred as MS panchayats, head these four panchayats. The basic indicators of four panchayats are given below:

Particulars	*Heenauti*	*Barunjhi*	*Rampur*	*Sikandarpur*
1. Area Sq. Km.	5	7	5	6
2. Density per Sq. Km.	325	219	320	244
3. Average Family Size	5.9	5.4	5.7	5.5

Contd...

Particulars	*Heenauti*	*Barunjhi*	*Rampur*	*Sikandarpur*
4. Number of households	291	284	281	293
5. Total Population				
Total	1627	1536	1601	1467
Female	761	723	738	668
Male	866	713	863	779
6. Sex ratio				
Female/1000 males	879	889	855	883
7. Literacy				
Total	31.59	34.29	42.34	35.19
Female	16.20	17.29	19.96	16.95
Male	45.13	48.64	62.19	52.46
	(In %)	(In %)	(In %)	(In %)
8. No. of voters				
Total	1071	958	1098	982
Female	460	418	529	545
Male	611	540	591	528

Sl.No.	*Particulars*	*Pradhan and Members in Panchayats*
1.	**Age (years)**	
	• 20-30	3
	• 30-35	5
	• Above 35	3
2.	**Marital Status**	
	• Single	0
	• Married	10
	• Widow	1
3.	**Caste Category**	
	• SC	3
	• OBC	4
	• General	4
4.	**Educational Status**	
	• Illiterate	4
	• Literate	3
	• Primary Pass	1
	• Junior High School	3
5.	**Occupation**	
	• House Wife	6
	• Agriculture labour	2
	• Farming	3

PROFILE OF PRADHANS AND MEMBERS

The profile of pradhan and members in Panchayats in the sample districts is tabulated and analysed below which gives their age, marital status, caste category, educational status, occupations and training received.

These women are the daughters of the 73rd Amendment of the Indian Constitution, passed in 1993. They had discarded the age-old custom of hiding their veiled faces behind home walls. They explained that they had to go to the bank to draw and deposit money, and to their district headquarters to attend monthly meetings. Agewise analysis of members show that majority of them were above 35 years old. All women were married but one woman lost her husband. There were four illiterate. Analysis of occupation of members shows that 6 are housewife, 2 were engaged in their own family farm and 3 were agriculture labour. The tenure of membership was 5 year in Varanasi district. Women membership in panchayat was nearly 33 per cent, which indicates that no women were elected from the unreserved seat. Pradhan and members in Panchayats had family relationship with ex-pradhan.

MEETINGS OF 'GAON SABHA'

Gaon Sabha is the basic grassroot level institution and it is the general body of Gram Panchayat. It provides a forum for all the residents of the village to participate in management of all activities proposed by panchayat. It provides an opportunity to all the people to participate in the development process by inculcating community spirit, which helps in strengthening overall development orientation by enabling weaker section to become a part of mainstream development. The number of Gaon meeting held in 1998-99 was 2, which increased in 1999-2000 to 3 per year. The average attendance of women in meetings was higher than men in both the years. About 80-90 per cent women pradhan and members attend the panchayat meetings regularly. Given their sheer numbers, one might conclude that democracy has become more effective than before at least at the grassroots level. This argument becomes strengthened because the socio-economic background of these women showed that the majority of them come from the lower income group. Thus, convening regular meetings of Gaon Sabha and the level of participation of various categories of people is an important indicator of not only the maturity of grassroot democracy but also of broad based participation particularly of the weak, marginalised and disadvantage sections of society in the development process to ensure equitable sharing of benefits.

Number of Meeting of Gaon Sabha Held and Average Attendance

Sl. No.	*Name of Panchayats*	*Number of Meetings Held 1998-99*	*1999-2000*	*Average Attendance of Members as % Age of Total Voters*					
				1998-99			*1999-2000*		
				Total	*Male*	*Female*	*Total*	*Male*	*Female*
1.	Heenauti	2	3	35	42	29	42	52	34
2.	Barunjhi	2	3	29	32	22	33	36	25
3.	Rampur	2	3	41	44	38	48	51	45
4.	Sikandarpur	2	3	36	42	31	39	43	34

Women not only take up issues relating to basic needs—drinking water, availability of doctors and teachers in the villages, which is dear to them, but also general developmental activities. This develops the understanding of women regarding their duties and rights about to be performed for the welfare of concerned village people and the role to play by them at household level and activities performed outside households. The physical progress in executing various types of development work made by the panchayat in the year 1998-99 and 1999-2000 helps to understand the progress made in creating necessary physical infrastructure in the panchayats. The entire work in panchayats has been executed by using local labour force and locally available raw material. Strict monitoring by panchayat members has ensured the quality of work.

Workunder Taken by Panchayat

Sl.No.	*Particulars*	*Work Undertaken 98-99*	*Work Undertaken 99-2000*
1.	Average construction of kharanja (meter/per Panchayat)	340.20	406.25
2.	Number of panchayats in which additional classroom was constructed	2	1
3.	No of drinking water tanks constructed/ handpumps installed	10	12
4.	Earth work (road repair etc.) avg. sq. meter per panchayat	8500	10500

SUB-COMMITTEES

Under the provision of Panchayat Raj Act, 6 sub-committees have to be constituted in Gram Panchayat namely:

Niyojan Samiti, Shiksha Samiti, Nirman Samiti, Swasth Evam Kalyan Samiti, Prashasnik Samiti and Jal Prabandh Samiti. The participatory with the member revealed that except Gram Shiksha Samiti all other samities are dormant. The pradhan and the secretary decided themselves about the composition of the sub-committees. These committees (except Siksha Samiti) were constituted, just in a day about 10-12 months ago and Pradhan nominated members in each committee in consultation with the secretary. The individual members were just ignorant about the functions of these committees and their own roles and responsibilities. Even the records of the meeting of the sub-committees were not properly maintained. Virtually all these committees were non-functional.

Beneficiaries of Schemes

Sl.No.	*Particulars*	*Beneficiaries*	
		98-99	*99-2000*
1.	IRDP	2	3
2.	Indira Avas	6	13
3.	Widow Pensions	21	18
4.	Old age Pensions	9	12
5.	Pensions to handicap	2	6
Total		40	52
	As % Total Voters	0.94	1.23

The ratio of beneficiaries of welfare and development schemes in 1999-2000 in Varanasi district worked out to 1:0.32. The on-going programmes included IRDP, Indira Awas, Widow pensions, Old age pensions and Pension to handicap for which beneficiaries were selected in the open meeting of Gaon Sabha in the panchayat. Although the percentage of beneficiaries may not reflect the efficiency of programmes scientifically because it should have been related to the total number of prospective beneficiaries. But since precise data on this subject was not available, number of voters has been used as common denominator.

MONITORING OF AGANWADI PROGRAMMES

ICDS programmes covering 0-6 years children and expectant and lactating mothers was operational in the GP. It was covering 165 and 41 expectant and lactating mothers. Pradhans and women members of panchayat are monitoring the activities of these centers every month. They supervise the distribution of nutritional supplement and number of children attending pre-school education. The MS members motivate mothers to send their children of 3-6 years age group regularly to these centers.

RECORD KEEPING IN PANCHAYAT

Although records of panchayat are kept by the secretary and pradhans, women members dictate the minutes of meeting of Gaon Sabha and panchayat. They often check up before signing the minute books.

FINANCIAL RESOURCES

The main source of financial assistance of panchayat include *JRY, Sunishchit Rozgar Yojana, funds allotted by 10th Finance Commission.* There was no flow of funds to these panchayats from Sunishchit Rozgar Yojana. In panchayat the detailed of funds received from different sources and their utilisation were generally made known to members of Gaon Sabha in open meetings. The financial records are kept with the secretary. The annual budgets are discussed at length and passed in the meeting of Gaon Sabha. This indicates higher degree of transparency in financial matters in panchayats. None of these panchayats has made any effort for mobilizing additional resources nor they have any idea as to how these resources could be raised. However MS members are operating women thrift and women credit group by mobilizing small scale saving which are used for internal loaning among the members, mostly for consumption purpose the objective behind it is to discourage the role of private money lenders and also to help women members to acquire productive assets. In the local newspaper published by MS has managed to procure and print the statement of allocation of funds for certain village, so that everybody should know about fund allocation. This also acts as a deterrent to the panchayat's misuse of funds.

IMPACT OF MS PROGRAMME ON GRAM PANCHAYATS

In MS panchayats, the workers of Mahila Samakhya Programme tried to access the impact of MS Programme on the empowerment of rural women and also on the overall functioning of panchayats, the details of which are as under:

- At the initiatives of MS. The felt need of the community is placed before the block and district level officials in the shape of proposals.
- In order to maintain self-image, pradhans and members perform their functions with honesty and there is high degree of transparency in their style of functioning. MS supported removal of a corrupt pradhans in MS panchayat by no confidence vote in Varanasi district.
- There is a marked decline in dependence of women pradhans on their male relatives in panchayat related transactions, There is a significant improvement in the mobility of women pradhans and members.
- MS programme has led to mobilisation of women irrespective of caste and creed in villages and their effective participation in the meeting of Gram Panchayat and Gaon Sabha.
- Pradhans and members have been made aware of their rights and duties motivating panchayat functionaries to perform better.

CONSTRAINTS

The members were asked to identify the major constraints in performing effectively pradhans and members of panchayat. The responses received from them in this regard given as under:

- Nearly 30 per cent illiterate women pradhans and members had to depend on husband, son or on literate women members for discharging there day to day functions.
- No knowledge of micro planning, project formulation etc. causes major problem in preparing projects.
- Lack of knowledge about budget, funds and its stipulation for utilisation, maintenance of financial records and financial management etc. are major constraints.
- Lack of knowledge about various on-going projects and programmes.
- Block level officials are not very responsive they do not give proper weightage to women's views and suggestions.
- Lack of wholehearted support from male members and their reluctance to accept women's leadership.

Most of these women came into the political system with several gender-related handicaps. These include illiteracy, responsibility of household work and childcare in addition to paid employment, social and familialy opposition to their involvement in the public life, a poor self-image, lack of self-confidence and ignorance about the political system into which they are included without any preparation. Male family members and colleagues actively prevent many women from participating in the activities of these bodies. They often take advantage of their illiteracy, ignorance of procedure, neglecting to send them notice of meeting, taking decisions in their absence, brow-beating them into becoming rubber stamps and so on. The socialisation at home, the lack of interaction of women and girls with outside development, the gender stereotyping and seclusion in political discussions, leave women often devoid of political information and training. Their subordinate status and culturally imposed constraints have made women diffident and fearful of taking part in the public affairs. Lack of adequate information and exposure about their roles and responsibilities all bar marginalised sections to function effectively. Women do not have closer interaction with the local bureaucracy as males dominate it. They have been discouraged by traditional taboos, bullied and used as proxies of men. Consequently, women's ineffective performance and inability to wield power has subsequently come under a lot of criticism. But these negative reactions over look the fact that male leaders who are from the grassroots have also had similar limitations. It is also based on the premise that there is some mythical state of readiness that women should achieve before they are allowed to play public leadership role and ignores the fact that experience and practice are often the best way of learning new roles. So any criticism that uphold the exclusion of a nity is placed before the block and district level officials in the shape of proposals.

- In order to maintain self-image, pradhans and members perform their functions with honesty and there is high degree of transparency in their style of functioning. MS supported removal of a corrupt pradhans in MS panchayat by no confidence vote in Varanasi district.
- There is a marked decline in dependence of women pradhans on their male relatives in panchayat related transactions. There is a significant improvement in the mobility of women pradhans and members.
- MS programme has led to mobilisation of women irrespective of caste and creed in villages and their effective

participation in the meeting of Gram Panchayat and Gaon Sabha.

- Pradhans and members have been made aware of their rights and duties motivating panchayat functionaries to perform better.

CONSTRAINTS

The members were asked to identify the major constraints in performing effectively pradhans and members of panchayat. The responses received from them in this regard given as under:

- Nearly 30 per cent illiterate women pradhans and members had to depend on husband, son or on literate women members for discharging there day to day functions.
- No knowledge of micro planning, project formulation etc. causes major problem in preparing projects.
- Lack of knowledge about budget, funds and its stipulation for utilisation, maintenance of financial records and financial management etc. are major constraints.
- Lack of knowledge about various on-going projects and programmes.
- Block level officials are not very responsive they do not give proper weightage to women's views and suggestions.
- Lack of wholehearted support from male members and their reluctance to accept women's leadership.

Most of these women came into the political system with several gender-related handicaps. These include illiteracy, responsibility of household work and childcare in addition to paid employment, social and familialy opposition to their involvement in the public life, a poor self-image, lack of self-confidence and ignorance about the political system into which they are included without any preparation. Male family members and colleagues actively prevent many women from participating in the activities of these bodies. They often take advantage of their illiteracy, ignorance of procedure, neglecting to send them notice of meeting, taking decisions in their absence, brow-beating them into becoming rubber stamps and so on. The socialisation at home, the lack of interaction of women and girls with outside development, the gender stereotyping and seclusion in political discussions, leave women often devoid of political information and training. Their subordinate status and culturally imposed constraints have made women diffident and fearful of taking part in the public affairs. Lack of adequate information and exposure about their roles and responsibilities all bar marginalised sections to function effectively. Women do not have closer interaction with the local bureaucracy as males dominate it. They have been discouraged by traditional taboos, bullied and used as proxies of men. Consequently, women's ineffective performance and inability to wield power has subsequently come under a lot of criticism. But these negative reactions over look the fact that male leaders who are from the grassroots have also had similar limitations. It is also based on the premise that there is some mythical state of readiness that women should achieve before they are allowed to play public leadership role and ignores the fact that experience and practice are often the best way of learning new roles. So any criticism that uphold the exclusion of a disadvantaged groups on the grounds of inadequacies arising from historical and social factors, is merely an attempt to preserve the status quo. So panchayat deals with all these disabilities and with the new challenge posed by her elective office in panchayat. Their empowerment has begun and will logically reach its fullness in the abolishing of inadequate, unjust laws and social practices.

BEHAVIOURAL CHANGES IN WOMEN PRADHAN AND MEMBERS

The officials and community members in MS Panchayat were asked to identify changes they could perceive in the women pradhan, panchayat members and BDC members. These are given below:

- Women members initially, were not interacting with officials but now they interact freely with them.
- They now directly approach block level functionaries to get additional schemes for their village.
- In block level meetings, the pradhans now go either alone or with women members and rarely with husband or other male relatives.
- They now conduct panchayat meeting with confidence.
- They participate effectively in BDC or other meetings.
- Increased in organisational capacity such as organising group work.
- Increase in managerial capacity like managing development works, monitor them etc.
- The now have greater understanding of gender issues, role of panchayat, their own duties and responsibility.

They believe MS has provided a forum to women for discussing their problems and gave an opportunity to develop common strategy to encounter challenges affecting their life. MS have made an effort to minimize the dependence of poor women on money lender by organising women's thrift and credit groups. However, a section of men believe that MS programme projects men as anti-women and anti-social, which is not a balance approach.

FINDINGS

"Power has become the source of growth. It has given something to people who were absolute nobodies and had no way of making it on their own."

- Women enjoy a respectable status within their families after getting elected to the *Panchayats*. They take decisions themselves in local affairs. These communities have exerted some influence after increasing the presence of the dispossessed people in these bodies. This has also given opportunities to them to grapple with local politics of development and learn the art of governance.
- The family has accepted the new role and even the relationship between husband and wife has been altered. The myth of being a proxy woman gets disproved. The husband-wife relationship has become relatively more egalitarian. This has led to a mobilisation of rural women to a great extent. Network members also feel that their status within the family and in official circles improves if they are members of such networks. The impact of network membership for women and the accompanying empowerment processes transcends public and private boundaries and enters the private and family spheres of the members, which in many cases has led to the reorganisation of relationships within the household.
- Women leaders in the Panchayati Raj are transforming local governance by sensitizing the State to issues of poverty, inequality and gender injustice. Through the PRI, they are tackling issues that had previously gone virtually unacknowledged, including water, alcohol abuse, education, health and domestic violence.
- The PRI has also brought about significant transformation in the lives of women themselves, who have become empowered, and have gave gained self-confidence, political awareness and affirmation of their own identity. The

panchayat villages have become political training grounds to women, many of them illiterate, who are now leaders in the village panchayats.

- By asserting control over resources and officials and by challenging men, women are discovering a personal and collective power that was previously unimaginable. This includes women, who are not panchayat leaders, but who have been inspired by the work of their sisters; it is this critical mass of unified and empowered women that will push forward policies that enforce gender equity into the future. The elected women prove to be the role model for the village women.
- Apart from this, due to spread effect of the MS, it is also expected that the participation of women would increase in the political decision making in adjoining areas of MS block as well. With increased awareness, the role and participation of women is expected to increase manifold.
- MS and women members of panchayats often motivate women to attend the meetings of Gaon Sabha. Women are encouraged and even prepared by MS to express their point of view openly and fearlessly in the Gaon Sabha meeting. MS working as a pressure group has led to resolution of many problems of panchayat at the block and district levels.
- Experiences gained so far in the functioning of *Panchayats* reveal that in spite of their social, educational, and economic backwardness, these communities have now a say in rural local governance. They have also noticed improvement in their life.

TRAINING OF ELECTED MEMBERS AND GENDER CONSCIENTISATION

The training of panchayats should be taken up as a national movement or a campaign. Training programmes should be developed to increase the political and management skills of women in politics, both as candidates and as elected officials. The objectives to design a training that is gender-sensitive, reflecting local as well as crosscutting themes relevant to all states. A gender balance in the selection of trainers and that the special needs of women should be considered while designing training programmes through *gender lens.* A critical understanding of the roots of women oppression and strategic interventions are required that can be result from gender awareness programme. Arrangements for the training of elected members of the panchayats at different levels, the administrative and technical staff attached to the panchayats, fall at present far short of requirements. An exponential increase in the quantum of funds made available for such training is required as well as deep consideration to the overall training requirements of both elected members and panchayat staff.

WOMEN SHATTERED THE MYTHS

Initially, women were hesitant to enter this whole new political arena, political parties and vested interest groups took advantage of the situation and proxy rule prevailed. Thus the power remained in the hands of the traditionally powerful groups. A new class of *'sarpanch patis'* also emerged where the husband of the woman sarpanch managed the affairs of the panchayat, while the woman acted only as a *rubber stamp.* Many women elected to the local bodies/ panchayats act like surrogates for husbands and fathers who could not contest because of reservation. Today panchayats which are headed by women, not only has the participation and leadership of women but also made an impact on grassroots governance, it has also shattered many of the myths regarding their inability to handle power and responsibility outside their homes. There is no lack of dynamism or leadership quality among rural women, nor is it true that they are unaware of their own needs and those of development. According to Devki Jain, *"Women's entry into local government in such large numbers, often more than the required 33.3 per cent and their success in campaigning, including the defeat of male candidates, has shattered the myth that women are not interested in politics, and have no time to go to meetings or to undertake all the other work that is required in political party processes.... PRI reminds us of a central truth: power is not something people give away. It has to be negotiated, and sometimes wrested from the powerful."*

Women's political empowerment in the last ten years through the Constitution amendments has exploded several myths, like the belief that they are passive and disinterested in political institutions; only the well-to-do, upper strata women will come through reservation; only the kin of powerful politicians will enter panchayats through political connectivity to keep the seats for them and lastly women are only proxy members and they do not participate in the panchayats. Even if women chiefs depend on their husbands, the power relation between husband and wife has already changed, the husband gets a chance to come to the public because of wife; the patriarchy is no longer monolithic. As a result the husband-wife relationship hasn't soured. Even the members of the family, including the husband, mother-in-law and sister-in-law help her to complete domestic chores. The community leaders of the same caste support the women candidates. As a corollary, the family members don't mind the women talking to the other men nor do they mind if they take off the veils and address the meetings. Even now half of the women are illiterate and their economic contributions don't get acknowledged. But a good beginning has been made to achieve the long-neglected gender justice. Without discounting the existence in panchayats of some women who do fit into this patriarchal oriented framework, one can say-that these myths have now been buried. Today the buzzword is that women can do it.

SUGGESTIONS

The quality of leadership amongst rural women has to be encouraged and allowed to grow so that women can develop confidence in decision-making, can identify their own problems, priorities and preference and use their wisdom, knowledge and judgement to suggest ways and means to resolve them. Certain concrete steps are required to make PRIs a real participatory democratic institution with increased, meaningful and sustained participation of women in the democratic process.

- In order to sustain changes in the working of panchayats, it is necessary that each and every section of society should participate in decision-making at the local level. For this proper institutional development should take place so that the decisions are taken by the majority and not by a few influential people. A culture should be developed in which there is no dependency on a chosen few. It should be based on consensus building particularly involving the weaker sections, which is the most important indicator of democratic functioning.
- Training in participatory planning should be organised at the panchayat level on repetitive bases. The methods of PRA/ PLA should be practiced by NGOs, through funding by Government Organisations implementing participatory and social development. PRA/PLA are very useful in awareness

building and empowerment of women through which they can be motivated to participate in Panchayati Raj Institutions.

- Training of village level functionaries in participatory planning and development should be organised on continuous bases so as to develop in them positive attitudes towards empowerment of people especially women. MS should take a capacity building programme not only of women but also of poor village men, to bring them into the mainstream of decision-making and develop participatory development and paradigms.
- Panchayati Raj Department should examine and if required do necessary changes in the rules and regulations or the law itself should be made so as to make it mandatory on panchayat to get all important decisions approved by the general body.
- Training and financial support should be provided to train members of NGOs, Mahila Mandal and MS workers in imparting training to women to promote social and political empowerment.
- Training should be given for capacity building of women pradhans and member in micro level planning, financial management and preparation of small projects.
- Different training agencies should collaborate for developing training modules. The Panchayati Raj Department with NGO's should design and conduct training programme on regular basis. Impact of training should be evaluated so that curriculum is received as and when required. Programme meant for leadership training should be carefully designed. Including women in designing training programme, projects-and schemes would reinforce quality.
- The rural development department needs to issues strict instructions to monitoring workers to ensure that the selection of beneficiaries under various development schemes should be done in open Gaon Sabha meeting.
- Women pradhans should make aware of the national and state policies of women empowerment should compile an inventory of on-going programmes of women development should be widely circulated.
- Women pradhans at block and district level should meet

periodically to review the progress of implementation of policies and programmes of women empowerment.

- Panchayati Raj Department should work out a system for providing some assistance to women who wish to fight election and have no support from the family. This system would act as a good incentive for women who are unable to fight elections because of non-availability of financial resources.
- MS philosophy needs to be extended in all areas as wide as possible. MS should extend its coverage both in quantitative and qualitative terms and should incorporate more women into its fold. Conscientisation of large numbers of women should be encouraged.
- In order to enhance the effectiveness of women pradhans there is a need to provide them opportunity to directly discuss their problem with key officer, Minister of Panchayati Raj Department, the Chief Minister and even Prime Minister. Tele-conferencing of women pradhans with them should be organised from time to time in order to bring their pressing problems in the forefront and find their solutions.
- To reduce the influence of money and muscle power in the elections of Gram Panchayats, stringent laws and effective implementation are required. Proxy representation should be declared illegal under the law.
- To enable women's effective participation the government should take certain facilitating measures such as child care facilities, escort during travel and financial support. Provision should be made to appoint Gram Sevikas with every woman Sarpanch.
- Women's study centers in the universities and colleges all over India, the agricultural extension institutions as well as agricultural colleges/universities, the social work departments in the universities etc. should be mobilised to play the vital role of being catalyst to mobilize the women and link up the Panchayati Raj representatives and women citizens with other activities, and help in resolving their political dilemmas, bring them the information and undertake to organise political education/training.
- To bring attitudinal changes in both men and women. The feeling that women are meant for home should be replaced

by a feeling of equal partnership. Both men and women should be made to feel that women's interest cannot be isolated from general social and political interest of groups, strata and classes in the society and that women should be recognised as equal.

- The financial dependence of women has a negative sense of bearing on women's confidence and vigor. Hence it is necessary to involve women in large numbers in economically gainful activities. Extensive use of mass media is also useful in bringing about fundamental changes. These efforts would facilitate the emergence of a new generation with new values.
- Education and contacts with the world outside make women more alert and active in the political process. There are two ways of establishing contacts between rural and urban women. One is that of facilitating exchange of views with others in the rural areas themselves, the second is that of the urban women visiting rural areas and exchanging views with the rural women.
- Indira Gandhi National Open University has evolved a multimedia model for extending training on a mass scale through the use of both traditional and innovative forms of mass communication. This multimedia model needs to be brought into play with all deliberate speed. Doordarshan too needs to take up the challenge of effectively training elected members and staff of Panchayati Raj.
- The Election Commission may be invited to review the experience of the conduct of panchayat elections in different parts of the country with a view to making recommendations that would promote free and fair elections, restraint on election expenditure, ending harassment of women candidates and other candidates belonging to the weaker sections, and the sharp curtailing of criminalisation in the Panchayati Raj system.

The lesson of PRI is clear: if the wisdom of grassroots organisations, especially the courage and clarity of women, is to become policy, it will not be through the art of intellectual persuasion but by the arrangements made within a political system for their voice to have power. Bringing women into power is thus not only a matter of equity, of correcting an unjust and unrepresentative system.

Focuses on feminism as a conceptual framework and proposes that women candidates develop a gender-based agenda. It maintains that increasing the number of elected women public officials per se is not what feminists should seek but the concretisation of this political empowerment into responsive and workable policies that will rectify inequality and injustice against women in a traditional, patriarchal society. It emphasizes that it is not enough that we get women elected to public office; more important is that their increased presence and participation in the formal political structures of political power in both the national and local levels will create a qualitatively leap in the transformation of the conditions of women in the home, the workplace and society at large. Broadening and deepening women's participation in politics, one has to look not only at the quantitative increase in elected women power holders but its impact on the qualitative transformation of women's lives.

CONCLUSION

Political empowerment is a process that enables women to increase their mobility and break their isolation, to develop their self-confidence and self-image and to establish their public presences whereby they participate in decision-making in an expanding framework of awareness and critical analysis to control and influence the direction of development. Political empowerment means women's representation in formal political institutions. Women's vision is rooted in grassroots realities; therefore the development initiatives taken by them have a bottom-up approach. Many studies and active work among the rural and poor women have repeatedly demonstrated this faith in women and trust in their leadership. They believe, hopefully correctly, that women would be more sincere, stable, committed, capable of hard work, and above all, not corrupt. They particularly view that women would worry about women's problems and hence would prefer them any day to men, as leaders. An assessment of women in the Panchayati Raj conducted by Professor *Susheela Kaushik* of the Women's Studies Center at Delhi University reveals *'Corruption has gone down and transparency greatly increased because of women's participation in panchayats. Women pradhans were generally uncomforgettable operating through illegal means while men were confident of accessing and using illegal channels of power.'*

It is true that women are gaining more self-confidence, while enhancing their managerial skills, administrative skills, and sharpening their decision-making capacities. Women have also realised the importance of literacy, acquiring more knowledge and learning by doing. In the process of gaining more self-confidence, being more assertive, achieving a sense of empowerment and by asserting control over resources, they have also generated a hope that their new perception of self will also influence the gender consciousness in their personal sphere. Women in panchayats leave many dreams and their self-perception changes when they realise the immense potential of the public sphere. Women have been given space in the public sphere, but have not been relieved from their personal responsibilities of household work and of upbringing their children, caring and nurturing the family members. The work burden for them has increased manifold. A set of strategies and actions, thus have to be evolved that might help remove the obstacles, redeem the deficiencies and help women play political roles effectively. It is also equally well recognised that any attempt that seeks to promote women's empowered roles has to combine multiple strategies that goes beyond politics into social and psychological, cultural and familial, economic and careerist, policy making and implementing levels; that the strategies should aim to reach beyond women to men, and beyond the women who are victims of discrimination and atrocities to men/women who perpetrate these; and above all its needs to empower women by ending their isolation by domestication, breaking their isolation imposed by socio-cultural barricades, by unifying them through common interest and by organising them on the basis of mutual trust, common goals and collectivity. Women's voice needs to be nurtured, through capacity building interventions. They need to feel able to express themselves. Patriarchy, caste and class dynamics in the power structure of rural society have prevented women from using political spaces provided to them by the constitutional amendment. The 73rd Amendment has an empowering impact on the women in a context where women's labour is still marginalised and the rural hierarchies remain unchallenged to a large extent, the entry of women into politics in such a big way is in itself a radical change. Despite the constraints, they are playing an extremely important role, which needs to be recognised. Training programmes for empowering women can weaken the barriers posed by patriarchy, caste and poverty. Women have been able to change the gender roles are not engraved on stone; they can and would change once women are able to play a more proactive role in it. Successful and effective women leaders have opened up gates for lot of women to come out as more confident, creative and courageous persons. It may be a slow process but there is a strong expectation and belief that the reality will improve in the days to come and will not be worse than the present. It is not as if women have succeeded in every panchayat but a large majority had and that is what makes it exhilarating. Women are now beginning to understand the system and are aware of their own innate strengths and capabilities. Some women have been able to encroach into the male dominated area of politics as successful administrator and decision makers, while for others there is still a long way to go.

REFERENCES

Ashworth Geogina, (1996): Gendered Governance: An Agenda for Change.www.undp.org/ gender.

Batliwala Srilatha (1996): Women's Empowerment in South Asia— Concepts and Practices, Asia-South Pacific Bureau of Adult Education (ASPBAE) and FAQ, New Delhi.

Batliwala Srilatha (1996): Transforming of Political Culture— Mahila Samakhya Experience, EPW, Vol. No. 31, Issue No. 21.

Bhandari Chitra (1997): Historical Background of Panchayati Raj System, in Panchayati Raj, Vol. 22 (1), 2-4, New Delhi.

Bouwhis Judith, (1995): Empowerment of Poor Rural Women, Monitoring The Mahila Samakhya Programme in India, M.A. Thesis, Development Studies, Third World Center, Catholic University, Njmegen, Utrecht.

Bulletin, Women in Panchayati Raj, (1995): The Ford Foundation, spring 1995, New Delhi.

Constitution (73rd) Amendment Act (1992) Reproduced in Panchayati Raj, Vol. 22 (1) 31-37, New Delhi.

Dayal Rajeshwar (1970): Panchayati Raj in India, Metropolitan Books Company, Delhi.

Freedman Jane, Feminism (2002): Viva Books Private Limited, New Delhi.

Government of India (1974): Towards Equality: Report of the Committee on the Status of Women in India: Ministry of Education and Social Welfare, New Delhi.

Government of India (1988): National Perspective Plan for Women 1988-2000: Ministry of Human Resources Development, New Delhi.

Institute of Social Sciences (1997): "Gram Panchayats at a Glance," In Panchayat Raj, Vol. 22 (1), p. 39, New Delhi.

Jain Devki; Panchayati Raj; (1996): Women Changing Governance; UNDP; September 1996, New Delhi.

Kabeer, Naila (1994): Reserved Reality: Gender Hierachies in Development Thought: Verso, London and New York.

Karl, Marliee (1995): Women and Empowerment: Participation and Decision Making: Zed Books, London and New Jersey.

Kaushik Susheela (1996): Women and Panchayati Raj, Har-Anand Publication, New Delhi.

Kaushik Susheela (1996): Women in Politics-Forms and Processes, Frederic Ebert Stiftung, Har-Anand Publication, New Delhi.

Kaushik Susheela (1995): Panchayati Raj in Action: Frederic Ebert Stiftung, New Delhi.

Mahila Samakhya an Overview (1997): Government of India, New Delhi.

Manikyamba, P. (1989): Women in Panchayati Raj Structures; Gian Publishing House, New Delhi.

Mehta G.S., Participation of Women in the Panchayati Raj System (2002): Kanishka Publishers, Distributors, New Delhi.

Ninth Five-Year Plan (1997-2000): Documents, Government of India, New Delhi.

Participation and Governance (2000): Vol. 7, No. 19, PRIA, New Delhi.

Phillips Anne (1991): Engendering Democracy; Cambridge; Polity Press.

Phillips Anne (1998): Democracy and Representation: or, Why Should it Matter, Who Our Representation Are? in Phillips Anne (ed.) Feminism and Politics, Oxford: Oxford University Press.

Pillai Sudha, Can Panchayati Raj Improve the Scene, Yojana Vol. 45 August 2001, Rakesh Press, New Delhi, Publishing House, New Delhi.

Ray Bharati and Basu Aparna (1999): From Independence Towards Freedom—Indian Women Science 1947, Oxford University Press, New Delhi.

Saxena Parul (2004): Population and Development—A Case Study of KAVAL Towns in UP., Human Resource and Economic Development, Singh J.L., Gaur K.D. (ed.), Sunrise Publication, New Delhi.

Sharma Kumud: Transforming Politics: Dimensions of Women Participation in Panchayati Raj: In Indian Journal of Gender Studies, Vol. 5, No. 1, January-June 1998, New Delhi.

Sharma P.N., and Vinayak Vani (2003): Women in Grassroot Democracy and Panchayati Raj, Mahila Samakhya, Lucknow.

Status of Panchayati Raj in U.P. (2002), Sahbhagi Shikshan Kendra, Anuj Printers, Lucknow.

Status of Panchayati Raj Institution (2000): A Report (Gujarat Haryana, Kerala, M.P., U.P., Rajasthan).

The Hindu (1999): Women Discuss Good Governance, November 07, 1999, New Delhi.

UNDP Report (1993): Planning Development with Women: Making a World of Difference, Macmillan, London.

Vidya, K.C. (1997): Political Empowerment of Women at the Grassroots, Kanishka Publishers, Distributors, New Delhi.

Index